A Holocaust Controversy

A Holocaust

The Treblinka Affair in Postwar France

CONTROVERSY

Samuel Moyn

Brandeis University Press
Waltham, Massachusetts

PUBLISHED BY
UNIVERSITY PRESS OF NEW ENGLAND
HANOVER AND LONDON

Brandeis University Press
Published by University Press of New England,
One Court Street, Lebanon, NH 03766
www.upne.com
© 2005 by Brandeis University Press
Printed in the United States of America
5 4 3 2 1

LIBRARY OF CONGRESS CATALOGING-IN-PUBLICATION DATA
Moyn, Samuel.
A Holocaust controversy : the Treblinka affair in postwar France /
Samuel Moyn.
   p. cm.—(Tauber Institute for the Study of European Jewry series)
Includes bibliographical references and index.
ISBN-13: 978–1–58465–508–4 (cloth : alk. paper)
ISBN-10: 1–58465–508–9 (cloth : alk. paper)
ISBN-13: 978–1–58465–509–1 (pbk. : alk. paper)
ISBN-10: 1–58465–509–7 (pbk. : alk. paper)
1. Holocaust, Jewish (1939–1945)—Historiography. 2. Steiner,
Jean-François, 1938– Treblinka. 3. Historiography—France—
History—20th century. 4. Treblinka (Concentration camp)
5. World War, 1939–1945—Atrocities—Poland. 6. World War,
1939–1945—Prisoners and prisons, German. I. Title. II. Tauber
Institute for the Study of European Jewry series (Unnumbered)
D804.348.M69   2005
940.53'18—dc22   2005012609

The Tauber Institute for the Study of European Jewry Series

Jehuda Reinharz, General Editor

Sylvia Fuks Fried, Associate Editor

The Tauber Institute for the Study of European Jewry, established by a gift to Brandeis University from Dr. Laszlo N. Tauber, is dedicated to the memory of the victims of Nazi persecutions between 1933 and 1945. The Institute seeks to study the history and culture of European Jewry in the modern period. The Institute has a special interest in studying the causes, nature, and consequences of the European Jewish catastrophe within the contexts of modern European diplomatic, intellectual, political, and social history.

Richard Breitman, 1992
The Architect of Genocide: Himmler and the Final Solution

George L. Mosse, 1993
Confronting the Nation: Jewish and Western Nationalism

Daniel Carpi, 1994
Between Mussolini and Hitler: The Jews and the Italian Authorities in France and Tunisia

Walter Laqueur and Richard Breitman, 1994
Breaking the Silence: The German Who Exposed the Final Solution

Ismar Schorsch, 1994
From Text to Context: The Turn to History in Modern Judaism

Jacob Katz, 1995
With My Own Eyes: The Autobiography of an Historian

Gideon Shimoni, 1995
The Zionist Ideology

Moshe Prywes and Haim Chertok, 1996
Prisoner of Hope

János Nyiri, 1997
Battlefields and Playgrounds

Alan Mintz, editor, 1997
The Boom in Contemporary Israeli Fiction

Samuel Bak, paintings
Lawrence L. Langer, essay and commentary, 1997
Landscapes of Jewish Experience

Jeffrey Shandler and Beth S. Wenger, editors, 1997
Encounters with the "Holy Land": Place, Past and Future in American Jewish Culture

Simon Rawidowicz, 1998
State of Israel, Diaspora, and Jewish Continuity: Essays on the "Ever-Dying People"

Jacob Katz, 1998
A House Divided: Orthodoxy and Schism in Nineteenth-Century Central European Jewry

Elisheva Carlebach, John M. Efron, and David N. Myers, editors, 1998
Jewish History and Jewish Memory: Essays in Honor of Yosef Hayim Yerushalmi

Shmuel Almog, Jehuda Reinharz, and Anita Shapira, editors, 1998
Zionism and Religion

Ben Halpern and Jehuda Reinharz, 2000
Zionism and the Creation of a New Society

Walter Laqueur, 2001
Generation Exodus: The Fate of Young Jewish Refugees from Nazi Germany

Yigal Schwartz, 2001
Aharon Appelfeld: From Individual Lament to Tribal Eternity

Renée Poznanski, 2001
Jews in France during World War II

Jehuda Reinharz, 2001
Chaim Weizmann: The Making of a Zionist Leader

Jehuda Reinharz, 2001
Chaim Weizmann: The Making of a Statesman

ChaeRan Y. Freeze, 2002
Jewish Marriage and Divorce in Imperial Russia

Mark A. Raider and Miriam B. Raider-Roth, editors, 2002
The Plough Woman: Records of the Pioneer Women of Palestine

Ezra Mendelsohn, 2002
Painting a People: Maurycy Gottlieb and Jewish Art

Alan Mintz, editor, 2002
Reading Hebrew Literature: Critical Discussions of Six Modern Texts

Haim Be'er, 2002
The Pure Element of Time

Yehudit Hendel, 2002
Small Change: A Collection of Stories

Thomas C. Hubka, 2003
Resplendent Synagogue: Architecture and Worship in an Eighteenth-Century Polish Community

Uzi Rebhun and Chaim I. Waxman, editors, 2003
Jews in Israel: Contemporary Social and Cultural Patterns

Gideon Shimoni, 2003
Community and Conscience: The Jews in Apartheid South Africa

Haim Be'er, 2004
Feathers

Abraham Grossman, 2004
Pious and Rebellious: Jewish Women in Medieval Europe

Iris Parush, 2004
Reading Jewish Women: Marginality and Modernization in Nineteenth-Century Eastern Jewish Society

Immanuel Etkes, 2004
The Besht: Magic, Mysticism, and Leadership

Ivan Davidson Kalmar and Derek J. Penslar, editors, 2004
Orientalism and the Jews

Margalit Shilo, 2005
Princess or Prisoner? Jewish Women in Jerusalem, 1840–1914

Samuel Moyn, 2005
A Holocaust Controversy: The Treblinka Affair in Postwar France

**Silence over the murder,
scandal over the books.**

—George Steiner,
on the Treblinka affair (1967)

Contents

Images

Preface

This little book is an experiment. Its subject matter is a Holocaust controversy that rocked French and French-Jewish life in the mid-1960s, set off by
the publication of Jean-François Steiner's book *Treblinka: The Revolt of an
Extermination Camp.* The project came about when I fell upon traces of the
forgotten dispute, quite accidentally, in the course of researching a different
study on the origins of the thought of the French-Jewish thinker Emmanuel
Levinas, now considered amongst the most important moral philosophers, in
any country, of the last century. Provoked by recent debates, then just beginning their rapid and voluminous accumulation, about the emergence of
Holocaust consciousness in different nations and across the world, constitut-
ing a new field of study at the time, I decided to look into the contextual origins of Levinas's major early article on the subject. It turned out to have been
inspired by—indeed, an intervention in—a controversy I had never heard
about but that my initial research suggested had been of major significance
in postwar France, in ways that the incipient historiography of "Holocaust
memory" completely omitted. I also discovered, initially in reading his spell-
binding memoirs, that the involvement of Pierre Vidal-Naquet with Holocaust studies—Vidal-Naquet eventually became perhaps the most significant
proponent in France of the importance of the genocide as an intellectual
topic, famous notably for his campaign against Holocaust denial—had been
catalyzed by this debate.

I began calling it the Treblinka affair, after the title of Steiner's book. This
fantastically successful text depicted one of the principal Nazi death camps—
a killing center, erected in 1942 as part of Aktion Reinhard, solely dedicated
to Jewish destruction, where historians safely estimate that perhaps 800,000
Jews were murdered over the year and a half of the camp's existence (of course,
estimates vary). In its climax, Steiner's book described the August 2, 1943,

insurrection by the Jewish inmates of the camp. Lasting for several months, the debate touched off by *Treblinka* tested popular understandings of World War II, cast light on the state of the Jewish community, and involved many of the most significant as well as numerous obscure writers of the day; the scope and range of the quarrel, surprisingly immense, are suggested by the cover of my book, where its dramatis personae are listed. I came to believe that a study of Steiner's enterprise and the furor that followed upon its publication, a *Rezeptionsgeschichte* of it, might have powerful ramifications for understanding postwar French cultural, intellectual, and political history, including French-Jewish history, as well as contribute to international Holocaust studies. Best of all, because the dispute involved a direct contest of the two major postwar constructions of the World War II past, its study casts needed light on the moral implications, debated even amongst Jews at the time, of the rise of the genocidal consciousness that has since become a hallmark of the contemporary era, in France as elsewhere. I chose, in summary, to elevate a background to Levinas, who still figures significantly in what follows, into a legitimate topic in its own right. This dispute, the Treblinka affair, is the subject of this short book.

It is an experiment for a number of reasons. Controversies are relatively new objects of historical concern, and what follows attempts to explore what it means to study one. According to Robert Darnton, writing in the *New York Review of Books* ("It Happened One Night," 24 June 2004), a large and increasing number of historians in recent years have tried their hands at telling the story of a personalized and local episode (as opposed to reconstructing, or rather with an aim to best illuminating, an anonymous and large-scale process). The goal of many of these works, as it is of this one, is to capture the fundamentals of an age or a problem through miniaturization. In that sense, the present "incident analysis" of the Treblinka affair—as Darnton usefully names the emerging genre—is part of a scholarly trend. But while murders, atrocities, riots, and trials have been the subjects of most of these recent studies, intellectual and cultural historians have worked on relatively few literary or philosophical controversies, and have narrated few of those in their unfolding dynamism, though literary events have many of the same structural features as more physically tangible occurrences.

The abstract reasons I think that controversies are valuable objects of historical scrutiny are enumerated in some detail in chapter 1 below, but there is little doubt that I became interested in the prospects of narrating this dispute—one of the earliest Holocaust controversies—because one of the major "incidents" of the years of my training as a historian had been the dramatic polemical battle (dramatic for historians at any rate) set off by the publication of Daniel Jonah Goldhagen's notorious book *Hitler's Willing Executioners* in the later 1990s, precisely when I initially came across the Treblinka affair and gathered most of the materials related to it. To that recent controversy, remarkable even in a field of study whose normal growth has been punctuated more than most domains by riveting and impassioned public and scholarly scandals, I found in the Treblinka affair an early analogue or even template: beginning with the important biographical circumstance of the victimized father, without reference to whom it is impossible to understand the young son's conduct, such Holocaust controversies typically involve massive (and for many, unseemly) commercial publicity, uncomfortably combine the rancor of professional experts with the esteem of the public, and often turn out to be as much reflections of contemporary politics and crises of current identity as debates about the past historical problems that furnish their ostensible content. Of course, there are significant dissimilarities. But it is out of a reflection that there are recurrent elements in the repeated public and scholarly furors over the Holocaust that have marked postwar history that I decided to anatomize the Treblinka affair as a model dispute, and to examine it not just on the grounds that it mattered in and of itself (though it did) but because the results might help illuminate a chronic, and enduring, phenomenon. Fierce arguments about the Holocaust are now practically a fixture of contemporary public and academic life, a fact that calls for recognition and analysis. Hence my title: "A Holocaust Controversy."

The study of such a controversy as a relatively self-contained event presupposes the possibility that a short-term but comparatively "deep" account may sometimes lead to different results than a long-term one that could only skim the surface. In spite of its potentially high price, the choice for depth can often reveal significant omissions in broad accounts; in Holocaust studies, for example, histories of Holocaust consciousness that depict "silence" and "delay" in the emergence of attention to the Nazi genocide—Peter Novick's well-known work on the United States is an important example—often do so only by slighting or ignoring local and often marginal subcultures whose texts and knowledge were not only vulgarized to vast audiences as time went on but also displaced by new kinds of productions, like *Treblinka* in the French case. There is no denying, of course, that Holocaust consciousness came late to the worldwide public, and this book tries to contribute to the study of when and how this occurred. But it did not come late to everyone: a model of vulgarization works much better, if the Treblinka affair is a generalizable case, to understand the processes by which the silence came to be broken and the delay ended in the formation of a more general post-Holocaust culture. For this reason, Yiddish-language actors and sources, both prior to and during the dispute, as well as the more general Jewish deportation community, are given full attention in what follows.

As for the terms of the controversy, they were local—and lasting. In what follows, I have striven for as rich a contextualization as possible of the historical problems that so divided the public. If many of them—and most especially the obsession with Jewish passivity and resistance during the war—seem almost morally unintelligible now, it bears recalling how central they were to the consciousness of a bygone era when the Holocaust first emerged as a public topic. I also suggest that both the content and the tone of the discussion reflected the peculiarities of the post–World War II era in France—notably the persistence of an antifascist appropriation of wartime victimhood—before the imminent transformation of that nation's renowned "Vichy syndrome" revealed the degree of its collaboration, including its implication in the genocidal events themselves. Still, throughout, I have tried to be sensitive to the ways in which there are certain enduring moral and intellectual difficulties in the post-Holocaust era, ones that outlived the Treblinka controversy in which they were given some of their earliest formulations. For that reason, throughout I consider obliquely, and close the book by examining frontally, what is living and not just dead in the Treblinka controversy's debates about how best to conceptualize Nazi criminality, the effect the Holocaust should have on the framing of Jewish identity, and, more generally, the relevance of such traumatic events in recent history as "lessons" to help guide one's response to current affairs, notably as generations change and biographical connections to the past become less and less direct and immediate.

The experiment of studying a controversy also involves the challenge of embedding intellectuals in more general cultural history, without making them suffer the trivialization that such contextualization can easily involve. In this kind of history, the texts emphatically have to be studied as part of a literary world, with its editors who roll out books, its journals that feature opinion-making reviewers, and its markets that require expert management; and it is not always the caliber of the figures as much as the importance of the cultural shifts they live through and bring about that matters. But as an intellectual historian, I try in this book to retain some of the focus on the highest and most rewarding of intellectual figures. Just as they have learned to see texts as events, so too, one might add, intellectual historians may occasionally have to study certain important "incidents" of thought, occurrences not simply internal to the individual mind but ones defined by public and collective dynamics. Like no other event, the Holocaust attracts the widest range of interest, and therefore commentary not up to its magnitude; but it also justifies the reflection of the most morally acute and intellectually penetrating figures, and in this book, and in Holocaust controversies generally, it is the sheer diversity of intellectual caliber that can seem both disconcerting and interesting. Indeed, the collision of abilities is one of the structural features, as it were, of the recurrent Holocaust controversies of the age. If the experiment of juxtaposition is successful, the point is not to abandon the study of incontestably major and internationally known intellectuals, such as Levinas and Vidal-Naquet, but to suggest that the forgotten traditions in or against which they have worked, the obscure writers with whom they interacted, and the vanished controversies to which they were parties, are sometimes critical to understanding the genesis, and perhaps the meaning, of aspects of their activity.

Finally, this book is an experiment because it is an attempt to *narrate* the controversy—to tell it as a story. Thus, I try in what follows to take the reader from the scandalmongering interview that first alerted the public to the book, and problems, at issue, through a note on the author and a reading of the text at the center of the dispute itself, through the large catalogue of responses to it that poured forth, to the belated reactions of the living historical witnesses whose experiences the text reinterpreted, ending finally with the controversy's aftereffects. In this media-driven affair, images played, and therefore play in this book, a role as well. Although I have tried to impose some order, especially on the huge number of printed responses, so as to separate them into categories and to argue for their transformative impact on public interpretation of lasting problems—specifically, I have divided them into chapters on general and intra-Jewish responses, which allows separate analysis of rival perceptions of Nazi criminality and alternative beliefs about the nature of Jewish particularity—the results nonetheless are likely to combine in equal measure the excitements and exasperations of any lived controversy. Such disputes are experienced as a totality, and thus have to be followed by historians where they lead, no matter how telling or tawdry the moments to which they give rise. Along with the idiosyncratic personages and sordid arguments, there is also the element of repetition, and even saturation and exhaustion. The methodological point is that the picture has to be presented whole.

By its end, if lived experience is to be trusted, the controversy may seem too trivial to have been worth the trouble; yet a reconstruction may suggest that absorption in it, not simply for the participants but also for spectators forced into involvement by the degree of its public intensity, may have been more pivotal, for the community and thus for the self, than may have originally seemed to be the case. Controversies show the extent to which, in historical reality if not in political theory, there is little distinction between public and private, as personal beliefs are revealed as constitutively dependent on public meaning. There is no interior place, sheltered from the exterior and collective production of meaning, to seek to take a stand by oneself and on one's own on the matters one finds vulgarized—often distastefully—in controversies. To stress this inevitability, finally, I have included, in the last chapter, a consideration of the next Holocaust controversy that occurred in French life—this one involving not Jean-François Steiner but Hannah Arendt. Whatever one's remorse at one's embroilment in such *affaires* after the fact, there is no way, in modern circumstances, and at least until the production and dissemination of public culture changes substantially, to avoid their recurrence, as one is implicated, willingly or reluctantly, once again. Controversies, in summary, deserve to have their histories told; this book is an experiment and case study in respecting this maxim.

■

I conducted the research for this book in Paris, in the personal archives of Jean-François Steiner, at the Bibliothèque Vladimir Medem, at the Institut d'études politiques, and at the Bibliothèque nationale de France. In the United States, I consulted archival material at the YIVO Institute for Jewish Research, the Library of Congress, and the New School for Social Research, and used the collections at Columbia University, Fordham University, Harvard University, the New York Public Library, and the Center for Jewish History in New York City. I would particularly like to acknowledge David Moore of Columbia's interlibrary loan department for his help in acquiring many obscure materials. In Israel, I relied heavily on the large number of relevant archival sources at Yad Vashem Holocaust Martyrs' and Heroes' Remembrance Authority, and would like to thank archivist Zvi Bernhardt for helping me find the right files and Dina and Paul Berger, my parents-in-law, for the many kinds of assistance they gave me on my trip. Finally, Gennady Pasechnik, archivist at the Diaspora Research Institute at Tel Aviv University, generously sent me some materials from the S. L. Shneiderman archive he runs.

I benefited materially from a Gilbert Chinard Prize conferred by the Institut Français de Washington, which funded the trip to France during which I embarked on this project, and from a Columbia University Junior Faculty Development Grant, which allowed me to compose a rough draft over the summer. I probably would never have written this book except for the instigation of two close friends and colleagues: Julian Bourg, who invited contribution of a piece of it in a volume of essays that he has edited,[1] in which I tried to isolate the story of Pierre Vidal-Naquet from the book that follows; and Eugene Sheppard, who not only provided critical stimulus to my thinking as I wrote and revised this study, but also put me in touch with Sylvia Fuks Fried, director of the Tauber Institute for the Study of European Jewry at Brandeis University and associate editor of the book series in which this text appears. I must thank Sylvia for responding with a revitalizing excitement to this book project at a time when my own energies had faltered and, in what I can now regard as an act of extraordinary generosity, for saddling me with the contract whose impending deadline finally forced me to execute it. Sylvia has shepherded this book through the different stages of preparation with great care, and I am deeply grateful. In readying the draft, I relied heavily on the research assistance of Albert Wu, who deserves my deep thanks, along with Alice Kessler-Harris, the chair of the Columbia University history department, who made it possible for him to provide his services during the summertime.

In France, I am first of all grateful to Jean-François Steiner, who welcomed me into his home and allowed me full access to the archival materials he has saved from his youth, and who lent me his automobile so I could find a photocopier (in the event, at a suburban pharmacy). Not least, he promised that I could use what I took freely and interpret it in my own way. Without this initial act of generosity, which I genuinely hope he does not regret, this book would not now exist; but I have not held back in framing my own reading of the events he set into motion. I also relied heavily on the extraordinary geniality of Pierre Vidal-Naquet, perhaps the other major protagonist in what follows, who likewise welcomed me into his home on several occasions and submitted to my questions; the opportunity to spend time with this admirable scholar and public intellectual is not one I shall ever forget. Both figures were generous enough, most recently, to read my draft and help me to improve it. I also owe the late Jérôme Lindon of the Éditions de Minuit for some extremely enlightening and useful conversations and information. Pierre Nora shared with me by correspondence some of his memories about the French publication of Hannah Arendt's *Eichmann in Jerusalem*. Experts in French-Jewish history Henri Raczymow and Annette Wieviorka met with and assisted me in the course of my early French research. Yitskhok Niborski provided much important information about the Yiddish-speaking world to me by correspondence as I completed this book. In the United States, Raul Hilberg and Michael Korda communicated with me about the American translation of Steiner's book.

I have decided to dedicate this book to two people. The first one is my former professor, Solon Beinfeld. When I was a young undergraduate, he introduced me both to French history and to Jewish history and contributed much to my decision, I hope a good one, to train for a scholarly career. Later, I relied on him countless times—benefiting from his providential presence in Paris the same year I spent some time there as a graduate student, and then again in Cambridge, Massachusetts, while I finished law school—for help in conceptualizing and executing this project and on his peerless knowledge of the historical cultures that overlap in this book. He also assisted me indispensably in gaining access to a number of sources, notably Yiddish materials. In the few years since then, he has read parts of what follows in several crude drafts and deserves the most credit for whatever there is of value in what I have made of this episode in the intersecting fields about which he has taught me so much. The parts that fail, of course, are my own fault.

Aside from those already mentioned, a number of friends and colleagues offered useful commentaries on the rough draft of this book, which guided my final revisions. I would especially like to acknowledge my teacher Martin Jay and my friend Paul Hanebrink, as well as the anonymous reader commissioned by the press, for their insightful remarks. I express my thanks to Phyllis Deutsch and her editorial and production team for seeing the manuscript into print.

This book is likewise dedicated to my grandfather, Henry Hutkin. He instructed me, from a young age, to remember the Holocaust and to be a Jew, directives that I found important enough to obey in life and perplexing enough to explore in what I have written. I owe most to my darling wife Alisa and the beautiful daughter, Lily Flore, she has given me. For the manifold blessings they have brought to my life, and the support they provided as I wrote this book, there is only my profound gratitude and abiding love—with no controversy whatever.

A Holocaust Controversy

1

The Interview: An Introduction to the Affair

It began in mid-March 1966, when Jean-François Steiner, then an unknown young man of twenty-eight, gave an interview to *Le Nouveau Candide*, a glossy, Gaullist magazine for which he had written as a journalist before cocooning himself away for a year and a half to emerge as the precocious author of *Treblinka: The Revolt of an Extermination Camp*.[1] Steiner's interview, timed to coincide with the book's publication, quickly became notorious, sparking a vituperative public controversy that lasted for a number of months as the book, with a preface by Simone de Beauvoir, and excerpts prominently published in the intellectual cynosure *Les Temps modernes* and the mass-circulation weekly *Le Nouvel Observateur*, vaulted to the top of the nonfiction bestseller list. (It sold over one hundred thousand copies in France by the end of the year.)[2] The text, once internationally well known as Holocaust studies first emerged, is now largely forgotten; but I shall argue in this book that it is centrally important to the emergence and development of post-Holocaust consciousness in France and beyond.

The cover of the issue of *Candide* in which the interview appeared, dated March 14, must have been designed to shock (though not necessarily to sell, for the magazine ordered an additional print run of the interview that it distributed free of charge). In large block letters, surrounding a swastika, the headline announces: THE JEWS: WHAT NO ONE EVER DARED TO SAY (figure 1). As of Steiner's response to the first question put him by the interviewer, Pierre Démeron, it is clear that an important moment of transition in French post-Holocaust discourse has arrived:

Q: Many books have been written on the death camps. Why a new one?

Steiner's answer is important because it denies the premise of the question.

A: There have been many books on concentration camps, on what used to be called the "camp universe" [*l'univers concentrationnaire*]. . . . And there have been thousands upon thousands of testimonies. But on the death camps specifically there has been very little, actually.

This answer heralds a shift in French post-Holocaust culture, to which the book made an important contribution, from a broadly universalist (and often antifascist) paradigm that assimilated the Holocaust to other Nazi crimes, including the internment of *résistants* so important in the French context, to a new regime of memory in which the Holocaust received specific attention as a phenomenon in its own right, separate from and irreducible to the continental war during which it took place or the more general Nazi system of terror that it consummated.

The phrase *univers concentrationnaire* to which Steiner referred dated from 1946, coined by David Rousset and used as the title of his early, internationally influential attempt to provide a unified conception of the Nazi internment system as a whole based on the author's specific experiences at the Western camp of Buchenwald.[3] It had become, thereafter, a stock phrase in antifascist but also Gaullist memory of the Nazi regime in France and beyond. Like any slogan, it implied an argument, one purveyed in the "many books" written about the Nazi regime in the twenty years after 1945. The argument assumed the unity of Nazi criminality beginning in 1933 with the repression and internment of the party's ideological (including political) opponents. For that reason, it risked occluding the eventual disproportion and specificity of Jewish victimhood at Nazi hands, marked institutionally by the rise of the death camps out of the concentration camp system in the midst of the war. This descriptive failure, shared by many contributors to the first international regime of memory, such as Rousset and many others, led to a massive explanatory loss in confronting the past.[4] Rousset, however, still living at the time *Treblinka* appeared and its principal critic in the debates it unleashed, believed that Steiner's new way of looking at things brought with it shortcomings of its own.

As in his interview, Steiner's inclusion of the phrase "extermination camp" in the subtitle of his book underlined his opposition to the dominant ten-

1. "The Jews: What No One Ever Dared to Say." Cover of *Le Nouveau Candide*, 14–20 March 1966.

dency. The book jacket, too, stressed that Treblinka differed from the concentration camps about which Frenchmen had already heard. "It was an extermination camp," it read. "Men, women, and children sent there were not asked to work themselves until they were reduced to animals or physically and intellectually exhausted. They were asked to die." Thus, Steiner's initial statement—novel at the time in France, repeated many times since, and still in need of occasional restatement—put the public on notice. Old myths were to be challenged.

■

As the interview continued, Steiner raised the two theses most associated with the controversy. The first argued—scandalously and for many offensively—for the shameful complicity of the victims of the genocide in their own death and the second for the necessity of finding heroes in the midst of an otherwise embarrassing tragedy. Henry Rousso has even suggested, in mentioning the controversy in passing in his classical work on "the Vichy syndrome," that the "furor" of the Treblinka affair occurred more thanks to these two theses announced in the interview than to the book itself.[5] Given their content, it is not surprising that this should be so. But in fact, the interview did not differ materially, except in its brazen and direct formulations, from the book whose sales it prepared.

When asked why death camps such as Treblinka had been avoided so far in favor of the concentration camps, Steiner replied that they had always been a sensitive topic and for good reason. For "in these camps the victims themselves, the Jews, made themselves into the accomplices of their own extermination. In Treblinka, as in all the other extermination camps, the Germans had designed 'the machine,' as they referred to the methods of extermination, in such a way that it would almost run itself. It is the Jews who did everything." In a manner reminiscent of parts of Raul Hilberg's *Destruction of the European Jews* or Hannah Arendt's *Eichmann in Jerusalem,* though with the zest of a controversialist rather than the sobriety of a political scientist or the acumen of a philosopher, Steiner thus claimed to direct his book at the "problem" of the Jews' complicity with the Nazis' homicidal plans. Of course, Steiner went beyond either of these figures in raising the specter, not simply of general passivity or elite compliance, but that of murderous participation too.

Though hard now to understand, such charges, in their various renditions, played an extraordinary role in the history of emerging Holocaust consciousness in the 1960s and into the 1970s. "Everyone takes up the subject without the slightest embarrassment," Elie Wiesel wrote in a text published in that same year of 1966, when he still counted mainly as a French-Jewish intellectual, although he had already begun to move between literary worlds. "[I]t is quite easy to blame the dead, to accuse them of the cowardice of complicity (in either the concrete or metaphysical sense of the term). . . . Who are we to judge them?"[6] But many, in this era, did so. It is therefore not coincidental that Hilberg, in whose masterwork of 1961 the phenomenon of passivity controversially figures, enthusiastically endorsed the English translation of Steiner's book for Simon and Schuster when it appeared in 1967. But practically nobody in France had ever heard of Hilberg's work (where it appeared in translation twenty years later).[7] Indeed, aside from Simone de Beauvoir, neither did many during the debate mention the Eichmann trial, which had contributed to transmitting what Hannah Arendt called the "cruel and silly" question posed during the trial, in Israel, about diaspora Jews: why had they died so willingly? This fact is probably explained by the importance of Arendt's own work in popularizing, outside Israel, the problems she thought the trial raised. In France, the *Treblinka* coverage in 1966 far outstripped the press coverage of Eichmann's trial in 1961.[8] And, save for a brief excerpt coinciding with *Treblinka*, Arendt's *Eichmann in Jerusalem* appeared in France in late 1966 *only after* Steiner's text and the controversy it occasioned, as the last chapter of this book will show.[9]

As a result, it is the Treblinka affair in France that may have the best claim to accomplishing in that country the "watershed in the public uses and public acceptance of discussion of Holocaust memory, a memory previously restricted to a relatively small, and relatively unknown coterie of scholars at the margins of the established disciplines."[10] The landmarks of Hilberg and Arendt, which make Steiner now seem redundant, when not reckless, in bringing supposedly uncomfortable truths about the period to light, and in the process bringing new aspects of the period itself into the public eye, did not yet exist or had little prominence in the French context. *Treblinka*'s brief moment of cultural priority on this major issue of the 1960s thus makes it unavoidable for historians interested in French Holocaust memory.

■

As his comments indicate, Steiner raised, for perhaps the first time before a large audience, the *Sonderkommandos* at Treblinka and the other Nazi death camps, squads of Jews who were conscripted laborers at genocidal killing centers. But Steiner did not merely want to identify the "problems" of the Jews' passivity, compliance, and participation, as epitomized in the—for him, unseemly—"collusion" in their own destruction. He wanted to work toward a solution to the persisting moral problem he thought such conduct, and even more its memory, presented. Indeed, Steiner's airing of the charge of Jewish passivity and compliance is impossible to understand except as a complaint against his own community meant to prepare the way for the revision of identity he hoped his book would help work.

In this regard, it mattered that Steiner, unlike Arendt and Hilberg, wrote as a self-consciously young man confused about the past, speaking for and to a new generation. "I wrote this book," he explained in his interview, "because I felt, not the indignation I had been taught, but the embarrassment of being a child of this people of whom six million allowed themselves to be led to slaughter like lambs. I am a Jew but I do not want to be pitied. And I am tired of hearing, each time a swastika is found scrawled on a urinal, that six million Jews were killed. I needed to find out exactly what happened." Out of dissatisfaction with one Jewish memory, in other words, Steiner set out to replace it with a countermemory—if he could find one. The surprise is that so many French Jews welcomed his proposal.

When Steiner investigated, he reported in the interview, he discovered that the well-known Warsaw ghetto revolt did not suit his needs in exhuming the past to suit his present-day search for identity. For the Warsaw Jews, according to Steiner, knew that their revolt would fail; ultimately, they chose death just as surely as those who simply let it overwhelm them. "Of course I had heard about the Warsaw ghetto revolt like everyone else," he told the interviewer, "but I did not find this hopeless revolt satisfying." In Jewish culture, he explained, what should really matter is not how one dies but whether one lives. "Pardon the expression, but [Warsaw] seemed very 'goy' as a revolt," Steiner commented with almost unbelievable and no doubt appalling condescension.

> The heroes of Warsaw chose the manner of their death but, in choosing death, they accepted it in a certain sense. There they sinned. The Treblinka revolt, on the other hand, seemed very different from the Warsaw revolt, from the first testimonies that I read. A man who wakes up in his barracks, who knows that it is today that his revolt will take place, he runs to the window and talks about what he sees in the distance beyond the barbed wire: the fields, the mist that rises between the copses and then, suddenly, the sun shining down. And then

he will say, "Today I will have those things." In this there is something exciting which warms you, whereas the stories of the Warsaw ghetto revolt leave you cold, so full they are of distress and hopelessness. The ghetto revolt ended in annihilation, whereas the Treblinka revolt ended in the escape of 600. . . . Many knew that they were going to die, but it was not in order to die that they revolted, but in order to live.

And that, Steiner explained, is why he chose the Treblinka revolt as a subject.[11] As well-known American journalist David Halberstam correctly summarized his point, reporting for the *New York Times* on the wide-ranging Parisian controversy that Steiner's theses had understandably provoked, "the more frail and less-known Treblinka uprising was Jewish in the sense that it was first and foremost for survival."[12]

Steiner certainly longed for commercial success—he conceived of his book as a popular "Western" about the Eastern European extermination camps—but he did not hide the personal and communal motive he intended, at least publicly or consciously, for his book to further; he explained quite clearly why he had come to the story of a few heroic Jews and their choice, so exceptional in light of the putative passivity of their coreligionists, of life in the face of extermination. Steiner never insisted that he had written a history, and while he would have rejected the label of "fiction" for his book, he freely admitted that parts of it had been imagined, to make the facts speak more truly. In the terms of the period, it was a "nonfiction novel" (Truman Capote's *In Cold Blood,* giving the enterprise of fictionalizing reality a famous name, appeared that same year). The fact that Steiner's book straddled genres, particularly on this most sensitive of subjects, and even more so than he acknowledged at the time, proved for many a serious mark against it. But it makes Steiner's work something of a counterhistory; he took as his most basic official aim to change the Jews' sense of who they were by retelling the facts in their own proprietary story with a new message. "The editor of my book asked me to delete a phrase, 'the professional mourners of history' [*les pleureuses de l'Histoire*], with which I stigmatized those who study history only to find material for hopelessness and lamentations," Steiner said in one interview. "But even if this phrase is gone, it is clear that this book is directed against those tearful ones who neglect heroism."[13] Ultimately, Steiner announced in the *Nouveau Candide* interview, his book's rude shift of emphasis would redound to the benefit of Jewish honor. Asked whether he feared that his campaign would backfire, in airing unseemly charges about Jews easily appropriable by antisemites, he replied: "Antisemites have never needed Jews to hate them and reject them, and therefore they did not need me." However much commotion it caused, his enterprise, he hoped, would, rather than ratify old prejudices, change not just the general but also the Jewish sense of the recent past.

■

From the incendiary point of departure provided in the interview, the Treblinka affair would rage for months before winding down in midsummer, as the praise and horror of multiple intellectual and cultural worlds rained down upon the young author. "It was Jeanne Moreau, drawing down the corners of her mouth," noted an American observer, "who spoke of the holiday crowds at Saint-Tropez: each winter-pale body turning gold in the sun and each pair of hands grasping at the covers of *Treblinka*."[14] The event provides new information against which to judge recent accounts of the transition in the 1960s between the two major regimes of memory of wartime—a transition about whose existence everyone agrees, but about whose moral implications practically no one does. Each of the factors that I examine in what follows— having begun with the interview, I will move to the author, from there to his book, and thence and in turn to various kinds of reaction—is worthy of attention in its own right. But only together do they add up to a controversy. And it is precisely as a *controversy* that I would like to examine this episode. The reasons for attempting this kind of treatment of Steiner's book—a kind of *histoire totale* from conception to publication to reception to aftermath— are perhaps obvious, but worth briefly enumerating nonetheless.

Most generally speaking, moments of crystallization and transition in public no less than in private life often occur as a result of precipitating conflict. The picture of how knowledge evolves offered in the recent philosophy of epistemological change is now practically second nature, but it is worth recalling the role usually conferred on the *dispute* in collapsing old paradigms and inaugurating new ones. "Historical instances of controversy over . . . intellectual practices," as a pathmarking book on such an event observes, "often involve disagreements over the reality of entities or the propriety of practices whose existence and value are subsequently taken to be unproblematic or settled."[15] It would not be too much to say that, like such high epistemic disputes, the Treblinka affair bore on the problem of how to describe the reality of the past and how to judge its consequences for life in the present and future. As in scientific affairs, so in other sectors of intellectual life: the controversy can mark the point when marginalized but troubling anomalies are brought to the fore, their discussion or resolution forced after long postponement. Accordingly, it is not coincidental that Steiner's book provoked some of the first statements on the genocide by new actors in the generation who would decisively shape what it would come to mean later in their country and indeed around the world—for example, Claude Lanzmann and Pierre Vidal-Naquet. In the end, a study of the Treblinka controversy is only a case study; neither the first nor the last of the Holocaust controversies even in France, the Treblinka affair, however illuminating, is in the end just one among others.[16] But while it is manifestly an error to collapse a long process of development into a single decisive moment, the importance of events in catalyzing gestalt switches is also worthy of attention and reflection.

An attempt to capture the totality of the positions in a public debate also allows a glimpse of a cross section of social actors in disparate milieux for whom the single event or production provides a brief and rare point of convergence. The very fact of the controversy, in a sense, creates evidence about the configuration of identities at a particular moment available no other way. A study of the Treblinka affair can help fix the state of knowledge at a particular time in France among different groups, from the "heights" of Jean-Paul Sartre's coterie to the "depths" of the immigrant communities who wrote and read Yiddish-language dailies. Indeed, it is potentially useful, in a sense, to interpret the objects of controversies as subsidiary in importance, since their function is sometimes almost purely occasional or pretextual: they simply provide the lightning rod for the preexisting but previously insulated energies that animate the dispute to be sparked. It is in this sense that the object of conversation may even turn out to matter less than the fact of the conversation itself—even when, as in the *dialogue de sourds* of the Treblinka affair, the voices of some are broadcast widely and others are too soft (or in the wrong language) to be heard. Above all, in this book, I have sometimes slighted the explicit subject matter of the debate in order to see what changes the discussion itself may have helped enact or at least reflect. Thus, in the chapters on the general and intra-Jewish debates about Steiner's book, I have focused less intently on the accuracy of Steiner's book or the painful charges of complicity he intended to raise. For it turns out that those discussions illuminate, more obliquely and often unintentionally, matters that were in my judgment of more enduring significance: one chapter, for example, attempts to use the Treblinka affair to examine how the post-Holocaust French-Jewish community searched for the truth about its identity, as a new generation arose.

But the Treblinka affair is not just any controversy. It is a Holocaust controversy. More than with any other event, perhaps, the meaning of "the Holocaust," as it began to be called in English around the time of the Treblinka affair, has been worked out through a series of contentious and often commercialized public disputes. It would take too much space to name them all, and in any case it is not necessary since they have been, as even the casual observer knows, wholly integral and indispensable to the way the Holocaust has come to be framed and understood. Aimed at a wide public, Steiner's book—like several more recent cultural productions on the topic of the genocide whose marketing incited and then depended on a whiff of scandal—succeeded in reaching it. "Silence over the murder, scandal over the books," as George Steiner's aphorism on the Treblinka affair had it, in a comment that would apply to numerous later events.[17]

The commercial aspects of the affair were not negligible. Later, Vidal-Naquet would reminisce that Steiner's book had been marketed as skillfully—in other words, as amorally—"as if it had been a new brand of soap."[18] A charge to which the author of the book in question, who agreed with Vidal-Naquet about little else, responded: "No, better."[19] The topic came to the attention of the public, then, through means that many observers understandably considered unseemly and hurtful in the extreme; for one observer, the publicity campaign for the book, though "perfectly mounted," also put the book under a cloud, since it required pedestrians to walk through a Paris in which thousands of swastikas—*Le Nouveau Candide*'s sensational cover image—covered the walls for the first time since the dark years of the German occupation. "For a whole week," this observer bitterly remarked, the swastikas

> were there honorably. It wasn't a matter of graffiti, scrawled illicitly by malcontented hooligans on urinals in pencil or chalk. No, these thousands of swastikas were very dearly printed up, and with careful premeditation. In large format, to pierce everyone's vision, even from a distance. Proudly displayed on a white background surrounded by red: as if they came directly from the workshop of Goebbels. . . . Even more striking, they were there accompanied by the screaming headline, reminiscent of *Der Stürmer*, of so vile a memory . . . [20]

The cover of *Le Nouveau Candide* provides only the first graphic element in the Treblinka affair, and the images reproduced in the following chapters do not merely illustrate the affair; they were part of its essential dynamics.

But such commercialism is only one structural feature of the recurrent Holocaust controversies of the age. Though no doubt unique in the extremity and tastelessness of its advertising, the Treblinka affair helped establish the now familiar pattern of success typically involving widespread publicity coupled with grandiose claims of staggering innovations and shattered taboos that, plausible or not, boost sales into the stratosphere. Popular success, in such cases, leaves behind not just the question why a work largely rejected by scholars was so victorious in public, and offers not just another occasion for criticism of the psychological and self-interested motivations of those who produced it. Whether deserved or not, legitimate or not, their success makes such works historical landmarks. The often partial, superannuated, or bizarre conceptual frameworks they may propose, made inescapable by public controversy, become practically unavoidable intermediaries even for intimate and private reflection on the controversial subject. It is this fact that makes the historical evaluation of public argumentation and rhetoric—in contemporary parlance, of discursive representation—so important. This consideration is applicable to the framing of all public meaning but, by virtue of the frequency of Holocaust controversies, provides an especially important justification for their study.

Finally, and most specifically, the Treblinka affair is a French controversy, and it is also important to view it accordingly. In postwar French culture, as already ought to be clear, it raised, intentionally, substantive issues very similar to those Arendt's *Eichmann in Jerusalem* raised elsewhere and inadvertently.[21] But it appeared in a critically different national context. It is mainly significant as a French controversy, I will try to show, insofar as it undermined the dominant universalist (and specifically antifascist) regime of memory that had proved especially powerful to that point. As noted, it was amongst the consequences of the dominance of antifascist, or more generally *résistantialiste* memory, to blur the central historical difference between the project of concentration camps begun shortly after the Nazi seizure of power and the program of Jewish extermination begun only during wartime. And so I focus with special intensity on the process of separation of the one from the other, a transition with weighty cultural ramifications. What is, I think, special about the Treblinka affair is that it occurred at a moment of pivot, and therefore it allows, perhaps better than any other episode, comparison and contrast of the two major regimes of memory of French postwar life.

It is true, of course, that this difference between concentration and extermination had to emerge everywhere for, as Peter Novick observes, even in American popular culture it took many years for the Holocaust to be understood as "a distinct and separate process, separate from Nazi criminality in general." In the first edition of his landmark *Destruction of the European Jews*, Raul Hilberg could decry "the constant emphasis in the literature and in speeches upon 'concentration camps,' often including the epitomization of Dachau and Buchenwald but rarely embracing any mention of Auschwitz, let alone the faraway camps of Treblinka and Sobibor or Belzec." It is emblematic of the pivotal change under study in this book that, late in his 1996 work exclusively on the Jewish fate, Daniel Jonah Goldhagen must remind the reader that "not only Jews inhabited the concentration camp system." Where once concentration subsumed extermination, now the reverse is sometimes true, making the need for the original distinction unnecessary.[22]

In France, however, the idea of the unity of Nazi crime proved especially tenacious, for a number of reasons, some morally attractive and some not. Even many Jews were wedded to the deportation interpretation that, for a long time, barred the emergence of "the Holocaust" as an isolable object of historical and memorial perception. So although—as multinational research has shown—this perceptual shift occurred in nearly all countries, the French case presents its own dramatic specificity; and its study illuminates a surprisingly long-lasting moral conflict that continues to be felt even in current historical and philosophical debates. Even more general causes for the isolation of the Holocaust, like the crucial if neglected factor of the Christianization of the Jewish tragedy that also entered decisively in the Treblinka affair, had their own locally French inflection. It is perhaps in these most basic of senses that the Treblinka affair counts as "a Holocaust controversy," for it contributed powerfully to the processes by which it became possible to perceive and describe the Holocaust at all. In France, the original construction of the memory of the war lingered long into the 1960s, and the Treblinka affair is one of the most significant signals and causes of its ongoing displacement during the crucial and transitional years in which the ways that contemporary societies understand the last global upheaval, and the crimes perpetrated during it, were entirely rethought.

2

Author and Text

No one had ever heard of Jean-François Steiner when his outrageous interview set the Treblinka controversy in motion. But his lineage—familial and ideological—is important. To understand the dynamics of the affair, much preparation is required. This chapter surveys what information there is about Steiner's background and personality prior to 1966, before turning to his text. It cannot purport to provide anything but a sketchy portrait of the author and young man, for unlike the controversy itself, the evidence for reconstructing his personality and thought is too spare and refractory, and interpretation difficult. Nonetheless, certain elements of Steiner's past and of his itinerary toward *Treblinka* stand to illuminate what the source of his ideas was, why he may have written the book, and how inextricably interwoven were intergenerational psychology and contemporary politics in the making of this specific controversy, as they were in the formation of Holocaust consciousness in general. More important, these personal elements deserve to be reviewed because, to the extent Steiner cut a public persona during the controversy (or people speculated about his motives), they became caught up in it. In the end, however, there is the text of *Treblinka* itself, open to close analysis now in order to understand how it could have been so open to alternative interpretations and rival appropriations then.

■

The future author and controversialist Jean-François Steiner was born in 1938 in France, the child of the Polish Jew Kadmi Cohen and his wife, a French

Catholic by birth who converted to Judaism before marriage. Cohen's importance is signaled in the dedication Steiner chose for the book: "To the memory of Kadmi Cohen, who gave me life and to Ozias Steiner, who taught me to love it." Who was Kadmi Cohen? Steiner's father proves on examination no less unusual a figure in the history of modern French-Jewish identities than his son and is in some ways almost as important to the scandal because of the intergenerational legacy he appears to have left behind. His own life, and especially his beliefs about the nature of Jewish particularity, consequently require some discussion for those of his son to be understood.

Born in Lodz in 1892, (Isaac) Kadmi Cohen first traveled to Palestine in 1910 to study (after World War I, his parents, who were early followers of Theodor Herzl, emigrated). As a young man, Cohen trained as a lawyer in Switzerland and, after military service on the French side in World War I allowed his French naturalization, became a member of the Parisian bar. He earned a doctorate in Oriental languages and cultures, writing his dissertation on Semitic studies, and in his maturity published a number of forgotten books that propounded an extreme version of the Zionist conclusion that modern antisemitism had bankrupted the emancipationist dream of integration.[1]

In this and other respects, Cohen's place in history is that of a rare follower and publicist of Vladimir Jabotinsky's Zionist Revisionist ideology in France in the interwar period (Jabotinsky and Cohen were personally acquainted from the former's time in Paris in the formative years of his organization). Nevertheless, Cohen's rhetoric is worth reviewing to understand his beliefs about Jewish heroism and particularity. In his *Nomades,* his "essay on the Jewish soul" of 1929, Cohen brazenly took the virulence of recent and contemporary antisemitism as proof of the existence of "Semitism" as a racial and spiritual set, not just as a past historical phenomenon but as a persisting set of collective traits. "The negative is irrefutable proof of the positive," he maintained.[2] Cohen's initial attempt to define Semitism as restless and eternal nomadism consisted in an inversion rather than a negation of antisemitic canards of the day. Around the same time as *Nomades,* Cohen published a controversial series of articles in the *Mercure de France* announcing the failure and advocating the renewal of Zionism, which he envisaged as "neither nationalist, nor economic, nor political, but metaphysical." For Cohen, Zionism ultimately drew "its origins from the profound faith in the particularity of the Jewish self, and the necessity of protecting it," and he spoke of "the necessity of preserving the originality of the Jewish essence from any adulteration."[3]

During the course of the 1930s, as the pressure of events created a huge diversity in Jewish ideology, and Revisionism itself evolved, Cohen extended these themes, becoming among the most radical propagandists for Jewish nationalism in a country whose Jews remained by and large allergic to all forms of Zionism through 1948 and beyond.[4] (Recently, Cohen has received attention for another of his passions, the hatred of America and its values, themes to which he devoted a venomous text).[5] In essence a counternationalist like Jabotinsky, Cohen eventually became, in his exaggerated dreams of a Zionist empire stretching from Iran to Egypt, *plus royaliste que le roi*. Cohen's furious search for a positive, enabling content to Jewish identity and his idiosyncratic attempt to invert the nationalist delirium of the Jews' racist opponents as if they possessed a power to be envied were, it would seem to some, part of a syndrome that he appeared to have passed on to his son.

Cohen's most audacious and revealing book for these purposes, perhaps, is the one called *L'État d'Israël*, which he published in 1930.[6] The book began by suggesting that, so far, Zionism had failed. For Cohen, the plans for a Zionist state as imagined in the prior few decades, because of their modesty and partiality, had simply added another ideological option for Jews without providing a complete and unanimously agreed-upon solution to the "Jewish question" of modern times. But for Cohen, a new Zionism would have to strive for such unanimity; by definition, any solution that further factionalized the Jews failed. To avoid this outcome, anticipating Jabotinsky's own sensitivity to the claims of Jewish religiosity, Cohen argued that the new Zionism would have to overcome the contemporary rivalry between religious and assimilationist European Jewries; the former were forgetful that religion amounted to a proxy in exile for Jewish particularity ultimately separable from law and ritual, while the latter simply refused to see that normality would not occur among strangers. For religious Jews, a return to Jewish political autonomy would make religion dispensable by creating conditions for Jewish particularity without it; for assimilationist Jews, Zionist politics would, likewise, provide the nonminority status that assimilationists wanted but could not have because of their stubborn resistance to leaving Europe behind. A vision of specifically Jewish normality would satisfy both sides, but only once transplanted to a new land.

More interestingly, perhaps, Cohen thought that a Zionist enterprise, while providing a European foothold in "reawakening" Asia, would actually return Jews to the Semitic roots they shared with Arabs, the roots he had uncovered in his dissertation, allowing (and forcing) their common participation in the creation of a renewed Semitic civilization, a kind of cooperative national rebirth. Indeed, Cohen supported a "binational" (in his word, "Pansemitic") state, in which Jews and Arabs would have parity (possible because world Jewry would emigrate and necessary because the grandiose scope of the project would perforce involve the inclusion of many Arabs in the state).

What these political and logistical considerations would make possible, Cohen averred, was a genuine forum for inexpungeable Jewish particularity, about the content of which, however, Cohen remained vague. It was clear enough, however, that, along with religion, he also rejected "gentilization" (associated by Cohen with David Ben-Gurion), in the name of a futurist and renewed version of ancient particularity. Of course, it could not take its old theocratic form. But, in a line reminiscent of other promises of those years that somehow fused loyalty to the past with a vision of a radically new future, Cohen suggested that "Zionism has something Nietzschean about it." For "[i]t involves the transvaluation of all the values on which Jews have been living for two thousand years. Without abolishing anything, it will have to transform everything—and is already doing so."[7] Such rightist, separatist rhetoric explains why Pierre Vidal-Naquet, whose career would run crucially through the Treblinka affair, later termed Cohen "an extremist Zionist of insane bent."[8]

The coming of World War II provided the last forum for Cohen's response to antisemitism with Jewish heroism. Initially rounded up in October of 1941 and interned at the camps of Drancy and Compiègne, Cohen secured a release, apparently for health reasons. Thereafter, in the midst of the Vichy years, Cohen became involved in a curious venture known as Masada, named after the fortress in ancient Judaea where the Zealot Jews who had defeated the Roman garrison retreated for their heroic last stand, and their suicide, in the first century. Cohen founded the Masada movement in the Compiègne camp, where he gave a series of rousing and illuminating lectures on its purpose and spirit.[9] Mostly, these lectures repeated his long-incubating ideas about the fate and future of the Jews and the radical solution to the Jewish question he recommended—except that, speaking in the grim forum of the camp, his pessimism about existing alternatives to his brand of heroism seemed ratified by the course of contemporary history. Very clearly now, assimilation had been bankrupted; open to individuals to attempt if they wished (a chancy experiment given its failure in all Jewish history), it could not, Cohen insisted, provide any definitive solution and might hurt as much as it helped resolve the collective quandary.[10] Cohen also repeated his response to the reduction of Judaism to religion. In Jewish history, religion had played the signal role of saving the Jews in response to their ancient defeats. Indeed, Zionism had erred in siding with secularism, since religion at its best inculcated in Jews "self-respect, confidence in their strength, certainty in their preeminence, and pride in their origins." To be sure, Jews would have to reject rabbinic religiosity once they founded their state, in the same way that the butterfly left its chrysalis, but only to return to and reinvent the marriage of politics and religion the Jewish nation once possessed and lost in defeat. In fact Masada, Cohen proclaimed, emphatically supported the rebuilding of the destroyed Temple, as part of a new *Culte Nationale* that would arise on the ruins of transvalued religion, just as the Talmud would disappear into the archives to be replaced by a new one, and Tisha b'Av, the day of Jewish national mourning, would give way to a celebration of national grandeur.[11] In response to newer ideological currents of the 1930s, and like many other nationalists of the day, Cohen emphasized that his ideology counted as the true socialism and the true populism.[12] For these reasons, the founding of Masada would represent "the turning point in Jewish history," eradicating antisemitism by abolishing its causes.[13] In the near term, Cohen felt that the movement's main mission had to be ideological: to convince as many Jews as possible (and Jewish youth in particular) to join up in order for it to be a force at the peace conference that would conclude the present global conflict. But it ultimately aimed at nothing less than the Jewish state with the expansive borders (and the Arab citizenship) that Cohen had been advocating for more than a decade.[14]

Cohen's rhetoric reached its peak, in his impassioned speeches in the internment camp, in his defense of Jewish dynamism and his identification of the shameful "spirit of the ghetto" as the movement's only genuine enemy. In explaining why the movement had taken the name of Masada, Cohen called those ancient Jews who had heroically resisted "supermen" (*surhommes*) who had saved the self-respect of Israel through war even as religious authorities ensured the physical continuity of the nation at a moment of political catastrophe. The heroes had died, but the new partisans of Masada would take up where they left off. "The Crusades, the Inquisition, the Black Death, the Chmielnicki and later pogroms and—why not say it?—these concentration camps in which we are suffering, have they ever succeeded in overcoming us and leading us to surrender?" Cohen asked rhetorically. "Our own enemies have been shocked and amazed that alone against the whole world we dared to resist them victoriously—and that we even succeeded in dominating them."[15] He finished:

> My dear compatriots, we must make our people understand what the creation
> of our movement in this concentration camp means. I do not know what the
> enemy's motive might have been in interning us. It may have been to terrorize,
> by the example of our fate, those who are still free. But if he intended to break
> us, to break our moral resistance, to annihilate our will to live and fight, the
> enemy erred greatly. The creation, precisely here, at Polizeihaftlager-Frontstalag
> 122, of the movement for complete national renaissance, provides the irrefrag-
> able proof and constitutes the undeniable testimony of this fact. I have no ha-
> tred against the enemy who shut us away in this hell. I even have gratitude to
> him for having revealed us to ourselves. That he did it unintentionally and in-
> voluntarily does not matter, since the result followed. In the hunger that tor-
> tures us, in the cold that makes us shiver, in the terror that weighs on us, we
> have been able to measure all of our true capacities. Trapped, without exit,
> without space, without even hope, we did not fall apart but instead took heart.
> If we took the name of Masada, it is because, like our ancestors of that illustri-
> ous central site in our history, we dared, in the midst of general destruction, to
> face up to our destiny.

In such circumstances, the true enemy could only be internal, the part of the
self that hesitated before fate, and cowered before opportunity. "After all,
there is something at once sublime and exalting to be declared the implacable
enemy of the greatest military power on earth," Cohen confessed. "Though
cowards tremble, I am proud."[16] Simply calling the Jews to their hopes,
Cohen explained, would "liberate the irresistible and all-powerful forces that
sleep in them and which they do not yet realize they have."[17]

After his serendipitous release, as the war advanced and the "Final Solution" began in earnest, Cohen acted on his plan to save his people from the
false alternatives of the day. He entertained the thought that the ruling right-
wing government of Vichy could be convinced to support a separatist Zionist solution to the Jewish question; and he befriended the Abbé Joseph Catry,
a former Jesuit who had left his order because he feared its philosemitic and
philo-Masonic drift, in order to collaborate in a common enterprise. In this
endeavor, Cohen may have been following Jabotinsky's own occasional advice to cooperate with enemies for a mutual resolution of the so-called Jewish question; already in the interwar period, Cohen had become close to opposite numbers in reactionary movements of the day, notably including
Xavier Vallat, the man, like Cohen a war-veteran activist and Parisian lawyer,
who would head the Commisariat général aux questions juives for a time
under the Vichy regime.[18] Cohen influenced Catry to see in Zionism a solu-

tion to the Jewish question haunting Europe, since it might "offer the possibility of getting Jews out of France no less effectively than the Germans were doing," but with a new destination: Zion. In response, Catry proposed to Pétain, through his circle, that "exodus replace assimilation as the ancient goal of French policy."[19] Their proposals, taken quite seriously by Vichy policymakers, were advertised by Cohen as a "positive, constructive antisemitism."[20] But with countervailing resistance from others at Vichy and eventual rejection from German authorities, Cohen's proposals, apparently relatively widely circulated, were ultimately rebuffed. He found himself interned once again; this time, he did not escape. Jean-François saw his father last at the age of five. Kadmi Cohen, deported from Drancy on March 27, 1944, died in Gleiwitz, one of Auschwitz's many subcamps, soon after.[21]

■

It is hard to say with perfect assurance, of course, what legacy the father left to the son. It is not simply that nuanced evidence is not available but that it would involve controversial psychological speculation. Still, it would be equally irresponsible to deny any and all link between Cohen's beliefs, activities, and fate and Steiner's mind-set in the period during which he composed his book. Indeed, Steiner's case, and the Treblinka affair generally, suggest that Dominick LaCapra is surely right to insist on how much is lost if one chooses decisively between the two main paradigms for studying individual and collective memory that have emerged in recent decades. According to one paradigm, the "psychological" approach, a traumatic event in the personal, communal, or national past leads to a syndrome that, depending on the case and the theory, might involve the forgetfulness of repression, the fixation of constantly reexperienced pain, acting out, working through, melancholia, mourning, and so forth (or some or all of the above in stages); the overall image is that of the past controlling the present. According to the second, or "political," approach, the present configuration of ideologies dictates the uses (and abuses) to which the past will be subject; the overall image is that of the present controlling the past. Where the one paradigm tends to hypothesize a weak agent in the grip of often debilitating memory, the other presents a strong agent manipulating history to suit his purpose. But LaCapra convincingly emphasizes that there is no "simple choice between acknowledging the pressure of the past and recognizing the ways present interests shape approaches to it."[22]

The Treblinka affair makes abundantly clear how necessary it is to combine both of these two manners of considering Holocaust (or any other) memory, beginning with its origins in the biography of Jean-François Steiner himself. The fact that much of what follows illustrates how fundamentally the function of contending solidarities (for example, leftist or ethnic) images of the past were, or that Steiner himself had a particular set of views, cannot obscure the crucial reality that many of the actors—again, beginning with Steiner himself—had a direct or barely mediated relationship with a deeply traumatic past. Politicized and media-driven though the controversy was, in a great many respects, one can easily interpret the author of *Treblinka* as undertaking in the writing of his book an extended and highly personal act of mourning (successful or not) for his father. In any case, a number of clear continuities emerge between father and son. First, both were committed to what one can call an ideology of heroism that prized strength over weakness and activism over abjection in response to threat. In the second place, they shared the view that humanist universalism and Jewish particularism are competitive and mutually exclusive ideologies: "there are two truths, two logics, and two moralities," Cohen put it at his most pithy, "the ones specifically Jewish and the others generally human."[23] These opinions would find themselves channeled, as it were, into Steiner's book, as if the father's principles allowed the son to reinterpret the circumstances of his family's tragedy, and that of the people his father had wanted, in his brutally foreshortened life, to redeem.

■

The dust jacket of *Treblinka* notes that Steiner's mother, "concerned to give her children the education that their father would have wanted, remarried with a Jewish physician." It referred, like the book's dedication, to Ozias Steiner, who helped raise her son and provided whatever familiarity with Judaism he had growing up. When Steiner legally adopted Jean-François Cohen, in 1952, his son became Jean-François Cohen-Steiner, later shortened in the military and as a pen name to Jean-François Steiner, as he was generally known during the controversy.

Already as a teenager, it seems, the future author of *Treblinka* began a search for a way to imagine Judaism, as his father had, as a heroic enterprise. In his late teens, Steiner decided to spend a year and a half in Israel, but he rejected the practical incarnation of his father's earlier Zionist fervor for reasons he would explain in public (along with the rest of his views about the options available for Jews in his own day) in the midst of the controversy's fury.[24] While there, it is clear, he imbibed, as a premise and a challenge, the stock image of diaspora Jews and Holocaust victims, often analyzed now, that circulated in Zionist ideology and Israeli life, especially before the evolution of Israeli attitudes toward the Holocaust that followed from the Eichmann trial of 1961 and the Six-Day War of 1967. "The Holocaust," Tom Segev reports of a fairly generalized attitude, "came to be seen as a general defeat. Its victims were censured for having let the Nazis murder them without fighting for their lives or at least for the right to 'die with honor.' This attitude in time became a sort of psychological and political ghost that haunted the State of Israel—reflecting scorn and shame, hubris and dread, injustice and folly."[25] Steiner clearly absorbed such perceptions in his teenage trip, but found them hard to reconcile with the activist defiance of his father.

Not long after, once having taken university classes, Steiner joined an airborne unit in Algeria during the war there, an experience he later memorialized in his remarkable literary debut in *Les Temps modernes*.[26] Already in this article, which is a study of the transformation wrought on young men through their induction in the military, Steiner showed a proclivity for the moral analytics of strength and weakness. "Before their military service, narrowly confined in the repose of their lives," he explained, "these young men who will become airborne troops often live mediocre lives, lowering their heads and submitting to the wishes of others." But their military training changes this obsequious compliance, for it gives them "the promise of taking part one day in superhumanity." They start to "dream of terrible fighting which lasts for days and days." And though initially the soldier in training "lives through an agonizing contradiction which tears him apart" between his fear of his enemy on the one hand and his desire for superhumanity on the other, the latter eventually wins out. "To choose 'superhumanity,'" Steiner supposed, "is to realize that fear is simply the first obstacle. It provokes a hatred for the enemy. . . . This hatred is violent, sovereign; it seizes one's being completely. A little like love, it fills one with a new power."

The alternatives of humiliation and power, and the psychological transit from one to the other, are striking anticipations of the dialectic of cowardice and heroism Steiner would claim to find in his study of the Treblinka revolt: "The enemy," Steiner wrote of the resulting transformation, "is no longer menacing and his existence ceases to be a source of humiliation; he is, on the contrary, the object which permits courage to reawaken itself, and the mold in which heroism is cast."[27] At this time in his life, Steiner considered himself on the left politically, as his stepfather, once a communist who had fought during the Spanish Civil War in the International Brigades, had taught him.

But there is no denying the continuities between Kadmi Cohen's rhetoric and Steiner's alluring portrait of paratrooper life, and there is little doubt that Steiner would soon read his Holocaust sources through the moral lens his airborne service had provided him, a lens that placed a premium on Nietz-schean overcoming and self-transformation in the crucible of violent conflict, as part of a struggle for survival against all odds.

After his military service, Steiner began work as a Parisian journalist, writing for *L'Express, Combat, Réalités,* and *Le Nouveau Candide* itself. In fact, many of his articles for the Gaullist magazine that would play such a role in the success of his book dealt with Algerian politics after the French departure, most of them not very subtly insinuating the conclusion that the new regime, controlled and staffed from outside (notably by leftists), represented no improvement on the French colonialism it replaced.[28] His editor—and former Gaullist spymaster—Constantin Melnik of Fayard suggested to him that he write a book on the subject of Reinhard Heydrich, one of the fore-most organizers of the Final Solution, assassinated in 1942.[29] In the period, Melnik cultivated young authors, frequently allowing them access, through his government connections, to secret information that would give their books the virtue of novelty and, often, the whiff of scandal that Melnik knew would boost sales. Around the same time, Melnik assisted and published an-other protégé, Gilles Perrault, likewise a former paratrooper, who wrote a number of successful books for Fayard with Melnik's help.[30] As for Steiner, in spite of Melnik's proposition, it turned out that Jean Cau, a much better-known writer and winner of the Prix Goncourt for his novel *The Mercy of God* of 1961, had resolved to write about the SS for the same publisher. Be-cause of the vague similarity of the subjects, Cau's project made Steiner's superfluous. As he cast about for a new topic, Steiner recalled an article by Abba Kovner he had read shortly before, translated in *Amif,* the journal of the French-Jewish physicians' association. Originally written and published in Hebrew soon after the war, the text, published in French in 1964, became the catalyst for Steiner's turn to Treblinka as a new subject. It movingly sketches the entire moral landscape the protagonists of his book would in-habit, and so is a critical document in its own right.[31]

■

A hero of the Vilna partisan movement, eventually amongst the most impor-tant Hebrew poets of the twentieth century, Kovner (1913–1987) is fre-quently credited as the first, while a young man in occupied Europe, to see in the scattered Nazi crimes against the Jews in fast-captured Lithuania an organized attempt at the extermination of his people. In a famous meeting at a Vilna public kitchen during the night of December 31, 1941, that Steiner would dramatize in his book, Kovner announced the need for resistance to avoid—in a phrase he coined and later said he regretted—"going like lambs to the slaughter."[32] He followed his own advice, participating in partisan activities from inside the ghetto and, after its destruction, leading the movement from the forest. In the immediate postwar reflections that so influenced Steiner, which were delivered as a lecture in prestate Israel at a Palmach meeting, Kovner broached the problem of the Jewish passivity he had witnessed and tried to combat, recounting how it had obsessed him mentally and emotionally throughout the war. As already noted, this "problem" became an international public and scholarly concern in the period of the 1960s and 1970s; that Kovner's historically prescient deliberations were revived then, in France through Steiner, is itself significant.

The lecture, which profoundly influenced Steiner's manner of thinking about the war, recounted the shame Kovner experienced, in spite of the heroism of his own survival, when he faced the question of why so many of his people had barely resisted their fate. In its opening sections, Kovner argued that the courage and resistance of the Jews had been underrated (in part because of their participation in partisan groups of various nationalities), just as the passivity of other populations had been occluded by their hagiographic celebration of the few heroes that emerged from the midst of their own basic compliance. "The [Jews] who disappeared did so like a herd, like sheep. But it would be an affront to their name if one did not add at least that everyone else disappeared the same way," he remarked. "Thanks to this parallel between Israel and the Gentiles, the memory of the passivity of our millions of victims should make no one blush." Yet, in spite of this basic insight, Kovner in the end insisted on the necessity of regarding Jewish passivity as a moral problem, special and different from the submission of other peoples. "It is necessary to plumb this darkness, not in the hope of finding a balm for our wounds, but to uncover and lay bare the mystery of that hecatomb, one which once uncovered will be a lesson and warning," Kovner said.[33]

What such an inquiry revealed, Kovner reported, is that the Jews died in spirit before they died in body, allowing themselves to be led to extinction because they had already been led to view themselves as worthy of death. The true tragedy, Kovner affirmed, consisted of an "abdication" of life. It had been arranged "satanically" by the Nazis, who trafficked in illusion and carefully withheld from the Jews the reality of their impending fate, always leaving them slender grounds, until the end, to rescue the delusion of hope from the reality of desperation. It was precisely because they never faced their enemy without mediation, in a diabolically arranged trap, that the Jews submitted to his design with such compliance. The Nazis were not new versions of the Cossacks of old or like Simon Petliura, the Jews' more recent foe and scourge. Kovner referred to the novel challenge that the Nazis threw up as "the art of murder." Somehow, in this atmosphere of illusion and abasement, of course, a miracle occurred: the idea of heroic resistance emerged. Hence Kovner's title: "The Miracle in Abdication." He closed his remarks with a parable, about a Vilna grave digger who discovered in the cemetery, amidst death, a woman who had escaped from Ponary (the nearby site where the Vilna Jews were being taken and massacred) and gave birth to a child before his eyes. The parable explained why Kovner could single out Jewish passivity from that of other peoples: in order to single out the reversal of their fate that followed as a sequel. "In this moment, here, in the midst of such a people," Kovner finished, "I also hear a cry—the cry of a newborn in a tomb."[34]

But while offering a redemptive, uplifting interpretation of the war years and the Holocaust, Kovner could not avoid the expression of an undercurrent of nagging doubt in his lecture. The minority who escaped the syndrome of abdication, he explained, were not dedicated to the goal of defeating the enemy or even ensuring their own survival. Instead, they adopted the goal of vindicating the Jews' honor, the project of dying in revolt rather than in passive submission. But what counted as honor, Kovner asked rhetorically, in this moral universe in which so many Jews trusted the Führer's assurances that they were merely in the midst of resettlement, in which Jews participated as police in anti-Jewish atrocities, in which Jews insisted on remaining quietly in the ghetto even in the course of its liquidation? The only ones who came to the decision to resist were those, Kovner said, who had given up their illusions of survival. But they were fighting for the stained honor of the thousands who had been led to abdicate everything. And so while he refused to concede that the choice of partisanship had been an act of hopelessness, no moral victory emerged with absolute clarity from the horror, in spite of Kovner's attempt at a rousing conclusion.[35]

As Steiner's *Nouveau Candide* interview testified, and an examination of his book will amply confirm, Steiner accepted Kovner's portrait of the moral challenge to which he would hold up the Treblinka revolt as a solution that the Jews in the midst of the tragedy only rarely found. In search of a subject,

Steiner saw the possibilities in Kovner's article, whose narrative of resistance conflicted with the dominant representation of the Holocaust in Israel and also, he thought, in the Europe of his father.

When Melnik accepted Steiner's proposal to write the story of the Jewish resistance in wartime, Steiner set to work to find a way of approaching the subject, searching in particular for a self-contained, dramatic episode that would make a workable book. After laboring for several months without success at the Parisian Centre de documentation juive contemporaine (the major French research center on the genocide then and now), Steiner traveled to Israel, where he hit upon the story of the Treblinka revolt. Kovner's article does not mention Treblinka except as a place of abasement and mortality, but Steiner came to believe its dramatization would both illustrate Kovner's propositions and point beyond them. Once Steiner had selected that revolt, he read the few published treatments of life in the camp and the revolt that destroyed it; then he relied on unpublished survivors' interviews—housed at the then decade-old Holocaust memorial, Yad Vashem, where Rachel Auerbach, director of its testimony collection, aided him both with written materials she had collected and with conducting a significant number of live re-interviews. Upon publication of the book, French audiences would be informed by a *Paris-Match* photographic spread, with a number of individual portraits, that Steiner had done so, a fact also noted in a text whose reliance on oral testimony seemed to vouch for its authenticity (it would not become known in the midst of the controversy but, as a later chapter will show, Auerbach and many of the survivors came to very much regret the help they had given the young author).[36] Steiner also drew on materials from the Düsseldorf trial in 1964–1965 of ten of the main Nazi perpetrators at Treblinka. This documentation in hand, upon his return from Israel, Steiner composed his text. (See figure 2.)

■

Jean-François Steiner's beliefs and motivations at the time he wrote *Treblinka* are perhaps impossible to fathom completely, and for a history of the book's reception, they are far from the most important concern. But there are some grounds for crediting his own understanding of what drove him. Schooled in Israel, as a young man, on a contemptuous attitude toward Holocaust victims, an attitude that his own father's case made seem limited if not mistaken, Steiner, it seems, wanted to show that both the abject passivity that Kovner deplored and the radical activism that would overcome it—whether

2. Jean-François Steiner in 1966. *L'Arche,*
April 1966.

in the Masada movement, Jewish partisanship, or in Zionist state-building—
were not so much mutually exclusive opposites as related and continuous. "I
knew this attitude," Steiner explains of the radical critique of the diaspora,

> from my time in Israel . . . [and] I wrote the book, among other reasons, to
> show that the "disgusting cowardice" that Israelis stigmatized was only an ap-
> pearance and that the Jews of the diaspora also knew, at Treblinka, how to show
> a courage perhaps even greater than their own—so there existed no break be-
> tween those there and here, between them and us, but rather a perfect conti-
> nuity, and that they did not invent the courage of which they were so proud but
> inherited it from their fathers and their fathers' fathers, that in short the Jew-
> ish people is one in space and time.

Though practically no one understood this avowed intention in its full dimensions in the course of the controversy, the text itself—we will see—suggests

that it played a major role in determining many of the book's features. The key is that Steiner's response to the charge of passivity and submission did not involve its simple denial but rather its "contextualization" within a vision of Jewish identity that would acknowledge its truth at the same time that it insisted on sources for its supersession.

If such is the case—and it is only one interpretation of the biographical origins of *Treblinka*, since authors, like everyone, are never fully in conscious and intentional control of their performances, and in any case it is a retrospective interpretation—it is a pity that the sensationalization and commercialization of the book, beginning with Steiner's rash interview, so distorted his intent, notably by so explicitly and one-sidedly presenting the passivity and "complicity" of the Jews during the Holocaust, with the *Sonderkommandos* as their symbol, as a matter of embarrassment. Put differently, Steiner's enterprise, if intending to show the limits of the Zionist denigration of Holocaust victims, actually made a major contribution to internationalizing that attitude. Aiming to overcome it, Steiner began by introducing it, and few recognized—his public statements no less than his text, along with the antagonism of his foes, made it difficult to see—that his narrative of the revolt was intended to reject the very opinion many attributed to him, by showing that passivity and compliance were inextricably bound up with the sources Steiner hypothesized of the activist revolt he, like Kovner, prized.

To understand the fate of the book, for this reason, it is necessary to understand not simply the author but also the journalistic culture that determined his work, and the cultural situation of the specific moment in which it appeared. *Le Nouveau Candide,* the organ that began the controversy and for which Steiner had once worked, had been directed by Pierre Lazareff, the outstanding journalist and impresario of postwar French culture, like Steiner Jewish in his origins, most famous for editing the newspaper *France-Soir* and for hosting perhaps the most popular news program of the era, *Cinq Colonnes à la Une.* Founded in 1961 in order to provide a Gaullist counterweight to the overwhelmingly left-wing press of the era, and apparently secretly funded by the government, *Le Nouveau Candide,* in spite of its ideologically diverse staff, frequently not only sensationalized but also singled out the topic of Jews for commercial consumption. In doing so, it helped establish an important public atmosphere in the period, one without which Steiner's project, or at least its reception, is impossible to fathom.

Not long before *Le Nouveau Candide*'s participation in the public rollout of *Treblinka,* the scandal around Roger Peyrefitte's book *The Jews* took place,

in which—not coincidentally—*Le Nouveau Candide* also played an important catalyzing role. As during the Treblinka controversy, the magazine made
much of the atmosphere of scandal it itself helped create, and there is little
doubt that the rollout of the earlier book—with its titillating charges against
and defenses of Jews in public—provided a template for the organizers of
the later one.[37] Peyrefitte's book presented itself as an attack on antisemitism,
officially aimed at the interrogation and rejection of a long series of time-
honored charges. But, as American observer Renée Winegarten argued at
the time, its announced intent allowed it to revive—just as Steiner would
with charges of Jewish passivity and complicity—many of the perceptions it
claimed to criticize, a fact responsible for much of its scandalous success.
Peyrefitte dignified antisemitism with a reply, as Steiner would with the
"problem" of Jewish compliance. "The discussions in this extensive tome
touch upon almost every conceivable theme related to Jews during the last
fifty years and more," Winegarten observed. "The malice of the book has to
be seen to be believed." Peyrefitte's text, Wintegarten wrote,

> written ostensibly in the name of truth but privately, one suspects, to satisfy an
> insatiable craving to shock and to make trouble, sets out to tear the bandage
> from every half-healed wound. . . . [I]nevitably, whatever the work's declared
> aim, the odious impression left on the reader is not dissimilar to the emotions
> aroused by Céline or any other myth-making anti-Semite who finds Jews lurk-
> ing behind every tree, and even wearing the triple crown. . . . Peyrefitte's aim
> in writing [*The Jews*] seems less a desire to combat racialism than to exploit the
> current French vogue for Jewish subjects.[38]

Not surprisingly, and not least because *Le Nouveau Candide* inaugurated his
controversy as well, Jean-François Steiner's enterprise could easily be assimilated to Peyrefitte's outrageous success, correctly or not. It could seem to
"exploit . . . Jewish subjects," and many Jews would see it that way.

For her part, Winegarten offered an interesting hypothesis about why
French culture in these years took the turn it did, a turn—strangely combining philo- and antisemitism—that alone explains, if not Steiner's enterprise, then many aspects of its reception. On the one hand, for the prior ten
years, the special fate of French Jews in the war, and the role of Frenchmen
in causing it, had begun to penetrate the culture—intermittently and hesi-
tantly, of course, as if in slow preparation for the more explosive effect of
Robert Paxton's rethinking of the Vichy period of just a few years later.

"Gradually," Winegarten commented, "an awareness has grown that the Occupation was very different for those who were Jews and those who were not, and this awareness has come to color much contemporary writing on the subject."[39] In 1967, for example, Jean-Paul Sartre would remind his readers that it had been French police who rounded up Jews, and Claude Lévy and Paul Tillard would publish a work on the *"grande rafle"* in which so many Jews had been taken away by them.[40] But, at the same time, antisemitic tropes and insinuations remained popular, acceptable at least in some quarters, and, in their public expressions, were even in the the process of becoming more commonplace. According to Winegarten,

> [A]t the dark and twisted roots of much of the sympathetic interest in Jews and Jewish affairs that flourishes in France at the present time, there lies an ineluctable sense of guilt and complicity. Guilt is the impulsion behind the new curiosity; guilt the shaky foundation on which that ill-named phenomenon, philo-Semitism, rests. . . . Alongside the now almost commonplace confessions of culpability, however, there runs a powerful current of indifference to, and reaction against, the assumption of complicity. . . . It is curious that roughly at the same time as the guilt complex appeared to be reaching its apogee, that is, during the last decade, there was a recrudescence in France of Fascist-inclined sentiment and atmosphere. Peyrefitte's book thrives on this antithesis; indeed, his book may even serve as its distasteful symbol.[41]

Jean-François Steiner's *Treblinka* never raised the issue—about to become culturally and politically convulsive—of French complicity in the genocide, though by focusing with such unusual intensity on the fate of the Jews at the expense of more familiar and local sufferings, he may have inadvertently helped bring about the conditions for such perceptions of national complicity to be possible. But Steiner emphatically did, if perhaps for his own special reasons, write about the Jews in ways—beginning with his focus on the allegation of Jewish participation in the murder—that fit a contemporary mood. There is thus little doubt that his book, if not a product of this atmosphere, could easily have seemed to participate in it and at the very least became caught up in it. Its marketing only abetted this association. Not on the extreme right—though the extreme right would certainly enthuse over its coverage—*Le Nouveau Candide* thus had a confirmed history of participating in "the vogue for Jewish subjects," and Steiner's enterprise provided grist for its mill.

■

A final biographical fact is relevant to the scandal. Shortly after it ended, Steiner married Grit von Brauchitsch, formalizing a relationship that, he had good reason to fear, would add to the atmosphere of scandal in which he found himself. Steiner had met his future wife, the granddaughter of the Prussian general who commanded Hitler's land army from 1938 until the tail end of 1941, when she had come to Paris in the late 1950s to study. (See figure 3.) "In the final analysis," Steiner explained at the time, once their relationship became more widely known, "it is just a beautiful love story between a man and a woman." But he attributed another meaning to it beyond simple romantic attraction: "It is as if she possesses the other half of the solution, like in those old tales of pirates in which it is just a matter of reuniting the two halves of a torn map in order to find the site of buried treasure." (Brauchitsch converted to Judaism shortly after their marriage.) Though never mentioned by his attackers, Steiner's relationship to Brauchitsch, to the extent it was known, undoubtedly added insult to the injury Steiner came to represent to a good many Jews during the affair, and many could easily draw from it confirmation of their interpretation of Steiner's true cultural politics and implicit agenda.[42]

Unquestionably an unusual example of what analysts now call "second-generation" consciousness, Steiner is not in an entirely different universe from more familiar exponents of the group. Consider, for example, Henri Raczymow's Esther—the figure who probably (along with David Grossman's Momik) counts as the most striking literary incarnation of second-generation consciousness in contemporary Holocaust literature. "The irony of history had it that I was born at Chatou," in France, "and not in Lodz, Vilna, Pinsk, Minsk, or Bialystok like my fathers and the fathers of my fathers," Steiner noted in one autobiographical essay from the period.[43] The irony of history is to thank—but also to blame—for a displaced birth that both saved his life but also deprived him of what should have by right been his experience, one that he would reconstruct in his novel—reliving it, he wrote, in the name of understanding it. Born, not coincidentally, on the very day of the Treblinka revolt, also in France, Esther provides a similar sense of deprivation, but with a critical difference: "I was born on August 2, 1943 in France," Esther is imagined thinking. "But it's in Treblinka that I would have liked to die, that day, that I should have died."[44] She relives Treblinka not by fantasizing about its successful revolt but by mimicking its victims, to the point of asphyxiating herself.

3. Jean-François Steiner and Grit von Brauchitsch. *France-Soir*,
13 December 1967. (Courtesy of Jean-François Steiner.)

Steiner's identification with Treblinka is exactly parallel, except that the entire purpose of his identification with Treblinka was to escape the morbid identity enforced on Jews like himself, he thought, by the fact of the Holocaust and the way it had been remembered. The difference is startling. But though Steiner represents another example of the complex relation between identity and memory, in his case it is difficult to know whether it was short-term politics—including those of the Gaullist intelligentsia of the years of Algeria and after and the cultural blend of philo- and antisemitism—or long-term psychology that dominated. Most plausibly, they combined. In any case, Steiner's idiosyncratic example of Holocaust consciousness would have been of strictly biographical (and therefore minimal) interest, except that his book sold so well and provoked a debate that resonated at length and with the cultural significance that what follows will try to reconstruct.

■

"Since they had not succeeded in deporting all the Jews of whom they wanted to rid their empire, the builders of the Thousand Year Reich decided to exterminate them."[45] So *Treblinka* begins. The rhetoric, here as in much of the rest of the book, is reportorial and dry, but also chillingly to the point. The text that follows, presented as a novelized documentation based scrupulously on Jewish testimony, is divided into two essentially unrelated parts. The opening section—approximately seventy pages—is a dramatic set piece narrating the fate of Vilna, the scene of Kovner's struggle. The narrative then turns to the abasement and triumph of Treblinka itself. Even this structural choice, it is worth noting, bore a message. Just as its first sentence makes clear that the subject matter of *Treblinka* is the specific fate of the Jews in wartime, the first section of the book implies that the antechamber to extermination at the heart of National Socialist horror is not, as for many writers of the time (and today), the concentration camp, to which many non-Jews in France as elsewhere were also sent as victims; instead, it is the ghetto, the specifically Jewish antecedent to the so-called Final Solution.

The set piece begins with the shocking discovery in Vilna of the fact that mass killings have begun at Ponary about four miles away. One day Dr. Marc Dvorjetski, a Vilna notable (and a figure still living in 1966, like many others in the narrative), is awakened by scratching at the door; it turns out to be Pessia Aranovich, a local young woman who arrives in desperate need of medical attention, claiming to have escaped from Ponary's horrors. In Steiner's presentation, Dr. Dvorjetski only slowly comes to believe her report of mass shootings. Dr. Dvorjetski, in turn, has trouble convincing the other residents of the ghetto. The dominant theme of the section is not simply the inability of the Jews to come to grips with the situation in which they find themselves, but also their tenacious belief that passive compliance is the best chance to survive. After her warnings are ignored, even Pessia rejoins ghetto society and keeps her mouth shut. Steiner comments that through this psychological syndrome the Jews unwittingly played into Nazi hands. The Nazis "learned of Pessia Aranovich's misadventures in the ghetto with the keenest satisfaction. It was the magnificent crowning of two months of effort and the proof of the excellence of their method. . . . Thirty thousand Jews had already been killed and . . . [t]he most perfect calm reigned in the ghetto."[46] As for Dr. Dvorjetski, he is said to feel almost like an accessory to the murder once he belatedly acknowledges its reality.

As the ineluctable fate of the Vilna Jews approaches in his book, Steiner shifts focus to the material that initially inspired him, the beginnings of partisan activity in and outside the city associated with Kovner and his compatriots. Steiner's dramatization of the internal partisan discussions, including Kovner's New Year's Eve declaration, allows him to broach the ultimate theme of his work before his narrative has reached the Treblinka camp itself. "They were not twenty years old," Steiner writes of Kovner and his friends, "and they talked about death like veterans or philosophers." One of them emphasizes "a moral threat which is even graver" than the physical threat they face, a spiritual danger that he defines as follows: "If not a single Jew resists, who will ever want to be a Jew again?" It is Kovner's question. But the secular partisans see no escape, Steiner recounts, from "this death [that] was neither a possibility nor a hypothesis; it was a certainty—only the manner of dying depended on their choice." The manner of their impending demise, shameful or proud, is the restricted subject of their deliberations. But another young partisan—standing in for Steiner's own position—rejects this alternative between dying passively and dying with honor. "[O]f two solutions," he says, "I always choose the third." The search for this further alternative is the subject of Steiner's book, a solution Kovner and Zionism had not found to the question about Jewish compliance that he and it correctly posed.[47]

As the Vilna ghetto is liquidated, and the German search for superior means of killing extends through the gas van and culminates finally in death camps, the scene in Steiner's book shifts to Treblinka itself. In their quest for a perfect mode of killing and throughout the text, Steiner refers to the Nazis as "the Technicians" (*les Techniciens*), a description that divided his readers.

It was intended to capture the sinister genius—already emphasized by Kovner in his article, whose description of "the art of murder" Steiner updated—of the Nazis, offered in a tone of macabre humor that some, like Simone de Beauvoir, found chillingly effective. Others, primed by Steiner's public statements to search the book for antisemitism or even self-hatred, understood the description—like several others in the book—as illustrating an admiration for the Nazis' organizational acumen. Both in their treatment of the Vilna population and, more remorselessly, in their planning of the Treblinka camp, the "Technicians" are depicted as obsessively devoted to making the Jews their own killers. They aimed, Steiner says, to be the deistic gods who set up a perfect universe that would thereafter run of its own accord without further intervention. "This method which consists in making the victims the accomplices of their own executioners," Steiner remarks, "was a kind of dogma to the Technicians." Writing in an almost theological register, Steiner explains how the Nazis' "desire for rationalization combined with a concern for detail clearly illuminates the grandeur of the machine and the disconcerting power of a technique which, in its constant and unsatisfied search for perfection, even utilized human imperfections for its ends. Carried to this level, technique becomes an art which engenders its own aesthetic, its own morality, and even its own metaphysic."[48] The technique, Steiner emphasized, worked to shame the victims before killing them.

Steiner's brand of prose, in this exemplary passage and thus throughout, struck readers differently: what some saw as the mark of a captivating storyteller, others found labored to the point of grandiloquence. Combined with those passages of apparent awe and wonder before the Nazis, however, it illustrated something else. The Germans, one of whom Steiner describes as "so handsome, so remote, so different from us," are not excoriated or rejected (except perhaps tonally), and were therefore easily interpreted as models of competence and self-confidence.[49] Such passages even suggested, to those readers who were willing to insinuate such attitudes to the author on the basis of his interview and thanks to the literary atmosphere in which the book appeared, a personal hatred of Jewish weakness and envy of German strength. It was possible to interpret other sections along the same lines, as when Steiner describes "the little despicable Jew, the little ghetto Jew, the vermin, the subhuman" who attacked "the beautiful edifice of the tall officer, blond and handsome and black who considered himself divine."[50] Though such views are always interior monologue and many are rooted in testimony Steiner had gathered—in particular, the admiring descriptions of Lalka, or

"The Doll," as the good-looking sadist Kurt Franz of Treblinka was known—some readers referred to such passages when they interpreted Steiner as an author scandalously divided in his allegiances in depicting this most black-and-white moral universe.

The rest of the book shows that Steiner believed that Jews could partake in heroism, only it had to be their own kind, one that overcame the restricted choice between different kinds of death. Against the background of Jewish destruction—again, a focus that made the book a mass-market novelty in its time—Steiner begins his well-paced narration of how the Jews who would revolt in Treblinka slowly come to understand the need for the moral effort they will eventually shoulder. The hellish setting of Treblinka enforces a bleak choice on those inmates not immediately marked for death in the gas chambers of the extermination camp. When he begins his depiction of the syndrome of passive compliance in Vilna, Steiner does not hesitate to raise the implication, just as openly as he did in his scandalous interview, that the Jews were in effect complicit in their destruction. Sometimes, he does so through sly alterations of the sources he ventriloquizes, as when he has Dvor-jetski (whose published memoirs Steiner cited in the original published version of his text) "realize that . . . he had been made [the Germans'] accomplice."[51] Once his narrative reaches the *Sonderkommando* of Treblinka, the allusions to the Jews' complicity—"monstrous complicity," as it is called at one point—only continue their accumulation. The most remarkable instance, undoubtedly, comes with Steiner's formulation that the members of the *Sonderkommando* "bought their lives with the lives of others. . . . The price of 'tenure' at Treblinka, calculated in Jewish heads, amounted to fifteen units per day. . . . [S]uch was the terrible arithmetic of a day's survival." Steiner does specify that "the work would have been done anyway" if the Jews had not complied; and, in an important qualification, he notes that in spite of "an element of cowardice in the attitude of the Jewish mass, which preferred to suffer the worst degradation rather than revolt," this "cowardice is more apparent than real, as the tragic end of this story will sufficiently demonstrate."[52]

He refers here to the revolt with which the book closes; for Steiner's point in stressing the complicity, he makes relatively clear, is that only out of humiliation and abjection could some alternative to them arise. This usually misunderstood paradox, which Steiner evidently considered the key to the proper memory of the Holocaust as well as to Jewish renewal, is the actual problem of the book. The bulk of the narrative, consequently, is given over to the slow discovery of an alternative to the syndrome of shame, compliance, and collusion that nonetheless arises out of them.

Agency comes to the inmates slowly. Reporting the decision of one Jew to help another one commit suicide in order to choose death on his own terms, Steiner suggests that this "demonstration of solidarity in death . . . seems like very little, and yet it is from this first gesture that everything would follow. On the basis of this solidarity in death, life would begin again." This act "represented a stage that may have been more important than the discovery of fire in our civilization."[53] Other acts of insurrection, from small to large, begin occurring, notably the assassination of the SS Max Biala with what Steiner described, relying on his collected testimonies, in a minor detail that would figure in the controversy, as a "great Sabbath knife."[54]

Nonetheless, Steiner stresses that the fiery spirit of resistance he wanted to praise did not spread quickly in the camp. He follows a few characters through their initial halting steps but equally emphasizes their own awareness of how hard it would be to awaken the whole camp in an all-out attack. "Something has broken in them," Galewski, the major organizer of the revolt, says to a friend about his fellow inmates,

> "which it would have taken a very long time to put back together. They are alive only by virtue of an old ancestral reflex, but unconsciously they are ashamed not to have died with their families. That is the extraordinary power of the Nazi system. Like certain spiders, it puts its victims to sleep before killing them. It is a death in two stages: you put men to sleep, then you kill the sleepers. This may seem very complicated, but actually it was the only way. Suppose that the S.S. had arrived announcing that they were going to kill us all, swearing it, starting to prove it. There is no doubt at all that the three million Polish Jews would have revolted. They would have done it with their backs to the wall, with the courage of despair. And it wouldn't have taken a few thousand men to beat us, but the whole Wehrmacht—and even then it isn't certain that all the soldiers would have obeyed! Then look at *us!* Not only do the Jews let themselves be killed without a gesture of revolt, but they even help their killers with their work of extermination. We, the accomplices, the employees of death, live in a world beyond life and death; compromised so profoundly that we can only be ashamed to be alive."
>
> "Monsters, in short?"
>
> "Yes, a new species of men in keeping with this new world."[55]

But only monsters can, in such circumstances, become heroes, Steiner wanted to show. He adopted the goal not only of accounting for the passivity but of finding the ultimate sources of resistance at the furthest reaches of submission. It is as if, according to Steiner's theory, the extremes of humiliation and mastery meet, and maximizing the one will inevitably force the surprising emergence of the other.

A main thesis of Steiner's book, then, is encapsulated in one of the two epigraphs he appended to it—the notion (attributed to a Hasidic poem) that "[a] man must descend very low to find the force to rise again."[56] Steiner explains this premise at more length as he turns, around the middle of the book, to the story of the revolt:

> Since the German invasion, [the Jews] had fallen from one renunciation to the next, until they had reached a state of physical and moral slavery which may have been unknown in the history of social relations. In the course of this vertiginous descent it seemed as if nothing would ever stop them. It was as if a spell had been cast over them which prevented them from recovering their balance. A kind of fatality made them fall into all the traps that the Technicians had set for them. The supreme masters of their destiny, the Technicians reigned over them like some otherworldly power.
>
> . . . And then, suddenly, came the miracle. Just when their abdication was total, when all values had ceased to exist, when their humanity had almost left them, the Jews, rousing themselves at the bottom of the abyss, began a slow ascent which death alone would stop.
>
> A few months earlier, these men had won back the right to die by committing suicide; now they were discussing the right to die by fighting. It was that night, in the buzzing barracks, in that insane world of Treblinka, that the miracle occurred at last: "the miracle in abdication."[57]

That Steiner incorporated Kovner's notion of the reversal of passivity into activism as the very pivot of his book—even as he translated it to the new precincts of a death camp—is indicated by his allusion to Kovner's title as his book moves from the portrayal of abjection to the beginnings of resurrection. Unfortunately, even Kovner had not gone far enough, for the "miracle" he found in abdication amounted simply to another form of death: death with honor. And in finding the true source for Kovner's wisdom in a Hasidic saying, Steiner changed the grounds for Jewish vitality from the Zionism that Kovner (like Steiner's own father) advocated.

Steiner's narrative begins to rush toward a climax different from Kovner's as a Jew named Choken, whose escape had been one of the Treblinka resistance committee's early experiments in opposition, returns to the camp, dying, to impart the moral lesson of the crushed Warsaw revolt. It failed, as Steiner said in the interview, in adopting the wrong end. "The plan was purely defensive," Choken says. "The defenders did not have the slightest chance of getting out alive." Choken had heard the Warsaw organizers—living out the solution Kovner's partisans discussed—speak of "the freedom of choosing between two ways of dying." But for Steiner the Treblinka Jews, like Jewry in general, needed and ended up offering a third option. Similarly, Steiner has Choken realize—quite strikingly, in light of Kadmi Cohen's wartime movement—that Masada, like Warsaw, is a useless precedent in Jewish history for moral action, for it was just happenstance that the ancient historian Josephus recorded the battle, which would otherwise have left no lesson and in any case amounted to no victory. It illustrates, like Warsaw, an alternative death rather than a new life. It is Choken, dying, who imparts the lesson of ancient and modern Jewish history to the Treblinka Jews: "There is no vengeance possible and hatred is sterile," he explains. "It's not to die in a desperate battle that we need, it's not to kill Germans that matters. What we need is a victory and witnesses to tell about it, witnesses, Shlomo, witnesses of the victory of the Jews over the S.S."[58] The fight for life, witnessed to the world, is the "third solution" Jewry needs.

The drama of the book is only superficially martial. It is, more fundamentally, moral. It is not just that the Treblinka Jews adopted an aim Steiner characterizes as "insane, grandiose, and almost unique in the history of the camps of Nazi Europe: an armed revolt." It is the spirit in which they adopted this purpose, for Steiner, that truly matters.[59] He makes this clear in the one of the numerous reflective (and occasionally pretentious) asides that litter his narrative. "For the Jews," he argues,

> the real enemy was not Hitler . . . , it was death. . . . Wars may be made with men, but they are declared in the name of principles, and the victor is not the one who has lost the least men, but the one whose principle is saved. The real stake of the war that the Nazis made on the Jews was life itself. When people talk about the war of 1939–1945, they confuse two wars that have absolutely nothing in common: a world war, the one Germany made on the world, and a universal war, the war of the Nazis against the Jews, the war of the principle of death against the principle of life. In their war the Jews were alone, but it could not be otherwise.[60]

Offered in perhaps the most important and controversial sentences in the book, this distinction is indeed one of the reasons Steiner wanted finally, against the overwhelming tendency of the immediate postwar period, to distinguish the Holocaust from the war that merely provided the occasion for

Holocaust to occur. The assault of death on life, Hitler against the Jews, counted for Steiner as the true conflict at the heart of the war, recognizable only through isolating the one from the other.

If the Holocaust is separated from the war, so Jewish behavior—both passivity and resistance—is distinguished by Steiner from the general run of human activity. One of the most striking aspects of the book is Steiner's regular concession to stereotype: the constant attribution of collective traits not only to the Germans, who are frequently described as technical geniuses with good looks, but to Jews as well. If this dimension of the Steiner's work is ignored, one of the essential reasons for the appropriability of his enterprise will have been missed. A variety of qualities are attributed to Jews, but a few examples of this remarkable tendency will suffice. Steiner announces early on that "the Jewish intelligence" is "more speculative than practical," for even if it "sometimes loses contact with reality," it is distinguished by the fact that it "attach[es] more importance to the manner of stating a problem and the manner of solving it than to the solution itself."[61] For Steiner, "the typically Jewish quality" of "always looking for the hardest way, always wanting to do better, never being satisfied with the possible, and undertaking against all odds what is logically impossible."[62] At times, clannish self-separation and love of money are suggested. Beyond these cultural predispositions, Steiner attributes a number of spiritual characteristics to his people. "[T]he Jew, the real Jew, raised only on Jewish culture, though he may be susceptible to anguish, is invulnerable to despair," he wrote.[63]

These last traits are, however, not just stereotypes, for Steiner meant them to combine into a full-blown theory of Jewish particularity that would explain first the passivity and then the resistance to which somehow it gave rise. Accordingly, they are linked, throughout the book, to a depiction of Jewish religious culture that presents it as integral, timeless, and, in the end, salvific. Numerous references to Abraham's passive submission to God's commands run through the narrative, as if in explanation for the Jews' passive compliance to their Nazi masters.[64] But Jewish identity is in possession of its own source of revolt, too, perhaps ultimately rooted in the Deuteronomic command to choose life. It is because they do not participate in it that the Zionist partisans, like Kovner, no matter how accurate their perception of the problem, are not presented by the book as the people in possession of a workable solution. Rather, Steiner argues, the response to passivity has to come from an authentically Jewish source, as part of a transformation of, rather than a break with, a putatively authentic Jewish culture.

It is Rabbi Isaac Nissenbaum of Warsaw, quoted early in the book, who gives the clearest initial indication of what this source is: "For a Jew, survival is more than a desire, it is a duty," Steiner has him say, in a citation meant to summarize his teaching.

> "To live is a *Mitzvah*," [Nissenbaum continues.] "When they attacked our souls, we joyously mounted the funeral pyres for the sanctification of the name [i.e., martyrdom]. But now that it is our bodies they are after, the time of the sanctification of life begins." . . . A revolt in the name of the honor of the Jewish people, which the young Zionists urged, did not touch the deepest chords . . . : the people of the Bible placed their self-respect on an infinitely higher level. But revolt may also be born of despair, of the feeling that there is nothing left, that life has lost its meaning. In this case, it is no longer a revolt for the sake of something, some ideal or other, but a revolt against nothingness.[65]

In particular, it is a desire not simply to live but to *witness* their destruction and survival that is the true Jewish response to the Nazi attempt at homicidal negation. This idea is related to religion, as Steiner's citation of Nissenbaum suggests, but even those Jews not believing or observant are led, somehow, to understand it: "A Jew is born a Jew. Child of the chosen people, his faith rests on two sanctifications: the sanctification of the name and the sanctification of life; *kiddush hashem* and *kiddush hachaim*. If the Inquisition had been the time of *kiddush hashem*, the Nazi era brought about the conditions for *kiddush hachaim*. In the Nazi era, the *mitzvah*, the act of faith, no longer consisted in dying for the glorification of the holy name, but to live for the sake of the first gift God gave: life."[66] Jewish martyrdom, to be practiced or prized in other circumstances, now gives way to Jewish insurrection, for a Jewish people become one. This is the revolt, out of a specifically Jewish imperative, that the Treblinka Jews will eventually undertake. It is also this collective will to survive that Steiner says, in a climactic passage, ultimately eluded the Nazi masters, who "did not understand that one can kill Jews, but not overcome 'the people with the stiff neck.'"[67]

The rest of Steiner's book tells, with the remarkable narrative élan that captured the imaginations of so many readers, how this revolt progressively became real. The slow unfolding of the insurrection, meticulously canvassed in the text, ultimately occurs very simply because of the difference between Jews and others. The Jewish refusal to submit to the fate Nazism had decreed for them, Steiner suggested, is a mystery . . . whose explanation can only be found in another and greater mystery, which is the survival of the Jewish people. Reason can enumerate a certain number of causes for this phenomenon—devotion to a faith, sense of solidarity, familial fanaticism, and so on—but other nations in which these same conditions applied have disappeared, at best leaving behind only a few fragments of stone. Heirs of this age-old mystery, the Jews of Treblinka revived it once again. And yet this time all of the conditions seemed to point to its not being renewed. Perhaps it is in this individual denial of death, this congenital inability to imagine it, that one can find the underlying cause of this miracle of survival. The Jew, more than any other man, realizes himself within his national community; as a Jew he can exist only insofar as he belongs to it. As soon as he leaves it he loses himself in the broader species of man. If the individual Jew remains mortal in spite of himself, his will to deny death renders the community immortal.[68]

His father's "metaphysical" views, transposed away from Zionism to be sure and rooted in a different source of Jewish authenticity, explain what happened. It would anger many respondents to the book, but Steiner thus identified the zest for life in the face of persecution as Jewish rather than human, available only on condition of communal membership—indeed it seems in Steiner's narrative to be the nation's ultimate and unanalyzable essence, a unique trait that explains the Treblinka revolt and emerges as a redemptive source of ethnic self-confidence to be emphasized in the face of the otherwise humiliating fact of the genocide.

Such premises affected Steiner's plotting of the revolt in many ways. It is an important implication of Steiner's interest in discovering a collective solution to what he saw as a collective quandary, for example, that none of the individuals in the *Treblinka* narrative—even in the leadership of the revolt—are granted any exemption from the syndrome of passivity and compliance. Their heroics are explained, rather, as transformations in the syndrome rather than as exceptions to it; they are simply the individual exponents of the collective mutation of abject submission to death into activist seizure of life. "They are heroes beyond compare whom circumstances snatched from anonymity," Steiner argues of his dramatis personae, "but there is no essential difference between them and the mass of prisoners." For "[l]ike the rest they allowed themselves to be led to slaughter, like the rest they became accomplices of extermination. Their virtues and their defects are Jewish virtues and Jewish defects." Accordingly, the "mad idea" of a central figure to stage the revolt "had germinated in a Jewish brain."[69]

After a failure to secure weapons through bribing Ukrainians in the camp with money taken from the bodies and possessions of arriving Jews, the insurrectionary band of inmates is helped by a fatal Nazi mistake and a stroke of luck: an armory is constructed on the grounds. The final preparations for revolt are made. Major roles in the initial steps of the operation are given to Heniek and Marcus, youths of thirteen and sixteen; the famous signature image on the cover of the French edition of the book must depict one of them. "Inside this child's body, behind this pathetic face," Steiner suggests of one of the youths, "a kind of wild animal now throbbed."[70] (See figure 4.) It seems that this child represents the Jews as a whole, unexpected heroism at the core of an abject weakling. He is therefore properly the symbol of the whole book.

The crucial stimulus for revolt is provided by the arrival and report of Yankel Wiernik from a mysterious part of the Treblinka installation where, Wiernik reports, the Nazis have begun digging up and burning bodies in preparation for the full liquidation of the entire camp.[71] The Jews only now realize that the time has come to act, because the few left alive for the functioning of the machine will not survive its dismantling; Steiner portrays the Nazi commandant as wistfully regretful that his fantastic creation will eventually have to come to an end.[72] Having reached the climactic day, August 2, 1943, Steiner cites Wiernik's testimony at length—the major direct citation in the book—in order to explain how the nearly derailed insurrection came to pass nonetheless thanks to Wiernik's fearless ingenuity in restoring communication between the two parts of the camp.[73]

In citing Wiernik, however, Steiner surreptitiously added to the spare text on which he drew, as he had with Dr. Dvorjetski's testimony, in order to achieve an overall thematic consistency in his book as it came to an end. Wiernik had written, "Each of us realized the importance of the moment and thought only of gaining freedom. We were disgusted with our miserable existence and all that mattered was to avenge ourselves on our tormentors and escape." Steiner entirely rewrote the passage, notably so that Wiernik says: "I knew that this day would determine the justification or condemnation of our long agony, our terrible complicity."[74] Finally, the weapons are distributed, and the battle is joined: a victory to affirm life and cleanse the Jews of their collusion with death.

Internalizing into the narrative, perhaps, the Treblinka Jews' own principle that the technique of preparation for the revolt is everything and the consequences that necessarily follow are of only subsidiary interest, Steiner devotes a mere ten pages of four hundred to the actual August 2, 1943, events.

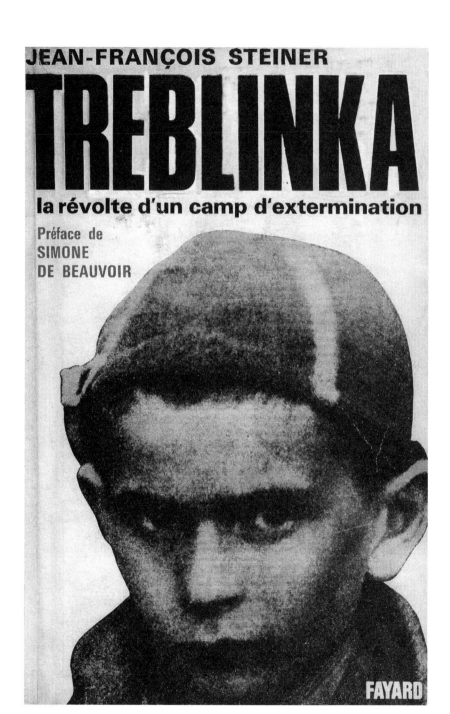

JEAN-FRANÇOIS STEINER

TREBLINKA

la révolte d'un camp d'extermination

Préface de
SIMONE
DE BEAUVOIR

FAYARD

4. Cover of *Treblinka*, French edition. (Courtesy of Dr. Josseline Rivière.)

Like "a force too long pent up," the Jews, "slaves, accomplices, sublime heroes or accursed people, broken, gassed, burned, killed a thousand times and
a thousand times reborn," through the fighting emerge as "one solid mass of
humanity, unleashed, blinded, catapulted by hatred, hope and rage," as they
"explode and flow and roll and charge and erupt; in a wild gale, a torrent of
hatred, hope and rage, they howl and run and leap, those who abandoned
their own, those who pulled their teeth out, who gassed them, burned their
bodies, and reduced their bones to powder, the Jews of abdication and the
miracle, the Jews of death and of life, of agony, of faith, and of desperate
hope."[75] They burn the camp to the ground and, though many die or are recaptured during the revolt, a number escape. The book ends.

Steiner's brief postscript indicates that of the six hundred who escaped
that day, only forty ultimately survived the war (a mistakenly low figure, as it
turns out). Most were either recaptured or killed at a variety of hands, Nazi
and local, in the year before the Red Army arrived in the area in the middle
of 1944.[76] But the survivors, scattered by the middle of the 1960s across the
globe, accomplish through Steiner's ventriloquizing book the primary objective of the insurrection: to bear witness to the sempiternal truth of Jewish
survival and to recount through their story not only why so many Jews allowed themselves to die in the course of the Nazi genocide but also how the
will to live and fight emerged out of, and depended on, the very extremism
of Jewish passivity and abjection.

■

In reconstructing—and partially reimagining—the history of the Holocaust,
Steiner must have believed that he had shown, in his *roman à these* based on
real events and rooted in genuine testimony, why there was no cause for
shame; a unified Jewish people could now be deservedly proud of the heroism even of its dark recent past. But books rarely fulfill their intended aims,
because of the way they are presented and the way they are received. The
story of a text is always also a history of reading (or, sometimes, not reading).
An interpretation of *Treblinka* only begins, therefore, with a portrait of the
author, his background and his environment, and an overview of his curious
book. No less essentially than the tangled circumstances of its production, its
reception by its various publics, to which the rest of this book turns, defines
it too. *Habent sua fata libelli.*

3

Nazi Criminality between Concentration and Extermination

On its appearance, *Treblinka* garnered the high-profile re- views, filled with exorbitant praise, of which many writers dream. In *L'Express:* "One does not ask oneself whether it is 'good.' It is un- forgettable." In *Paris-Match:* "This book bowls over the conscience of men." In *Le Nouvel Observateur:* "The most atrocious, most fascinating and, if one may say so given the subject, the most exciting and most beautiful book ever written on the camps." In *Le Journal du Dimanche:* "It is one of the most im- portant books ever published on the concentration camps, and on man in general, Jewish or not." In *Nouvelles littéraires:* "Steiner recounts [it all] with consummate reportage, dialogue, suspense, and direction. Without ever giv- ing in to sentimentality, to indignation, or to lyricism, . . . he has evoked one of the greatest dramas of all time." In the new *Quinzaine littéraire:* "He has the air of a former deportee. . . . I thought I was reading the testimony of a Treblinka survivor." In the communist *L'Humanité:* "Jean-François Steiner describes with an extraordinary power of evocation what this massive exter- mination was like. . . . Never before has there been so systematic and detailed a description of the horror, so evocative, or it could not have bowled over the former deportee that I am." In *Le Canard enchaîné,* the satirical weekly: "Steiner not only amazed me; he convinced me. . . . His four hundred page book reads with anxiety and fervor, and one is carried away as of the first chap- ter." In the leftist Christian *Esprit:* "If I did not fear big words, I would say that this book should not become the object of controversy amongst literary men, historians, or politicians, but that it justifies a quarrel of prophets."[1] And so on. For all that, the praise was not uniform, and the debate not random.

This chapter begins an analysis of *Treblinka*'s reception by attempting a survey of the most prominent and substantive public discussions focusing, insofar as possible, on the challenge the book posed to widespread contemporary perceptions of the nature of Nazi criminality. (The next chapter finishes the analysis by turning to intra-Jewish discussions of the book, interrogating their assumptions about the past and future of Jewish identity.) The reason to focus on this issue, aside from its intrinsic importance, is to make the point that controversies often matter because of their unintended consequences. Though the manifest content of the debate often involved Steiner's claim about Jewish complicity or his enemies' counterclaims about the book's accuracy, its latent and more important result may have been the beginnings of a gestalt switch in the construction of the World War II events in French public discourse.

To understand the significance of *Treblinka*'s effect on the framing of Nazi criminality, much context is necessary, so fundamentally has perception of the cataclysm of World War II moved since its end. Writing in 1995, the eminent historian Pierre Vidal-Naquet pointed out a fact noticed by many other observers in recent years. In 1945, few—next to no one in Vidal-Naquet's France—drew a distinction between concentration camps and extermination camps, between Western sites like Buchenwald for the diverse range of Nazi enemies and Eastern ones like Treblinka for the execution of the Jews alone. (Many of the reviews just cited, for example, refer generally to "the camps" or to "deportation" as unitary phenomena.) Now, such a difference is deeply ingrained in the consciousness of historians and, to some extent, even that of the public. But, as Vidal-Naquet emphasized: "The distinction, now strongly drawn, between the system of concentration camps and the exterminatory project is an accomplishment of contemporary history."[2] It is the considerable historical puzzle of when (and why) such a distinction began to be drawn in France and when (and why) it took hold that an analysis of the Treblinka affair helps solve.

■

A description of the background from which the Holocaust had to emerge is a necessary preliminary. Postwar French political culture, as many studies have shown, propagated a myth of heroic resistance, both to explain the origins of the new polity (which set the terms for the battle between left and right over its leadership) and to distract attention from the potency of native fascist currents in France and that country's collaboration with the Nazi occupation—including, of course, with the deportation and murder of a quarter of France's Jewish population. With the myth of resistance, a discourse of "deportation" came to be linked, amalgamating many different categories of victim. A way of constructing the past that marginalized the brute fact of disproportionate Jewish victimhood, this early representation of World War II folded Jews into a more general category of patriotic French martyrs, possible since a great many Frenchmen had suffered under Nazi rule. Accordingly, all victims of Nazi criminality were presented as victims for a powerful collective cause, whether the native French resistance (especially on the Gaullist right) or the antifascist fight (on the communist left). A host of politically powerful associations sprang up shortly after the war, all with a claim on the attention and assistance of the French public and government, including an *amicale* for every camp. The umbrella organization of the Fédération nationale des déportés et internés résistants et patriotes (FNDIRP) summed up, in its name, the ideology of the (sometimes uneasy) coalition of victims officially acknowledged by the state and by the dominant culture.

There were many reasons why the past came to be selectively reconfigured in ways that elided the specificity and enormity of Jewish victimhood.[3] First and perhaps foremost, the many non-Jewish deportees who returned to France upon the liberation were visible and vocal, unlike the Jewish victims of deportation. While roughly equivalent numbers of Jews and non-Jews were deported from France, nearly all of the former perished during the war whereas about half of the latter survived. For these two reasons, non-Jewish deportees to Western concentration were simply physically present, after the war, compared to the Jewish deportees to Eastern extermination who vanished in the death camps. In the second place, the Western concentration camps (in some contrast with the Eastern extermination camps) were highly publicized—indeed, spectacular—in their liberation and in the graphic (often photographic) documentation produced immediately afterward illustrating their horror.[4] Some of these camps, it is true, had been reception sites for surviving Jewish prisoners who were relocated, many in the infamous "death marches," from the Auschwitz region in early 1945; but many of the longer-term inhabitants of the Western camps interpreted the arrival of these Eastern victims as evidence of the further extent of the unified Nazi project, not that their own suffering in the West had to be classed as resulting from a different, and lesser, crime. Finally, of course, there may have been persisting antisemitism, which certainly played a role in the occlusion of the nature of victimhood, as well as the penchant of Jewish survivors and communities, in all countries, for avoiding a topic that (they believed) might obstruct their reintegration. The pedagogy of Allied war crimes trials about the nature of Nazi criminality confirmed these trends.[5]

The result of these overlapping factors is that, in the years leading up to the publication of Steiner's *Treblinka*, the main political strife amongst victims of the Nazis occurred not over the existence and implications of the Nazi genocide but between Gaullists and leftists over the more general phenomenon of deportation (on the unity of which both sides tacitly agreed). In intellectual or conceptual terms, it was David Rousset, Steiner's most vociferous antagonist in the Treblinka affair, who founded this configuration, one perhaps epitomized a decade after the end of the war and a decade before Steiner's intervention by Alain Resnais's *Night and Fog* (1955), the gripping film about Nazi criminality in which Jewish victimhood is barely mentioned. It was the lasting dominance of this way of thinking that made the shift in France toward a "genocidal" paradigm of memory of the events of World War II so spectacular, and the reception of Steiner's book sheds much light on this shift.

■

As already indicated, Steiner saw himself, in the very choice of the Treblinka camp as his subject, as reminding the French public that what they saw as a unified phenomenon—a single universe of crime—in fact required differentiation, and he strove to separate the Nazi project of extermination and thus the Jews' fate from the overall Nazi enterprise against its different enemies. Examining Steiner's book by itself, however, does not explain whether his attempt to alter perception succeeded. Only a study of the controversy that ensued can chart the fortunes of Steiner's descriptive attempt to distinguish extermination from concentration.

Initially, it was not clear that *Treblinka* would have the effect it did on the conceptual terms used to that point in France to interpret the war (and the place of the genocide in it). The left and the right concurred on the importance of the book, but only in ways that confirmed their own worldviews. The study of its reception suggests that the appropriability of the book is the most striking thing about it. That the intellectual left could find something of value in *Treblinka* is indicated by the enthusiasm of its first reader, who wrote the preface, Simone de Beauvoir.

Beauvoir had met Steiner through his article in *Les Temps modernes* and made a pact with him before his book's publication to lend it her support—especially if it should come under attack. In her preface, she interpreted *Treblinka* through the lenses provided by the current state of her partner Jean-Paul Sartre's existential Marxism (an interpretation not disturbed by her love affair with Claude Lanzmann, who would later become the most influential French spokesman about the genocide). As she observed, in beginning her few influential pages of introduction, it had been known since David Rousset's immediate postwar work that the Nazis had both sapped the will to resistance of their victims and divided them against one another. That she invoked Rousset on this point is no surprise: it had been Rousset who had provided the terms by which European intellectuals had deciphered the meaning of Nazi criminality from very early on in the postwar age. In citing Rousset on the Nazi *univers concentrationnaire* as a single phenomenon, however, Beauvoir appeared to ignore the essential drive of the book before her, its particularizing agenda, according to which one cannot understand either the Jews' victimhood or the terms of their ultimate resistance except as a syndrome that occurred to Jews in particular during the war rather than humans in general. Rousset, the Treblinka affair would show, knew better than to ignore the novelty of Steiner's enterprise on this point; but in citing him, Beauvoir indulged the illusion that Steiner's book provided evidence for her own universalizing belief that Nazi criminality had affected Jews as it had non-Jews, abasing the ones like the others.

In her preface, Beauvoir had a ready explanation for why. According to Sartre's most recent major exercise in theoretical philosophy, *The Critique of Dialectical Reason,* people do not revolt against their dehumanization in bourgeois, capitalist society, because they are "serialized."[6] By this, whatever the complexity of Sartre's theory, Beauvoir meant little more than that they are divided in order to be conquered. No one can resist—Jews in concentration camps or workers under capitalism—because all the oppressed are deprived of the enabling conditions of solidarity. Like Steiner, Beauvoir insisted she was interested, not in the "complicity" of the Jewish elite, but in that of all Jews so submissive in their deaths. (Of course, in the preface she justified her dismissal of the Jewish elite in more formulaic terms: "The collusion with the Germans of Jewish notables forming the *Judenrat* is a known fact which is easily understood. In all times and all countries, with rare exceptions, eminent persons have collaborated with the victors: a matter of class.")[7]

But, unlike for Steiner, the problem of the failure of the Jewish masses to

resist, for Beauvoir, turned out to be a version of the problem of false consciousness and voluntary servitude over which Marxists perpetually worried.
"In the curious world in which we live," Beauvoir explained,

> aggregates of individuals who share a common way of life in a dispersed state—
> Sartre calls these aggregates *series*—show behavior in which they become en-
> emies to one another and therefore enemies to themselves. . . . As long as the
> workers remained isolated within their class, the employers had every oppor-
> tunity to exploit them. Each worker saw the next one as a competitor who was
> ready to accept slave wages to get hired, and tried to sell his labor at an even
> lower price. . . . The skill of the Germans was to *serialize* the Jews and to pre-
> vent these series from becoming groups.[8]

But if this interpretation left aside everything particular about the Nazi "serialization" of the Jews, it also ran up against the fundamental reasons why
Steiner believed they had revolted. Nevertheless, Beauvoir continued by suggesting that, in their resistance, the Jews at Treblinka were not categorically
different from workers under capitalism in their attempt to overcome serialization. As she put it, "For the demands of labor to become possible, groups
had to be formed in which . . . each individual regarded the next one as the
same as himself." And Steiner had showed in *Treblinka* that, similarly, "it
takes only a few heroes to make people recover confidence in each other and
begin to dare." But then (though she did not immediately draw this implication from her remarks), there was nothing special about the Jewish resistance in Treblinka, contrary to what Steiner himself declared in his interview
and throughout the book. The Jewish fate under the Nazis, for Beauvoir,
seemed merely an instance of the general problem of submission to unde-
served oppression, just as their heroic refusal of death at Treblinka illustrated
the general potential of what Sartre called the "group in fusion" to form.

Otherwise, Beauvoir's preface sang the praises of Steiner's book. That
such a preface, with its remarkably appropriative reading of the book it introduced, adorned the text is hardly explicable, except thanks to the prestige
of the existentialist intellectuals and the crucial endorsement Beauvoir's
reflections and her advocacy gave it. But if Beauvoir contributed to Steiner's
success, she also did much to conceal his message. (Beauvoir recalls in her
memoir, without a trace of irony, that when she met with Steiner after reading the draft of his book she "surprised him very much by asking whether he
had had *The Critique of Dialectical Reason* in mind when he was writing *Treblinka*. He had never read a word of it.")[9]

■

There are creative misreadings, and then there are abusive ones. More troubling—especially to the Jewish public, which feared that Steiner had provided fodder for antisemites—was the appropriation of the book by the radical right in France, still culturally powerful in these years though stripped, after the ideological and actual purgation of the liberation years, of the legitimacy it had often had in French history. Eloquent testimony to the perverse appropriability of Steiner's interview and text is provided by the malicious enjoyment with which the extreme right greeted Steiner's charge of Jewish complicity in the genocide as well as the Jews' internecine squabbling about the meaning of their own experience. The reactionaries of France were willing to particularize the war years through and through, interpreting Jewish particularism, however, in an offensively negative sense.

In an article in the reactionary and nakedly antisemitic *Rivarol,* Étienne Lardenoy greeted Steiner's book for airing views that "are, one must say, rather heterodox in their relationship to the official 'truth' of the past twenty years."[10] Steiner's achievement, Lardenoy said, had been to shatter the mythology that the Germans were terrible villains and the Jews were innocent victims, for (as Steiner showed) the Jews had collaborated in their own deaths. The *Rivarol* writer characterized Steiner's thesis as "audacious, but one that, as soon as one considers it, calls for a few observations and reflections." Lardenoy wrote with special anger that it had been the sensationalistic, albeit right-leaning, *Le Nouveau Candide* that had opened the debate, for the magazine itself, directed by the Jew Pierre Lazareff, illustrated the problem of Jews stooping to anything, even right-wing populism, in the name of wealth. Reviving the anger of the right because of the vengeance visited upon it by the empowered left just after the war, Lardenoy explained that Steiner had erred only in imputing to the revolting Jews the theological motive of witnessing, a motive Lardenoy rejected as a high-minded fiction hiding the low-minded quest for power and money. "We all knew these unscrupulous opportunists," he wrote, "on familiar terms with the Germans, banqueting with them and producing for them the signs of the most indecent servility." He commented: "We found them again on the barricades of the Liberation . . . plundering, torturing, and killing their compatriots, then continuing and getting rich during the hard postwar years, just as they had done during the occupation."

No wonder they had remained silent then about what they had done, Lardenoy argued, and Steiner's coreligionists would "regret that questions that had remained hidden in esoteric places are now thrown into the light of the public square." Such questions involved not only their behavior at the liberation but also their clamoring for compensation from a regime with which they had—as Steiner had now shown—criminally collaborated in the camps. The *Rivarol* writer did not mention the fact that the crime in which they "collaborated" had been the mass death of the Jewish people. As a result, *Rivarol* concluded, "Steiner's book has a much greater chance of interesting those who, without necessarily opposing the Jews, nevertheless have noticed . . . that in all times and places the concentration of Jews has led to the same brutal and pitiless responses." If the Jews suffered in wartime, they had themselves to blame. Steiner's book showed, not that antisemitism remained a persisting quandary in French postwar life, but only that "the Jews have always been their own worst enemies." In this way, *Rivarol* provided a denigrating particularism to match the laudatory particularism that Steiner had attempted to purvey in his book. The task of what follows is to inquire into what effect Steiner's brand of particularism had on the most venerable and important universalism of postwar France: the patriotism of the deportation community, in both its leftist and Gaullist variants, which turned out to be crucially different in their reception of his book.

■

Only when *Le Nouveau Candide* opted to capitalize on the scandal it had itself created did the Treblinka affair actually become a genuine affair that split the deportation community, like France as a whole, in two. On March 21, a week after its publication of the inflammatory interview with Steiner, it ran a long and diverse series of letters. Then it published a spectacular, lengthy analysis and critique of Steiner's book over two weeks (the April 18 and April 29 issues) written by the journalist and author David Rousset, in many respects the founder of French discourse about Nazi criminality.

So interesting a figure and so significant in his time, though now largely forgotten, notably in the English-speaking world—a brief digression on Rousset's life and works is appropriate, not simply in order to understand his role in the Treblinka controversy, but also to restore him to his rightfully critical place in the history of the interpretation of the European fascist era. A Protestant by birth and a Trotskyist by interwar political formation, Rousset (1912–1990) quickly became a celebrity after the war thanks to his testimonial works.[11] His famous *L'univers concentrationnaire* (published in the United States as *The Other Kingdom* and in England as *A World Apart*) was one of the first reports on the camps to be published after the war and became, without question, the foundational French text on the subject. Dated August 1945, it appeared in 1946. A friend of Sartre during the period and a Marxist, a founder with Sartre of the abortive Rassemblement Démocratique Révolutionnaire, Rousset published two fragments of his testimony in some of the initial numbers of *Les Temps modernes*, before ultimately choosing to divide his narrative into two books, the report and the vast successor "novel," *Les Jours de notre mort* of 1947.[12] He also published a collection of documents, *Le Pitre ne rît pas*, in 1948; this last book, consisting of documents gathered at the fledgling Centre de documentation juive contemporaine (CDJC) and published in collaboration with the historian Léon Poliakov, who also participated in the Treblinka affair, engages more directly with the Nazi persecution of Jews.[13]

Rousset did not coin the expression "concentration camp," but he contributed decisively to its currency; and in the title of his best-known book, *L'univers concentrationnaire*, he inaugurated the notion of a separate and isolated world constituted by the archipelago of exclusionary institutions constructed by the Nazi regime to contain its enemies.[14] Like Eugen Kogon's *Der SS-Staat*, the other report of the period that had major international resonance, *L'univers concentrationnaire* was written by a non-Jew and extrapolated from personal experience in different Western camps, notably Buchenwald, to dwell more generally on the system as a total phenomenon.[15] As Annette Wieviorka has put it, Rousset

> introduced to the larger public the idea of a "concentration camp," no longer simply a repressive tool like a prison, but a world apart governed by its own laws. He thus allowed the concentration camp system to be conceived globally, and made it possible—going beyond the testimonies on the Nazi camps published already before the war and, in numerous quantities, after 1945—for common principles of organization to be perceived. . . . It was not a matter any longer of the mere evocation of individual tragedies or of limited insights into a given camp—Dachau or Buchenwald—but of a global reflection. Even if David Rousset's analyses can seem partially obsolete today, a whole mode of reflection still operative is owed to him.[16]

Rousset's book, like his subsequent *Les Jours de notre mort*, aimed to capture the sheer immensity of the camp system that grew up in Europe from shortly after the Nazi seizure of power. It also presented the Nazi camp system as in principle iterable in other times. Indeed, Rousset epitomized, in France, the broadly universalist and specifically antifascist interpretation of Nazi criminality.

Rousset's work influentially described the camp experience as absurd and fictitious. The closest parallel he found to the camp was in Alfred Jarry's absurdist play *Ubu the King:* "Ubu and Kafka lost their original literary association," Rousset wrote, "and became component parts of the world in which we live."[17] In terms that became central to contemporary (and persist into very recent theoretical) interpretations of the camps, Rousset emphasized the prisoners as not only literally but also existentially naked as a result of their internment and in the midst of a life no different from death—on the border between them.

It is striking, however, in rereading Rousset's work in light of Jean-François Steiner's later enterprise, how much they shared, how close they were, even as they believed they so fundamentally diverged. Steiner, of course, claimed that the notion of a *univers concentrationnaire* obscured the exterminatory enterprise of the Nazi state; but interestingly, Rousset showed himself more than happy to admit inward differentiation within the overall *univers concentrationnaire,* almost to the point of acknowledging the fundamental difference between concentration and extermination. "The camps," he wrote, "were not all identical or equivalent. The *univers concentrationnaire* was organized on different planes. . . . Buchenwald, Neuengamme, Sachsenhausen, Dachau, each and all fitted into the same plan, and were types of the 'normal' camps which made up the essential framework of the concentration camp world. In utterly different latitudes lay the reprisal camps . . . for Jews . . . in the shape of Auschwitz. . . . The camps for Jews . . . were a large scale industry for torture and extermination." The fact that Rousset could, in his main text, in effect introduce the distinction between concentration and extermination himself suggests the fact that the claim of unity of and not differences in Nazi criminality is at bottom not an empirical one to be resolved by appeal for factual resolution. In any case, the empirical distinction Rousset willingly drew did not lead to any more serious analytical fragmentation of the universal syndrome he depicted. "Between these extermination camps and the 'normal' camps there was no fundamental difference: only a difference in degree," he affirmed.[18] His core theory of the camps, and not just his politics, led to this result, for the erasure of the distinction between life and death in concentration—emphasized in the phrase *Les Jours de notre mort,* the title of his second book—also, of course, led him to see camps devoted to actual killing as fundamentally similar.

The result of Rousset's unitary interpretation was to rule out any and all of Steiner's later localized theses about specifically Jewish extermination camps. But, like Steiner, Rousset showed great interest in the problem of the "collaboration" of camp inmates in the functioning of the Nazi enterprise and the attendant moral problems such conduct might raise. Among the most vivid sections in *L'univers concentrationnaire* (as of course in other, more obscure camp literature) is the one that describes the relative marginality of the Nazi masters to the experience of camp life, and the existence of hierarchies of rule amongst the prisoners. "The Gods do not make their dwelling here on earth," Rousset put it in one of his chapter titles. "It was a fixed principle that, within the organization, the running of the camp lay entirely in the hands of the prisoners themselves," Rousset explained.[19] From Rousset's perspective, already in his early depictions, the work of the *Sonderkommandos* in the death camps—the later subject of Steiner's book—simply obeyed this more general principle. Rousset did not, however, believe this principle reflected an unseemly collaborationism. In a famous statement from *Les Jours de notre mort*, cited immediately by Georges Bataille (and much later by Giorgio Agamben), Rousset suggested that this structural fact about the camps abolished easy juridical distinctions between master and victim: "Victim and executioner are equally ignoble; the lesson of the camps is brotherhood in abjection."[20] But for Rousset, this abjection simply illustrated the horror of the camp—and the world that could give rise to it—rather than shaming the inmates who suffered it and requiring the search for some uplifting alternative.

Finally, if Rousset shared Steiner's perception of the moral difficulties that internees faced in the camps through their "collaborative" activity, he also focused on the zest for staying alive. But the "ludicrous determination to hold on to life" was for Rousset no ethnic or religious principle, reserved to the Jews in particular, but a human need that operates everywhere. Long before Steiner, he endorsed a "principle of life" that warred against the "principle of death" unleashed by the SS camp masters, referring to "a dynamic awareness of the strength and beauty of being alive, self-contained, brutal, entirely stripped of all superstructures, of being able to live even in the midst of the most appalling catastrophes or the most serious setbacks."[21] For Rousset, however, the drive to life did not have to be found as an antidote to humiliation and abjection; rather, it explained why they were tolerable.

But where Rousset differed perhaps most radically from his later antagonist, of course, was in the moral consequence that flowed from his depiction of the camps. It did not lead to the affirmation of a particular identity but to universalistic vigilance. Rousset intended the unforgettable portrait of the camps he had achieved to serve as a "warning" to the present of the probable and perhaps imminent iterability of the evil that the Nazis had unleashed most spectacularly but that lurked in any modern (capitalist and imperialist) society. After the border between life and death and between fiction and reality had been crossed, there was no easy return. "It would be duplicity, and criminal duplicity, to pretend that it is impossible for other nations to try a similar experiment because it would be contrary to their nature. . . . Under a new guise," Rousset concluded his work, "similar effects may appear tomorrow."[22]

■

Rousset's conception of a unified system of Nazi criminality that combined concentration and extermination had an enormous impact, within antifascist circles but also far beyond them. And his work found illustrious readers both in France and beyond.[23] Indeed, though her many commentators have failed to note it, Hannah Arendt depended very largely on Rousset's interpretation as a source on camp life in *The Origins of Totalitarianism,* which is worth examining in order to understand the drift of Rousset's universalizing and homogenizing views. Arendt praised Rousset for perceiving the radical novelty of the camps in European history. There was a caesura in European history, only it was the camps as a whole and not simply the particular fate of the Jews in them. The Nazis had, Arendt argued, realized in practice the scope of possible human crimes that European moralists and immoralists had first achieved in theory. Ordinary social life excluded the terrifying fact that Rousset had been (Arendt said) "the first to understand"—that "everything is possible." Far from denying the extremity of Nazi crime, as Steiner in effect charged, Rousset first captured its dimensions. Fiction, she repeated from Rousset's presentation, had become reality. (Arendt herself used the word "fictitious" several times to describe the world of the aims and achievements of totalitarian regimes.)

Most important, Rousset's analysis pushed Arendt to a striking and explicit argument that the suffering of the Jews in the extermination camps needed to be understood as *continuous* with the rest of the Nazi camp system, its natural outgrowth or furthest consequence rather than a phenomenon in a different and alternative category. Very rarely, it is true, she absolutely distinguished the phenomenon of extermination, for example in her comment in the immediate aftermath of the war that "by a criminal lack of imagination, we did not differentiate between persecution and extermination."[24] In general, however, Arendt softened or abolished, following Rousset, any distinction between concentration and extermination, as in her review of Poliakov's early work on the Nazi genocide, in which she commented that "[c]oncentration and extermination camps are the most novel and most significant devices of all totalitarian forms of domination. . . . The differences between [the Nazi and Soviet camps] are real but not radical; both systems result in the destruction of people selected as 'superfluous.'"[25] She could say so since, drawing on Rousset's depiction of living death, she understood extermination camps such as Treblinka as a consequence of concentration camps, not as a new and different formation. As Arendt put matters, it is the camp system, rendering human beings superfluous through killing them juridically and morally, that deserves the most attention; having become "living corpses," it is as if they are already dead.[26] Only a regime that produces living death, she suggested, can reach the last consequence of producing actual death. Arendt's extraordinary rendition indicates some of the originality and fecundity of Rousset's intervention. And it suggests what could have angered Rousset about Steiner's attempt to distinguish concentration and extermination, as he did in his title and throughout his text.

The interpretation of the World War II events that Rousset offered crystallized with its age, and it is important to consider why it proved so long lasting. It certainly struck a continuity with interwar antifascist discourse, notably important in postwar French politics, reviving its interwar themes without allowing the novelty of genocide the force of interruption. Just as important, in France, the antifascist narrative that Rousset provided gave a left-wing inflection to the interpretation of events shared by left and right, which presented the search for a postwar patriotic order as the principal legacy of the victory against "concentrationist" regimes, and offered up a set of protagonists who, by virtue of their experience, could testify about the past and lead into the future.[27]

Did this interpretation always and by definition "suppress" the terrible fact of the Jews' victimhood in the Holocaust? It is possible to say so, except for the fact that, at least some of the time, Jewish persecution is given a great deal of attention *as part of* a more general and fundamental "theory and practice of hell" (the English title of Eugen Kogon's book). Arendt actually gave an argument—persuasive or not—for why the camp system explains the genocide (the superfluity to which totalitarianism reduces human beings also makes their elimination an expectable next step). And by and large Rousset and some of the other contributors to the discourse, like Arendt, never denied the disproportionate Jewish victimhood in the war, even as they integrated it into a larger picture of Nazi criminality. The thesis of continuity coexisted perfectly well with that of epitome: as Rousset put it in an early postwar article published in the Jewish journal *Évidences,* funded by the American Jewish Committee, the Jews' fate in the genocide, epitomizing the horror of the more general *univers concentrationnaire,* showed the need for more change to avoid for others in the present and in the future what the Jews had suffered in the past.[28]

The origins of the Cold War, it is true, left Rousset in a kind of no-man's-land of the left. Though always committed to revolutionary change, he responded to the news of the Soviet gulag with rage, like many Trotskyists and ex-Trotskyists, and assumed all victims of fascist camps would follow him in their denunciation. In late 1949 he published an open letter to deportees to join the militant fight against the Soviet camps.[29] In this sense, his universalist interpretation of Nazi criminality prepared him to see new and similar kinds of criminality elsewhere, to draw on his own experience in combating them, rather than attempting to distinguish them as different. In the period, he led a Commission internationale contre le régime concentrationnaire, and his activities suggest the lapse of memory of today's historians of antifascism, because the universalist interpretation sometimes led leftists to an attentive awareness of communist barbarism rather than an ideologically motivated repression of such knowledge.[30] Rousset's denunciation of the gulag led to a celebrated libel trial on this issue in which Rousset sued Pierre Daix and *Les Lettres françaises.*[31] (It was at this moment that Sartre broke with Rousset and, with Maurice Merleau-Ponty, took Daix's side, publishing an ambiguous piece in *Les Temps modernes* justifying Stalinism in response to Rousset's accusations.)[32] Subsequently, in the name of his committee, Rousset published exposés of Stalinist concentration camp practices.[33] As a result of this controversy, Rousset lost some influence among the deportee community whose experience he had helped crystallize in *L'univers concentrationnaire;* the Cold War redrew lines among deportees, dividing them between communists and anticommunists. Nonetheless, Rousset's "universalist" interpretation of Nazi criminality remained normative.

■

True to his beliefs, he stood up for his interpretation once again against the unexpected challenge of Jean-François Steiner. Rousset's double-issue review in *Le Nouveau Candide* (a magazine to which he occasionally contributed) tasked Steiner with a "mystical, racist, and confusing" thesis.[34] What vexed Rousset into so enraged a reply to Steiner, of course, was that *Treblinka's* particularizing interpretation, both of Nazi crime and Jewish inmates, denied the actual universalism that a study of the concentration camps should, he thought, promote. He opposed, most fundamentally, Steiner's charge that "two wars that have absolutely nothing in common" were still being confused: "a world war, the one Germany made on the world, and . . . the war of the Nazis against the Jews, the war of the principle of death against the principle of life."[35] For Rousset perfectly recognized that Steiner's attempt to *entirely separate* Jewish from other victimhood at Nazi hands, coupled with Steiner's emphasis on its comparative horror, also undermined the entire basis for postwar French solidarities of both left and right.

One erred, Rousset therefore claimed, in absolutely distinguishing the Jews from other kinds of victims, though of course the Jews suffered particular straits before the Nazi enterprise came to grief: "The anti-Jewish enterprise of the Nazis," Rousset averred, "was integrated in their general enterprise against fundamental liberties. It was one of the means of spreading terror and enforcing subjugation. They also eliminated the Gypsy people. They wanted to exterminate the Slavs. They pretended to make of the French a minor population."

This core difference led Rousset to a completely different approach to all the features of Treblinka that Steiner had wanted to see as Jewish in some specific sense. He began by taking aim at Steiner's controversial argument that the Jews had collaborated in their own extermination. But, Rousset stressed, he and many other deportees had shown long ago that the Nazis deployed such a "technique" everywhere in their *univers concentrationnaire.* "The pretense of breaking a silence is ridiculous," Rousset argued, under a banner headline explaining that "there was collaboration in every camp." Rousset called this "collaboration" the "permanent theme of all literature on the concentration camps. The management of the camps by the detained is the entire concentration camp system. It occurred to all of the concentrated prisoners, whether Jewish or not. From the point of view of the camp administration there is thus no difference between the racial and other camps."

Rousset argued in two (apparently incompatible) ways about the significance of this fact. On the one hand, he stressed that there was nothing morally specific about the Jews' collaboration because all prisoners everywhere were the victims of the Nazis' organizational genius. There was no moral problem to be discerned in the failure to resist; acts of resistance had been few and far between precisely because they were possible only in rare and fortuitous circumstances, because only rarely did mistakes and lapses lead to gaps in the Nazis' grid of control. The Jews' failure to revolt thus illustrated nothing negative about them; just as the Treblinka victory, though of course courageous, reflected rare and special circumstances rather than some Jewish existential logic.

On the other hand, Rousset went so far as to argue that, in some respects, the "collaboration" that took place at concentration as opposed to extermination camps seemed more ethically questionable if it involved selecting people for death rather than simply implementing their death.

> From a moral point of view it was indisputably less grave to take gold teeth from corpses, to empty gas chambers, and to operate the gas chambers than to choose who would leave on a transport and who would not, who would be allowed into the infirmary or not. To send a detainee from some work unit meant sending him to a certain death. To refuse him medical assistance too. Living in a *Sonderkommando* of the gas chambers involving living in psychologically horrible circumstances but not at all in a morally terrible condition. The moral state of a doctor, a kapo, a functionary of the *Arbeitsstatistik* or the *Politischabteilung* could involve far more anguish.

As Steiner had himself emphasized, the Nazi "Technicians" had devised the circumstances for all, and in some sense had robbed Jews of the ability to choose their destiny, even more than the nonracial prisoners. In any case, Rousset stressed, "[i]t was never a question of deciding whether or not to collaborate. The system was established." One simply played the absurd role appointed by Nazi designs. Rousset summed up by saying that "it is simply not possible to pose the critical problem of cooperation with the SS as if it were exclusively or principally a Jewish phenomenon. To do so means that one is either an antisemite or a Jewish racist." In making this interpretation, Rousset did not commit himself to the view that the Jews did not suffer disproportionately, only that their "collaboration" posed no new or different problems than the literature on the concentration camps—his own not least—had already exposed.

From there, Rousset went on from Steiner's claim of Jewish "abjection" to the Jewish antidote Treblinka supposedly illustrated. Even if the Nazis were particularists in singling out the Jews (a fact Rousset never flatly denied, though of course it did not occupy the center of his thinking), this fact did not suggest, as Steiner fantastically supposed, that the Jews responded in kind, and that the motives for their resistance involved the mystical drive for communal self-perpetuation. In this, most charitably read, Rousset did not so much deny the *fact* of special victimhood as the *significance* of this fact for making sense of the Nazi years as well as for crafting a moral program in response.

The difference he staked out from Steiner also implied a completely different image of Eastern European Jewish life. Rousset vehemently rejected the romanticized and sentimental view of Jewry on which Steiner had based his book, and emphasized instead the diversity of their political identities in the years prior to the genocide, most especially their participation in radical politics. Rooted in the workers' movement, Jews according to Rousset were primed, not for the mystical perpetuation of their communities according to a religious or national imperative, but rather for playing their role in the antifascist fight common to all mankind. "The struggle against Nazism was first of all and fundamentally an antifascist enterprise in which tens of thousands of Jews in Europe engaged because they were communists, socialists, and democrats," Rousset averred. It would be hard to say who erred through exaggeration more in the name of his ideology, Steiner or Rousset. But Rousset's view led him to complain that Steiner's "confused lucubrations regarding the mystical necessity of the biological survival of God's people," which had motivated his attempt to categorically distinguish the European war from the Holocaust that the war merely made possible, falsified not simply the unity of the Nazi enterprise but also the unity of the resistance to it. "Without underestimating the effects of an undeniable antisemitism, the Jews did not fight alone, in Poland or elsewhere: . . . Their motivations were just as diverse as those of non-Jews. All the same, many, and not the least important, battled on behalf of a social and political ideal that they shared with all those who presented themselves in Europe as democrats, as socialists, and revolutionaries." In this way, Rousset read the wartime in a manner that, rather than suppressing Jewish resistance, understood it as part of the larger war between the Nazis and their enemies.

One of the most important and culturally significant facts about Rousset's complaint in *Le Nouveau Candide,* beyond the substance of his arguments, is that it served as the conduit into the wider public sphere—more or less the only one—for informed Jewish critics of Steiner's book. He cited their attacks, otherwise only circulated in private or published in obscure places, in extenso in his two-part article. (This led *Le Nouveau Candide* to sensationalize Rousset's piece by printing a cover with the massive headline "The Treblinka Affair: The Jews Accuse." See figure 5.) That many Jews should

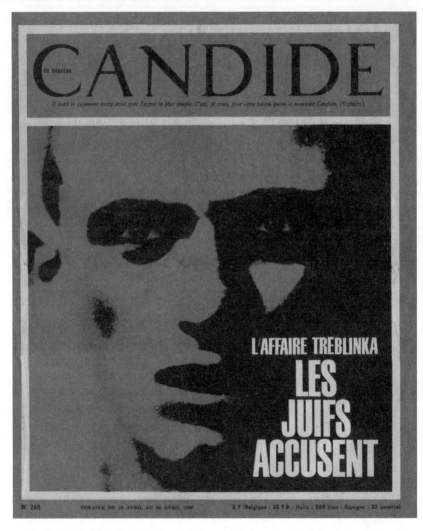

5. "The Treblinka Affair: The Jews Accuse." Cover of *Le Nouveau Candide*, 18–25 April 1966.

have sided with Rousset, particularly with his integration of the Jews' suffering with that of all Europe under Hitler's domination, may seem puzzling—a problem the next chapter will take up. But side with him they did. In particular, the knowledgeable historians of the genocide Georges Wellers and Joseph Billig, whose reports on *Treblinka* were privately circulated, found a voice before a large public only through Rousset's citation.[36] Wellers, for example, agreed emphatically with Rousset's argument that "collaboration" occurred in all camps. Another Jew, whom Rousset cited anonymously, argued Steiner had been mistaken to see in the syndrome of Treblinka's Jews anything particularly Jewish: "To read this author, all of the feelings experienced by the Treblinka deportees, all of their acts, and all of their responses, were specifically Jewish. They were not the feelings, acts and responses of men and women, placed in a specific situation. No. . . . In M. Steiner's mythology, Jewish particularity devoured the Jewish human being, an operation that, while rooted in different motives, is exactly parallel to the corresponding antisemitic practice."

What for Rousset and his cited authorities was worst about Steiner's enterprise, then, was that it separated the Jews from the other victims of the Nazis, not simply in the way the Nazis treated them factually, but in how the Jews responded morally. For Rousset, and his sources, Steiner had rooted the Treblinka revolt in a mysticism of Jewish particularity, rather than the vision of human universalism, ignoring the Jews' "feeling of solidarity with the struggle of other men against the Nazi horror," their sense that everyone had been (and remained now) in it together. It was as if one could not admit the Jews were special victims, except at the price of destroying the alliance of all humans against the persistent forces of hatred and domination.

■

Among the ironies of the Treblinka affair is the strange bedfellows it made. Converging with Rousset, in a comparatively obscure intervention without public resonance, yet worthy of coverage nonetheless, was the man now best known as the founder of Holocaust denial: Paul Rassinier. A former member of the Communist party, then a socialist, in the interwar years, Rassinier became a *résistant* before his apprehension by the Germans and his internment in the camps of Buchenwald and Dora. When he returned, after a brief foray into politics, Rassinier began airing the views that led to his canonization by the extreme right as the original source of "negationism" (as the French call Holocaust denial).[37]

The fact that it could have been a man interned in the Nazi camps who invented Holocaust denial has perplexed many over the years. After publishing his own, initially ignored memoir of camp life on his return, Rassinier published a "look at the literature on the concentration camp" titled *Ulysses's Lie* in 1950, which, it happens, devoted an entire acid chapter to Rousset for his alleged distortions of what had occurred in the Western camp experience they had both suffered through. Missing in Rousset's account, Rassinier charged, was the role of communist inmates in controlling the camps, and the pitiless brutality with which they ruled, in almost a moral equivalence with the SS, who were only the titular masters of the camps.[38] Rassinier raised the "problem" for which he would become famous, that of the existence of gas chambers, briefly and en passant in his first two works, denying in the first (correctly) that there had been any at the camps in which he found himself, noting in the second that the numbers of gas installations and gas victims had been overestimated and remained to be finally determined. The chief idea of his early works, Rassinier's idée fixe, was that the rulership—in effect, the collaboration—by communist internees in the camps had been obscured because of the extinction of their enemies in the camps and because of their postwar hegemony once they returned. He took this thesis to such an extreme that his enlargement of the communist role in effect and sometimes explicitly excused the Germans, relegated to the background of camp life. Some during the Treblinka affair in effect read Steiner as having done something similar, so intensively did he focus on Jewish "collaboration" at the expense of Nazi rulership.

Rassinier took the publication of *Treblinka*, fifteen years after his first works, as occasion to voice this thesis yet again, though by the midsixties the detail of his earlier discussions, the (antisemitic) hestitation about the gas chambers, had grown into the more full-blown denial for which he is now notorious. As Rassinier usually presented himself as the greatest historian of the camp experience, doubting the false memories and criticizing the partisan histories of other former inmates, he treated Steiner's book with dismissive condescension. (See figure 6.) Rassinier, who typically repudiated the testimony of all witnesses other than himself, did not need to bother indicting Steiner's mistaken memory, since Steiner merely transmitted the falsehoods of others rather than invented ones of his own. Of course, *Treblinka* had gotten one point right, Rassinier acknowledged. "Steiner's book would present little interest if . . . one did not find in it a thesis about the structure and essence of the camps—about their practical functioning—that I have defended in all of the writings published by me for twenty years . . . : that the deportees who managed, administered, and policed the camps . . . were the cause of the straits of the mass of the deportees, mistreated them, pillaged their rations, sent them to death, whether they were Jews or not."[39] The Germans were part of the picture, but in the background.

Where Steiner had erred, in spite of this insight, was in failing to see that

6. "The Jews and the Concentration Camps: Paul Rassinier Responds to Jean-François Steiner." Cover of *Le Charivari*, June 1966.

the collaboration affected only some of the interned prisoners and in making any distinction between the non-Jewish and the Jewish experience and, thus, between concentration and extermination. Steiner went wrong first of all since, in his obsessive thesis of the Jews' complicity in the camp and by nature, he identified the wrong target, for it had been mainly communists—Jewish and non-Jewish—who were to blame. "For it is not true that the Jews as a whole were complicit with their assassins," Rassinier maintained,

> only those who administered, ran, and policed the concentration camps were, only those who agreed to take part in the "self-government" that the Germans called *Häftlingsführung* (government of the deportees by the deportees themselves). These men agreed to everything in order to save their own skins and I repeat that they were, in their majority, communists or sympathizers: the communists, having been arrested first, occupied all the places when the others arrived. We others in the mass, we despised them more than the S.S. themselves since, given the zeal that they demonstrated, going beyond the hopes of their masters, asking from us more than they were asked to exact, they were for us, in fact, much more terrible and murderous than the S.S. were. But the others were only victims, not accomplices, and they are to be infinitely respected.

His biographer, Florent Brayard, has shown that this early element in Rassinier's thought persisted even as he moved more and more toward his more famous, "negationist" views.[40] Rassinier's "correction" of Steiner was really a matter of one idée fixe against another.

But, having insisted that only some Jews were open to Steiner's charge, Rassinier otherwise—and surprisingly—converged with Rousset in insisting that Jewish victimhood needed to be seen as a mere variation on the more general theme of Nazi camp life, no matter who was targeted or to what end. "Here again," he wrote in distinguishing between the collaborators and the victims, "this is true in all of the camps, not solely in the Jewish ones." Like Rousset, whose putatively exculpatory treatment of the *univers concentrationnaire* collaborators he nonetheless excoriated throughout his career, Rassinier judged the totality of Nazi criminality against what he had himself witnessed in Western camps. In attacking Steiner's conclusion that there had been something distinctive about Jewish passivity and activity in the extermination camps, insisting that "though it is quite true that the Jews went to the slaughter like lambs, Steiner can reassure himself that they were not alone," Rassinier ironically converged with Rousset again. Waxing autobiographical, Rassinier continued: "As resisters, Jewish or not, we let ourselves be arrested and sent to the camps with docility. Thus taken, against power there was no possible resistance and all sacrifice of life, in that circumstance, was perfectly useless. Myself a resister, I feel no embarrassment in so acknowledging."[41]

Much more radically than in Rousset's books and Treblinka affair essays, in Rassinier's thought this insistent point about the way the Nazis ran the camps obstructed any admission of the specificity and disproportionality of Jewish victimhood in them. And in the rest of his article, Rassinier gave antisemitic innuendo full play, doubting the testimonial evidence on which the history of the genocide in the east reposed, referring to his general evidentiary rule that eyewitness testimony did not count, a "principle" that would have a long career ahead of it in the history of Holocaust denial. Minimizing the numbers of Jewish victims by selective citation of evidence, Rassinier finished by relativizing their fate, narcissistically comparing it to the camp depredations that had permanently destroyed his own health. "Those [Jews] who could not flee," he made a show of acknowledging, "went to the slaughter like lambs. But I will repeat: we all did, and I did too." Finally, Rassinier made much of Steiner's Jewish identity and suggested there were ethnic reasons for the celebration of his book, which he saw as announcing partial truths available whole only in the works of Rassinier, the non-Jewish truth-teller. "No, we are not yet at the hour of truth," Rassinier confessed mournfully to an admirer at the time in a letter, "but I still believe that it will come. Last week there appeared, in Paris, a book that confirms my theses on the concentration camps. It is the work of a young Jew, so it is the toast of the town, whereas I stand condemned for having said, twenty years ago now, exactly the same things. For here is the truth: if the communists who reigned as masters in all of the concentration camps had been just, we would, almost without exception, have all returned. This is what flows from the book of my young Jew on the Treblinka camp."[42]

Of course, Rassinier simply ignored, in converting Steiner's book into an occasion for another lesson about the concentration camps in general, his attempt in *Treblinka* to introduce and to establish the difference between concentration and extermination. Rassinier died the next year, but not without having read *Treblinka* in a way that confirmed, as for so many others, his own point of view, to the detriment of the most culturally consequential point that the text actually contained. The question is: if figures as different as Rousset and Rassinier could reject the distinction between concentration and extermination, who would defend it?

■

The answer is: many people. Steiner's emphasis on the separability of the genocide caused a division among French deportees, and it helped that Beauvoir continued to protect the young author she had introduced with a stalwart, albeit confused, defense. As the terms of the protection to which she had committed herself fell apart under Rousset's assault, she lived up to her word nevertheless. In an interview conducted by the French-Jewish scholar Richard Marienstras for *Le Nouvel Observateur* (in which a young Lanzmann also participated), Beauvoir insisted that Steiner had produced a "visionary" text.[43] (See figure 7.)

Of course, in response to Rousset, she had to modify her position slightly. Marienstras politely suggested the limitations of seeing the Jews at Treblinka as "collaborators" (since, as Rousset had argued, inmates at all camps were). For his part, Lanzmann argued that, for someone older than Steiner like himself, there was no need to prove the heroism of the Jews by thinking of their collaboration before they revolted as a problem. To which Beauvoir responded that Steiner, younger and less informed a Jew, needed to prove to himself what older Jews could take for granted, thereby doing a service not simply for himself but all the youthful and ignorant.

This fact, however, could not change Steiner's original emphasis but only defend against its perverse misappropriation. And so, attempting to rebut the claim of *Treblinka*'s enemies that it had provided grist for the mill of antisemites at *Rivarol*, Beauvoir noted that it was *Rousset's* article—and the Jewish figures whose views he presented to the public—that had in the meantime led the satirical publication *Le Canard enchaîné* to claim that *Treblinka* was a "hoax." (The *Canard enchaîné* writers had explained: "Some historians just as Jewish as Steiner, though infinitely more serious, have started to say, even write, that this whole 'history' is nothing more than an atrocious hoax and that to present this little book as historical is to collude in a swindle.")[44] This argument clearly did not reach Rousset's main claims, however.

For Rousset's problem, of course, was that Steiner had proved the wrong thesis; and Beauvoir, unable now to ignore the central animating intent of the book she was defending, simply disagreed with it. "Each time that Steiner describes the attitudes of the Jews of Treblinka as specifically Jewish, I can no longer follow him, because this attitude was shared in common by all concentration camp inmates, who all lived through the same events," Beauvoir noted. On this point, Lanzmann, some years yet from *Shoah*, the brilliant documentary on the Holocaust that would make him internationally famous,

7. "The Jews of Treblinka: Simone de Beauvoir Responds." Cover of *Le Nouvel Observateur*, 27 April 1966. (© *Le Nouvel Observateur*.)

agreed with her, repeating her Sartrean perspective: "The Nazi concentration camp system was arranged to divide [the Jews], just like all the other deportees." Indeed, Beauvoir claimed that she had followed the opposite path from Steiner: beginning with the perception that most deportees were political prisoners, and later coming to learn that so many among them were deported as Jews, she soon came to identify the victims of the genocide not as a forgotten category but rather as subject to the same analysis—now the updated Sartrean analysis, which she repeated, of serialization and group formation (the eight hundred thousand murdered at Treblinka were, for Beauvoir, simply people serialized to death and thus beyond any chance to form a group, victims of no analytically different crime than were the rest of the deportation community or even humanity under capitalism). "Whoever the victims were (Jews, gypsies, Russians, resisters, communists), the system was always the same," Beauvoir affirmed. The diversity of ends to which the Nazis subjected their opponents apparently did not disturb this conclusion.

The striking fact about Beauvoir's defense of *Treblinka*, then, is that it reposed, like her preface, on universalist and homogenizing foundations that were in the final analysis identical to those which led Rousset to criticize the book. Beauvoir claimed, through strenuous appropriation, that *Treblinka* illustrated a lesson "not simply beyond the Jewish problem but beyond the concentration camp problem. It accurately presents one of those limit situations in which men were, thanks to the impossibility of living a situation, driven to transcend it." It followed that *Treblinka* bore a lesson not about the particularity of Nazi animus toward the Jews (to say nothing of Jewish cultural particularity) but rather about the general nature of domination, a lesson that conformed perfectly with Rousset's point of view, or ironically went beyond it in wholly denying the particularity and specificity of the Jewish fate in the genocide. It was predictable, perhaps, that Beauvoir's angry response in *Le Nouvel Observateur* provoked a further debate between Rousset and her in its pages two weeks later, but no amount of ink could fill the chasm between them. Nevertheless, Rousset was correct to point out, in his letter, that, if Beauvoir rejected Steiner's particularity arguments, then "she rejects Steiner's whole work. One is led to conclude that she did not understand the book she prefaced!"[45]

■

It must have come as a shock to Rousset—and perhaps even to Steiner—that many of the leaders of the deportation community endorsed Steiner's book, even as it undermined the historical basis for their homogenizing ideology. Sometimes, they attempted to praise the book while rejecting one of its central theses and its attempt to distinguish concentration and extermination. A good example is the laudatory review published in *Le Figaro littéraire* by the literary scholar and former Mauthausen inmate Louis Martin-Chauffier (author of a famous camp testimony).[46] What Steiner had narrated, Martin-Chauffier claimed, "did not concern the Jews alone. Some millions of other deportees died as well, and did not revolt either. Mr. Steiner knows this fact and does not hide it, but he perhaps does not understand to what extent it so tragically applied." Other prominent deportees, however, welcomed Steiner's book not in spite but because of its central thesis, thus laying the ground for a substantial split in the deportee community over the interpretation of their experience.

Edmond Michelet (1899–1970), a Dachau survivor, a former government minister under Charles de Gaulle and member of the Conseil constitutionnel in 1966, and perhaps the most politically significant exponent of the postwar deportation community, weighed in most consequentially in this regard. Having been given the proofs by Steiner's editor, Constantin Melnik, on the Gaullist right like himself, Michelet responded first in a letter that deserves to be quoted at length: "I have just spent most of the night reading this shocking *Treblinka* that you sent," he began. "*You are to be congratulated* for having wanted to make known this testimony—not the testimony of a witness properly speaking but, even better, of a child (if I dare call him that) of so many witnesses who are no longer here." Rejecting Beauvoir's leftist preface, Michelet showed himself nevertheless partly open to a universalizing interpretation that entirely sidelined the specificity of Jewish victimhood by emphasizing the commonalities of camp life for all: "Let us not delude ourselves. Treblinka (which was a new discovery for me) confirms my conviction that [Jacques] Maritain was right, that there exists a 'mystery of Israel.' But it also reminds me that, just as important *all* of the *univers concentrationnaire* could be called 'Treblinka.' How many phantoms I had to see again last night!"[47] The lines suggest an initial and understandable incertitude about how exactly the "new discovery" of Jewish extermination could fit with the patriotic Gaullist memory Michelet so influentially epitomized (especially since, as his language shows, Gaullism had its own adaptation of the ideology of the *univers concentrationnaire*). Nonetheless, out of interest in the book's fortunes, Michelet contributed a front-page review to *Le Monde*, and resolved the ambiguity of his letter about the terms in which he could endorse Steiner's book.

In his piece, printed in France's flagship postwar newspaper, Michelet admitted that the name Treblinka remained practically unknown, even in the deportee community, thanks to the endless talk of camps with numerous survivors like Bergen-Belsen, Buchenwald, and Michelet's own Dachau.[48] In some respects like Steiner's other readers, Michelet attempted to appropriate his text, in this case for the Gaullist deportation community that ironically shared so much, in spite of its many disputes, with the antifascist interpretation. Michelet emphasized that Steiner had been correct, and wise, not to indict the German people (the reconstructed Germany counted as an essential Christian and Cold War ally), just as *Treblinka* actually suggested the limits of deriving a revolutionary message from the book, as Beauvoir's "curious" preface tried to accomplish. Indeed, the true opponent of concentration camps opposed the left, since "those who judged the Hitlerian outburst from on high have since shown themselves capable of using Nazism's disconcerting methods." Unlike Steiner's other readers, however, Michelet agreed with the insistence he found in *Treblinka* on differential victimhood, albeit thanks to an interpretation that could countenance the particular fate of the Jews only through their subsumption into a universalizing narrative, Christian rather than leftist. Nonetheless, the distinction is crucial. Acknowledging the difference between concentration and extermination, Michelet wrote, "The people of the stiff neck," who continued to suffer so much in a sinner's history, "remain an incomparable model of the best and the worst for the world of *goyim.*"

To explain such a turn, blending universalizing appropriation with particularizing acknowledgment, Michelet's allusion in his letter to the Catholic philosopher Jacques Maritain is of extreme importance. Maritain, who provided the ultimate grid authorizing Michelet's interpretation of Steiner's book, had been one of the several Catholic intellectuals renovating their faith in the direction of friendly condescension rather than hateful contempt for the Jewish people, and Michelet alluded to Maritain's influential thesis that the Jews were not so much Christ-killers as Christ-givers (both Michelet and Maritain had moved away from integral nationalism in their youth). Glossing Paul's Epistle to the Romans (11:25)—"For I would not, brethren, that ye should be ignorant of this mystery, lest ye should be wise in your own conceits; that blindness in part is happened to Israel, until the fullness of the Gentiles be come in"—Maritain interpreted Jews' continued presence as a "mystery" full of theological meaning. Murderous antisemitism failed to acknowledge this mystery, attempting to extinguish the bearers of a precious message. "Six million Jews were *liquidated* in Europe," Maritain wrote in the text, republished in 1965, to which Michelet alluded in his letter, "and it is Moses and the prophets, and the Savior to which they gave rise, who were pursued in them. . . . It is the dignity of Israel, which the Catholic Church prays to God to spread throughout the nations, that were ridiculed in the Jews mistreated like the world's vermin. It is our God that was harassed and tortured through his fleshly ancestry before persecuting Him openly in his church."[49]

Maritain's acknowledgment of specifically Jewish suffering allowed Michelet, in 1966, to see Steiner's presentation of the wartime in a new way. Steiner—who, it is important to recall, likewise referred to the persistence of the Jews as a "mystery" at a crucial point in his text—helped make Michelet's beneficent Christian appropriation of his emphasis on the Jewish mission, an appropriation rooted in Maritain's conception of the Jewish mystery, easier.[50] The Treblinka affair, then, forces a reflection on the different historical implications of leftist and Christian universalisms for reimagining the past. It is surprising, but undeniable, that Michelet's allegiance to the official conservative ideology of the period—Gaullist and Catholic in a larger European atmosphere of conservative Christian democracy—allowed Steiner's emphasis on the special fate of the Jews in wartime a comparatively genuine hearing.[51]

That it may have been right-wing Christian assumptions that first allowed the specificity of the Holocaust that Steiner championed to be publicly acknowledged is a reality confirmed by the laudatory endorsement of *Treblinka* drafted by François Mauriac in his *Bloc-Notes* column, a testimonial that cemented the literary triumph of the book. It is hard to grasp the significance of such an endorsement by the Catholic novelist and Nobel prizewinner today, when he is rarely read and his commanding stature in French letters during the Cold War has been forgotten—indeed, never to be occupied again by a comparable Catholic intellectual. But like Maritain, Mauriac played an extremely significant role in his time both in the evolution of Christian attitudes toward Jews as well as in making the Holocaust a subject of reflection and debate.[52] As Naomi Seidman has stressed in a controversial article, for example, he involved himself in the publication of and wrote the preface to Elie Wiesel's *Night* when it first appeared in French in 1959.[53] And in the Treblinka affair, he intervened again.

Begun in 1952, and a landmark cultural indicator of the age, Mauriac's *Bloc-Notes* commanded a wide readership throughout the era, one very different— Gaullist and Christian—from Beauvoir's leftist audience. The *Bloc-Notes* took the form of a journal, and Mauriac's entry on Steiner, dated April 29, 1966, appeared in *Le Figaro littéraire* on May 5.[54] "What *Treblinka* reveals to us, in a manner that gives us the strength and the courage to relive in thought what these men, women, and children suffered," Mauriac wrote, "is Israel's mission, which is to remind the West the abomination of which it was the witness and thus the accomplice, and to forbid it from forgetting it." (Apparently, the West related to the genocide merely as a passive bystander to a crime.) Crediting Steiner for "giving for the first time a total picture of the Nazi technique applied to serial and mass death," a fate reserved to Jews in particular, Mauriac claimed that through his novelization Steiner had not really falsified anything but rather achieved a panoramic reconstruction available to no particular witness and reflected in no specific document. "This young writer," Mauriac concluded, "benefited paradoxically from not having been there and having learned everything."

Strikingly, extending his prior interpretations of the genocide, Mauriac attempted to find, like Maritain and Michelet, the principle that would make its recognition compatible with the Christian philosophy of culture and politics that he advocated. In the postwar age, like many other Catholic spokesmen, Mauriac struggled to understand the suffering of the Jews in the Holocaust as an event in a sacramental history intelligible within his own Christian faith. Seidman has charged that Mauriac's intervention helped determine the "Christianized" manner in which Wiesel reframed his earlier Yiddish memoir for eventually vast audiences in Europe and America; this Christianization suppressed, Seidman says, the authentically Jewish point of view, forced into conformity with alien premises. But there is the question of baseline in any judgment; and, from another perspective, the historian's question ought to be why, of all ideologies, only (or first) Christianity proved publicly open to the particularity of the Jewish fate in the war, helping end the marginalization of the Holocaust that Mauriac merely inherited. The Christianizing appropriation, in other words, is less surprising than the limited recognition that appropriation allowed. Mauriac's reading at least reversed the traditional Catholic teaching of contempt toward the Jews and recognized the specificity of the Jews' victimhood in the war. It could do so—unlike Beauvoir's preface, for instance—because Catholicism presented a kind of universalism that understood itself as a supersession of, but also perpetually dependent on, the prior and abnegated particularism of the Jewish people.

Like Michelet's piece, then, Mauriac's interpretation made more room than Beauvoir's Marxism or Rousset's antifascist leftism for the specificity of Jewish victimhood and, in a way far closer to Steiner's intent, the Jews' specific role in world history. In Mauriac's interpretation of Steiner's book, as in Michelet's essay, the suffering of the Jews thus became analogous to the suffering of Christ, tragedies reflecting human sinfulness but also portending Christian redemption. *Treblinka*'s ending, Mauriac stated, narrated "the exit of the Jews from hell," but this exit remained reversible so long as redemption remained in the future. "May Israel itself not lose faith in its election, in this choice that glorifies and crucifies it forever," Mauriac wrote, recommending the spirit in which to read the book he analyzed. "God's presence resounds throughout this history written by a young Jew, son of a Catholic mother, but himself faithful [to his Jewish roots]." In his emphasis on the Jews' mission in history, Steiner had precociously and inadvertently made the insight that his people are "a people of preachers." Mauriac knew, unlike Steiner, that what they preached transcended their own understanding and actually anticipated Christianity and the return of its redeemer.

Similar interpretations were available throughout the Christian press, which on balance welcomed Steiner's enterprise with the most warmth of any category of respondents. Another Christian writer, contributing to the Jesuit journal *Études* one of the more sensitive readings of the book, drew on one of Steiner's character's internal reflections about God's intention in bringing the Holocaust about, his feeling that the Holocaust must have a meaning in the plan of creation, a meaning in which the suffering of the Jews in particular amounted to "a warning to the world, that God was using His people to say something to the world." This writer recognized that the text recorded multiple conflicting interpretations of the meaning of witnessing, but that at its most authentic *Treblinka* recalled the prophetic and redemptive universalism of Judaism, overcoming Steiner's drive to particularism, making an invidious choice between Jewish and Christian readings of his book almost (but not quite) otiose. Steiner had unveiled the innate barbarism of human beings without God's promise of universal peace—and that "the most religious and lucid of Israel's members at Treblinka wanted themselves to be the instrument of this implacable news, and therefore the suffering servant, the prophet crucified because of his message."[55] The implication of the Christian praise for the history of Holocaust consciousness is therefore clear. As Pierre Nora has recently observed, the Christian appropriation of the Holocaust, bound up with the Vatican II attempt to cleanse the Church of the era of antisemitism, surely played a major role in the initial generalization of Holocaust memory, shaping the conditions of possibility for what came later. "Without the mobilization of Christian guilt and the transmission that it assured," he writes, "it is hard to understand how a memory about Jews alone could have had such an echo."[56]

Amongst more left-leaning Christians, it is important to record, praise for Steiner ran high too.[57] Nonetheless, it was the endorsements of Michelet and Mauriac, on the right, that mattered most. It is perhaps most plausible, in summary, to attribute their generosity—for in context generosity it was—to the fact that Christian universalism is premised on Jewish particularity. Along with the many left-wing deportee endorsements of *Treblinka* (including many cited at the beginning of this chapter), Michelet's review gave the all-important imprimatur of the other major wing of the deportation community to Steiner's book, even as Rousset attempted to awaken them to Steiner's attack on the basic organizing paradigm through which the phenomenon of deportation had come to be understood in French culture. Mauriac, speaking for conservative Christianity more generally, lent his extraordinary cultural authority to a similar view. It is true, of course, that the Christian reading of *Treblinka* departed hardly at all from the strict universalism of the leftist reading of Beauvoir and others. But ironically, it may have been the Christian admission of Jewish particularity for the purpose of its supersession that allowed the specificity of the Jewish fate in the war to be first "seen."

■

As a result, a general, intense debate about the nature of their experience, with crucial implications for collective perceptions of Nazi criminality, ensued within the deportation community and in France at large.[58] "In Paris this week," a *Time* magazine writer reported in late April, "survivors of the Nazi death camps marched up the Champs-Élysées to mark the annual day of mourning for those who died in the more than 2,000 camps that were scattered throughout German-occupied Europe." But this time, "the memory of the dead was clouded by a controversy that, nearly a quarter of a century later, still raises deep and bitter questions."[59] Patriotic memory of French martyrdom was under siege.

Aside from repeating his basic notions, however, Steiner did not himself intervene in the debate set off by Rousset's article, except to write a letter to *Le Nouveau Candide* in which he insisted "that this whole tumult should not lead anyone to forget the essential. My work is not simply an evocation of the martyrdom of my people, but is also and above all an example—among many others—of the resistance of the Jews to Nazi persecution. *Treblinka* is nothing else than the history of a revolt that, before breaking out at the end of the book, is in process in it from the very beginning."[60] Climactically, from the Comité d'Action de la Résistance, Steiner won the prestigious Prix littéraire de la Résistance, along with its twenty-five thousand-franc purse. It was a contested choice—five to four—of a split prize committee, and the first time an author had won for writing of events he had not himself witnessed.[61] In a triumphant moment, Steiner received the award from Marie-Madeleine Fourcade, former Resistance spy and celebrity president of the committee, at a ceremony. (See figure 8.)

Both in large fora and, no doubt, in the intimacy of local *amicales* of deportees, the book was discussed passionately. One large debate, initially organized so that Steiner could debate Rousset, took place on June 7, at the Théâtre des Ambassadeurs (now the Espace Cardin); but Rousset did not appear, and apparently the event, which also featured Fourcade, favored Steiner's presentation.[62] Some of the more prominent Jewish experts on the genocide— Georges Wellers and Olga Wormser among others—along with Marcel Paul, the FNDIRP's president, were organized to debate the book by the communist Union des Juifs pour la Résistance et l'Entraide (UJRE) at the Salle Lancry, but in this case Steiner did not appear (one report notes that his friends spoke up on his behalf in the midst of general denunciation). Harmonizing with Rousset's message, Paul emphasized the active participation of Jews in the more general resistance in the camps he had known, Auschwitz and Buchenwald, and, according to the reporter, "rejected any notion of a putative special conduct by Jews in the conditions of the *univers concentrationnaire* in the camps." Though acknowledging that "the deported Resistance has been completely embroiled in the debate set off by this book," he repudiated Steiner's attempt to isolate Jewish conduct—and Jewish victimhood—during the war. "It is not possible to divide the deportees into two blocs," he exclaimed.[63]

He needed to deny a divide in the deportation community, however, only because *Treblinka* had created one, winning breathless praise from some of its members just as it invited contemptuous opprobrium from others. The split within the deportation community—and the stress on its consensus ideology, so important to postwar French politics—meant that, far from unifying the deportees against Steiner's book in order to continue their old left-right disputes, the book had created an opening through which an entirely new paradigm made its way into French culture: one that did not uni-

8. Jean-François Steiner and Marie-Madeleine Fourcade at prize ceremony. *La Voix de la Résistance,* May 1966.

versalistically insist on the common fate of French patriots but instead on the special victimhood of European Jews in the wartime events. From Rousset's *univers concentrationnaire,* then, to Steiner's Jewish genocide.

■

And yet it may seem that the dominant, if not the only, result of this survey is that Steiner's particularizing argument, not simply about Jewish identity but about Jewish victimhood, faced difficulties in emerging—thanks often enough to his book's friends. Is the Treblinka affair testimony, then, to the sheer persistence and endurance of a generalizing interpretation of the war, or was the controversy one of the important events in its unraveling? It is impossible to judge with pinpoint accuracy, of course, just how powerfully *Treblinka* showed the factual limits of universalizing memory that did not adequately distinguish between Jewish and non-Jewish victimhood during the war. Even Steiner's staunchest defender, Beauvoir, essentially missed his point. And yet it is clear that in the strength of his advocacy that extermination differed from concentration—a central premise of the regime of memory that was to follow—Steiner's book helped mark a caesura in French perceptions of wartime criminality.

Indeed, having begun with Pierre Vidal-Naquet, this chapter concludes with his own ideological activation as a scholar of the genocide, for it was in the Treblinka affair that he *lived through* the origins of the distinction whose emergence he later identified as one of the principal events of recent thinking. Along with Lanzmann perhaps the central figure among intellectuals in the new regime of memory in which the Holocaust emerged as an object of study relatively separate from the larger war, Vidal-Naquet nevertheless became this actor slowly and over time. A study of the Treblinka affair is, then, also an inquiry into the origins of Vidal-Naquet's second career, an examination of how he became eligible to author his justifiably famous attacks on the Holocaust denial of Robert Faurisson and to act as ubiquitous and knowledgeable French commentator on the Nazi genocide.[64] And what strikes one as so remarkable about this career, in spite of his parents' deportation and murder at Auschwitz, and in spite of his own flight and hiding in the French countryside during the war, is the sheer priority and force of public preconception on his private memories and personal commitments. It was no intimate event close to him, but only the very public shock of Steiner's book, that made Vidal-Naquet the Jewish historian and public intellectual on Holocaust problems that he became.

Consideration of his career is also a bridge to the debates over contemporary Jewish identity catalyzed by the affair, examined in the next chapter, for it is impossible to separate Vidal-Naquet's historical perception of Nazi criminality from his response to Steiner's attempt to reactivate Jewish particularity. Vidal-Naquet is, of course, now retrospectively aware that it is impossible to grasp his mature identity without reference to his Jewish background; but the universalist, republican, and *dreyfusard* content of his own self-understanding initially led to the suppression of the Holocaust as an important theme in his life and work. As he describes this background in his memoirs, although endogamy had persisted until his generation, Vidal-Naquet, born in 1930, had no introduction to the spiritual or practical content of Judaism as a child (including circumcision). He remembers his father as "what Raymond Aron called a 'de-Judaized Jew,' a perfect example of the abstract citizen." In 1940, Vidal-Naquet gained a sense of himself as a Jew, but only as a target; and his father, in an affiliation that would profoundly mark the son, responded by introducing him to the Dreyfus affair, which most French Jews understood as a confirmation (not, as in much Zionist literature, a falsification) of their inherited Jewish republicanism.[65] "I am still proud," Vidal-Naquet wrote in his memoirs, "to affiliate with this tradition (which does not mean that I did not at times mistakenly apply the categories of the [Dreyfus] affair to causes that did not fit them)."[66] Indeed, he came to see his famed engagement during the Algerian War largely in these *dreyfusard* terms; Vidal-Naquet reflects that he may have singled out torture for his early interventions out of patriotic anger as well as in response to his memory of his father's torture at the hands of the Gestapo before his deportation.[67] His republican-style identity, rooted in a defense of the rights of man, conformed perfectly with the long tradition of French-Jewish universalism. As a result, insofar as he considered himself to have a Jewish identity in his early life, Vidal-Naquet considered himself one of those whom Sartre's *Anti-Semite and Jew* (published in 1946 and immediately purchased and read by Vidal-Naquet as clarifying his own sense of himself) had called the "inauthentic" Jew "whom other men take for Jews and who have decided to run away from this insupportable situation."[68]

Even as his interest in Jewish history arose, of course, Vidal-Naquet remained true to the universalistic and *dreyfusard* spirit imparted to him by his father. But a turn there was in Vidal-Naquet's life and career, in both his private researches and his public interventions, a turn most clearly marked— indeed, precipitated—by his reading of Steiner's *Treblinka* in 1966 and his participation in the controversy it unleashed. In an archival letter, written before the controversy allowed *Le Monde* to solicit a further review of the book from him beyond Michelet's report, Vidal-Naquet apologized to Steiner that he would not publish the article he had envisioned writing upon reading the book. "I read your book with admiration—admiration for the men who revolted, of course, but also admiration for the author." He explained that "professional historians (and as you know I belong to their guild) would criticize you, asking, for example, how you were able to reconstitute dialogue and interior monologue." But this professionalizing objection could not really impair the success of Steiner's project, Vidal-Naquet observed. He also expressed exasperation about Simone de Beauvoir's preface, for it had in a sense betrayed Steiner's central purpose. "I fail to grasp," Vidal-Naquet suggested, "how her rather rudimentary Marxism can succeed in explaining how it is that the revolt was organized precisely by those whom the Germans put in charge of the camp. But what your book makes so clear is that it is only these actors who could have achieved anything."[69] From the beginning, Vidal-Naquet believed that Steiner had shown that the Treblinka Jews revolted as Jews (rather than as a group-in-fusion).

When, as a result of the controversy, he published a review in *Le Monde* after all—thus becoming one of the few Jews writing on *Treblinka*, unlike those considered in the next chapter, before a wide public audience—Vidal-Naquet offered an all-out defense of Steiner's text. It is revealing about the book's strange fortunes and, more important, reflects Vidal-Naquet's conversion to one of the book's central premises: the factual difference between concentration and extermination. "This book which others have violently criticized, I read with admiration," Vidal-Naquet began. He politely disagreed with those who rejected it on the grounds that it falsified the past. One needed the proper standard to appreciate it, for though "it narrates history," *Treblinka* never pretends to be "a book of history." Nothing invalidated the project of novelizing history in order to make it more vivid and instructive, Vidal-Naquet commented, citing John Hersey's *The Wall* and Rousset's own *Les Jours de notre mort.* Anyway, he continued, "I have examined fairly closely Jean-François Steiner's 'sources' . . . [and] I can vouch for the fact that, in spite of the occasional distortion in the direction of the epic, Jean-François Steiner has respected the spirit of the testimonies he used. . . . To call it a 'hoax,' as some have, is a disgrace."[70]

More important, however, Vidal-Naquet defended not just the "novelistic" form but also the moral content of Steiner's project. The charges that the Jews had allowed themselves to be led to death were real and important, Vidal-Naquet reflected; and Steiner had correctly decided to "see the extent to which they were valid and, in the end, to refute them." In the major section of his review, Vidal-Naquet affirmed that Steiner had perceived the aims and nature of the camp inmates' actions with great moral exactitude. He agreed with Steiner—implicitly against Rousset's attack—that the Treblinka inmates were not "simply combatants in the antifascist fight." Instead, they were specifically Jewish in their submission and, finally, in their rebellion too. "Even a French, Marxist, and atheist Jew like myself will have noticed such tendencies in his own family traditions," Vidal-Naquet noted. Steiner had succeeded in documenting the limitations of the antifascist point of view, Vidal-Naquet insisted. For "[n]o doubt some of the men and women at Treblinka followed the progress of the Red Army and rejoiced at Mussolini's fall," finding grounds for revolt in left-wing resistance; but "[t]he immense majority [of the Treblinka inmates] had no refuge but the pride in being Jews that they slowly regained. . . . The sources show that it is only in returning to their function as *witnesses,* the role in which the medieval church had thought to imprison them, only in wanting to make themselves witnesses of horror in the world and to play Israel's role among the nations that the Jews of Treblinka found the strength to survive. Let us not make them 'Antifascist

Poles of the Mosaic Confession.'" It was as particularist Jews, not as universalist citizens or as antifascist resisters, that Steiner had properly captured the intent and success of the Treblinka insurrectionaries.

The next chapter will examine, more directly, the response of the Jewish community as a whole to the possibility of Jewish particularity that Steiner claimed alone explained the revolt. But perhaps most importantly, Vidal-Naquet felt he also had to draw from the implication that the victims were not universalists another, and in postwar France (and his own career) epoch-making, implication: the perpetrators were not universalists either. The genocide of the Jews occurred in some category different from Rousset's *univers concentrationnaire* or Beauvoir's serialization. Not just the revolt of the Jews, but the genocide visited on them, escaped the dominant generalizing rubric of the time, notably its antifascist variant. "To imagine Treblinka, Sobibor, Majdanek, Belzec, Chelmno, Auschwitz just as particular cases of the *univers concentrationnaire*," Vidal-Naquet insisted, referring directly to Rousset's paradigm, "is to betray the reality of the Nazis who organized [the genocide as well as] the free world that allowed it." For this reason, he finished, "The Treblinka revolt (like that of the *Sonderkommando* at Auschwitz) is no longer...[comparable] to the seizure of power by the Buchenwald deportees on April 10, 1945, any more than the Warsaw ghetto insurrection of April–May 1943 is comparable to the Parisian insurrection of August 19, 1944. The Nazis attempted, with the Jews, a complete and final obliteration [*une mise en condition totale*]." These were, in the context of the times, striking affirmations. The emphasis in Vidal-Naquet's homage to Steiner is, if not on the singularity of the genocide, then at least on the difference between concentration and extermination, a difference that by and large eluded the antifascist paradigm. But it emerged as one that Vidal-Naquet believed the act of witnessing of the Treblinka Jews—abetted by Steiner—allowed. Steiner's emphasis on the particularity both of the genocidal acts and of the identity of their victims was one that converted even this "French, Marxist, and atheist" Jew.

A debate organized by *Combat,* in which Vidal-Naquet and Rousset participated, makes a fitting conclusion to this chapter because it casts light on the contest of paradigms that the Treblinka affair encouraged. (See figure 9.) Vidal-Naquet affirmed, once again, that "the Hitlerian massacre of the Jews is without any common measure with any other crime committed by them," and that this point, the one "on which David Rousset criticizes Steiner most violently," survived all the other difficulties of the book.[71] The next chapter

9. David Rousset and Pierre Vidal-Naquet at the *Combat* debate. *Combat,* 10 June 1966.

will revisit—though it is obvious already—the extent to which Vidal-Naquet accepted Steiner's particularizing account of Jewish identity; for now what matters is his endorsement of Steiner's description of the bifurcation of the Nazi project between dominating the entire world and eradicating only one of its groups. But it is worth noting that Vidal-Naquet accepted Steiner's descriptive point about the Nazi enterprise only because of his openness to Steiner's moral project of insisting on Jewish existential particularity. "If the Treblinka revolt reveals the truth about the nature of this horror," Vidal-Naquet had asked in *Le Monde,* "is it too much to ask that the Jews receive the credit?" For his part, Rousset, in reply, dismissed Steiner's book as "a serious step backwards. Steiner returns us to the conditions of a world which was a world entirely focused on the Jewish question, and in which the Jew always felt he was the particular victim of particular circumstances." (To which Vidal-Naquet replied: "That's because he was!") Above all, while claiming that he had never denied that Jews and non-Jews had experienced different suffering, and that the terror visited on the first group had been "still deeper" than for the second, Rousset nevertheless concluded that *"this difference should not create any distinction in the moral problem under debate."* Vidal-Naquet replied that "there was not a difference of terror, but of nature, the ends [in different camps] being different"—*la finalité n'étant pas le même.*

Vidal-Naquet's conversion did not fade away; it proved the turning point in his career and, more broadly, in French culture. Soon after the controversy, Vidal-Naquet's evaluation of Steiner's book changed drastically. Pro-

voked by the controversy into studying the genocide with the same academic
and scientific rigor he brought to ancient Greece, his professional specialty,
Vidal-Naquet soon came to feel that he had been badly fooled by Steiner and
his book. He reacted, principally, to the fictionalizations and sensationalizations in *Treblinka,* its reckless novelization of a topic that he came to feel
needed to be treated with absolute historical probity. But the degree of his
reversal is startling. When Steiner's next book appeared, Vidal-Naquet told
its author that he would not allow himself to be duped by the same person
twice in a lifetime.[72] In "A Paper Eichmann," his celebrated attack of 1980
on the Holocaust denier Robert Faurisson, Vidal-Naquet grouped *Treblinka*
together with the "vast subliterature representing a truly obscene appeal to
consumption and sadism" that had to be "pitilessly denounced."[73] In a note,
Vidal-Naquet wrote that he "fell into the trap laid by Steiner's book," and
though he did not "retract the substance" of his *Le Monde* review, he insisted
that he had atoned for his mistake by attacking later sensationalizations and
falsifications of the genocide.[74] It remains true, all the same, that it was the
"trap" laid by Steiner that proved the decisive catalyst for Vidal-Naquet's
entry into his celebrated and far-reaching career as a scholar (and public intellectual) of the genocide, a subject so long ignored in the French academy
but ever since increasingly central, thanks in part to his work. What is so
ironic, then, is that the book he eventually rejected played such a significant
role in catalyzing his interest in the subject he accepted.

It played this role, it is fair to say, not just in a general way but on a specific
point. In a pregnant and important passage in his recollections, Vidal-Naquet
observes that it was Steiner's book, for all its faults, that pushed him to insist
on the difference between the antifascist conception of a unitary system of repression and the particularist insistence that, whatever the horrors of Rousset's "concentration camp universe," the extermination camps were in a different category. "The text I wrote differentiated," Vidal-Naquet recalled of his
Le Monde intervention in the Steiner affair, "between the concentration
camps and the places which were just for killing pure and simple." This insistence, he remarked, "proved to be a nodal point, even if my own researches
on it became much richer."[75]

One of Vidal-Naquet's reflections about this very episode, then, can serve
as the concluding remark of this chapter as well:

> The formation of a historian does not happen simply thanks to magisterial stud-
> ies. Even in the work of a historian—and, naturally, in his life—the irrational

plays a role. When I speak of the changes in historical consciousness, I cannot pretend that the history of the destruction of the European Jews has progressed in a linear fashion beginning with the simple gathering of testimonies and documents through the scientific elaboration to be found in the most recent edition of Hilberg's book. That would be a totally oversimplified picture of the evolution of the historiography. The idea of progress has to be put in question in the study of historiography just as it must in the study of history.[76]

But was Vidal-Naquet questioning the possibility of progress or only underlining the unexpected ways in which it may occur? In light of the centrality in the memory of World War II of the distinction between concentration and extermination—a distinction originally lacking in it but that the debate promoted—it is only fair to say that Steiner's book counts as one of the factors catalyzing an epoch-making revolution in thinking about Nazi criminality. The distinction faced a struggle in its emergence during the controversy itself, but there is no doubt that on the road through the decomposition of universalist (and especially antifascist) memory and the rise of genocidal memory, the affair is amongst the principal landmarks.

4

Jewish Identity in Question

As Vidal-Naquet's case suggests, it is difficult to separate the implications Steiner's book had for conceptualizing Nazi criminality from the consequences the author of *Treblinka* hoped would follow for the Jewish sense of self. But to turn now from the first to the second of these issues is to turn to a different—or at best overlapping—set of actors and commentators, and a relatively distinct set of problems, which must begin with demography. For the controversy over Steiner's book also provides an unusually revealing aperture on the evolution of French-Jewish identity, and Jewish identity more broadly, in the postwar period, at a moment when the generation of contemporaries (and victims) of World War II gradually began to be displaced by a younger generation with only childhood memory as a means of direct connection to the war—or no connection at all.

Indeed, it is striking that the Jews who commented publicly during the Treblinka affair often framed it, in spite of its historical topic, as a drama of generational change. They saw Steiner speaking to, and perhaps for, a new cohort with different attitudes than its predecessors, and a range of Jewish interlocutors appealed to the same new group to abet or to resist the lure of his presentation. This chapter surveys the disparate responses to *Treblinka* from the intra-Jewish dialogue. It begins, after an examination of Steiner's own self-fashioning before his community, with the acerbic (but comparatively little-read) criticisms in the Yiddish-language press catering mainly to the middle-aged and elderly working-class populations that remained from the waves of East European immigration of the prior decades—including newer arrivals from the immediate aftermath of World War II, victims of the Holocaust in its most intense precincts. Their responses are worth particular scrutiny, given the important sociocultural overlap between the Yiddish-language Jews—still hardly present in images and histories of French Jewry either before or after the war—and the communities most victimized by the Nazi genocide. What is surprising is not really how little "voice" such a community had in the wide-ranging general public debate over *Treblinka* surveyed in the previous chapter, but that it also managed to have little impact in the intramurally Jewish world, in which, I suggest below, responses often were highly favorable to Steiner's proposed revitalization of Jewish identity for the new generation of the postwar era.

Of course, as the bulk of the chapter shows, there were dissenting voices. There were, first of all, the leftist Jews of the French-Jewish deportation community; as a result of changing times and politics, they threaten today to disappear from accounts of modern Jewish history, but the Treblinka affair reveals that they had crafted their identities in a way that fit rather than challenged the antifascist political mood of the postwar years. But their dissent, too, failed to affect either the general conversation or even convince Jews not already close to their views. And then, perhaps most interestingly, particularly in the present day, the French-Jewish moralist Emmanuel Levinas, soon to become famous himself for his own moving advocacy of a renaissance of Jewish identity (and also as a precursor of deconstruction and a member of the canon of academically influential French theorists), intervened in the disputation.

To Steiner's proposal to make the memory of the genocide spiritually uplifting and empowering, Levinas responded by also addressing himself to the problem of the new and comparatively innocent generation in search of orientation, but by prizing the very Jewish abjection and passivity that Steiner had posed as a moral difficulty. It is important enough that Steiner's book provoked Levinas, unbeknownst to his scholarly interpreters, to speak more directly and explicitly about the contemporary significance of the Holocaust than he had before. But in offering, like Steiner, a proposal for the revision of Jewish identity, directed at the problem of the new generation and through an appropriative interpretation of past events, Levinas ended up, in many ways, sharing a great deal with the foe whom he intended to reject. Their climactic antagonism—and their unexpected commonalities—may reveal something more general about the polemical war over the nature and future of Jewish identity, as the generations changed, that the Treblinka affair set into motion.

■

What was the state and nature of the French Jewish community in the mid-1960s?[1] Over half a million persons in size, the community had more than doubled in the prior decade thanks to waves of immigration from North Africa (capped, most spectacularly, in 1962 with the migration of Algerian Jews with the collapse of the French colonial project). At this time as still today, French Jewry counted as the largest West European Jewish population and featured considerable diversity. Its religious, political, and intellectual institutions remained solidly controlled by a long-integrated core, to which new arrivals, in the 1960s North Africans as in the earlier decades Eastern Europeans, were invited to "assimilate." Unshaken in the long term by the waves of East European Jewish immigrants from the later nineteenth century through the interwar period, groups whose children were integrated into a preexisting French-Jewish identity, what Aron Rodrigue has called the "Judeo-republican" model would face serious cultural challenge only with the resistance of the new North African immigrants of the postwar era, and then not immediately.[2]

That Steiner's book could be respectfully—indeed even warmly—received by the dominant Jewish publications in French life, all while the subject of vitriolic criticisms in the Yiddish and Jewish deportee press, reflects what the sources reveal as the more serious and significant demographic fact about French Jewry in these years: the rise of a new generation. The French-Jewish community, after experiencing an expectable decline in births in the later interwar and wartime years, went through the more general postwar baby boom, lasting two decades, which produced a perceptible cohort of Jews reaching their teenage years and early twenties by the mid-1960s. The Jewish birthrate in France increased more than 50 percent between Steiner's cohort, born just before and during the war, and the immediately following cohorts, born in the late forties and early fifties, so that when Steiner wrote *Treblinka* in his late twenties he could address the larger group of Jews up to a decade younger than him, on the brink of maturity, informing them of his vanguard discovery of problems they might face and solutions they might try.[3] Thus, the demographic facts licensed the general perception in Jewish publications that a generational changing of the guard was at hand, and that Steiner's endeavor raised now what would become a serious communal question: what the children would make of their parents'—and their people's—recent past. If Steiner's public declarations resonated even partly with Jewish youth, the Jewish community faced a major challenge.

■

Already in his *Nouveau Candide* interview, for a mass public, Steiner had explained that his project had been born of the confusion—and the shame—about the past that he felt precisely because, as a youth, he had only learned about it secondhand. Steiner's interlocutors in the Jewish press specifically accepted, and in fact amplified, his self-presentation as a spokesperson for and to the new generation. This occurred first in the preeminent journal of French Jewish life, *L'Arche,* the publication of the Fonds social juif unifié (the central advocacy group for French Jews since the war).

In its pages, the Yiddish translator and man of letters Arnold Mandel—ironically, he had a decade before translated the Yiddish testimony by Marc Dvorjetski on which Steiner heavily relied and whose author complained of the theft of his voice—spoke up for the embattled young writer. Steiner's book, Mandel wrote, could not be dismissed as the response either of "Neo-Nazis of the likes of [Paul] Rassinier" or of young Israelis who repudiated the diaspora. "For I think that with *Treblinka* the questions of the *how* and of the *why* [of the genocide] have been posed for the first time amidst this literature of testimony and of description of the supposedly 'unsayable'—it has posed the true questions."[4]

In the interview that Mandel conducted with Steiner, and in Steiner's later publications in *L'Arche* (as well as in the intellectual journal of the Alliance Israélite Universelle, *Les Nouveaux cahiers*), the young author had the opportunity to clarify his position to his understandably wary coreligionists. Indeed, in these intra-Jewish sources, Steiner offered his clearest presentation of the ideas that, in the earlier wide-circulation piece for a general audience, had caused so much scandal. According to Mandel, the results were clear: this young man, far from hating his people, or unwittingly providing fodder to their enemies, "is in fact a religious type, and a Jew harking back to an ancient era." The editorial headnote to Steiner's later piece said the chief significance of the controversy, at any rate for the Jewish world, was "an exciting phenomenon: it suggests the way in which Jewish youth, those who did not directly know the martyrology, now interpret it and receive it. Since, in the final analysis, the 'Steiner affair' turns out to be a conflict of generations, another quarrel of the ancients and the moderns." (For such reasons, *L'Arche* chose the headline "Jewish Youth in Search of Itself" for Steiner's article.)[5]

In presenting his authentically new, and authentically Jewish, message, Steiner insisted that the new generation of Jews needed his book, as controversial as it might appear to his elders. "After a long period of apparent disaffection, turning away from what could seem like an abandonment," Steiner wrote, "Jewish youth are coming back to the search for a certain specific personality."[6] And yet, they were confronted, the moment they returned, he wrote, with the shame that had originally provoked them to leave Judaism behind. His quandary, however discomfiting, had to be faced, reflective as it was of a search for identity common among youth.

In one piece, Steiner raised the childhood source of such feelings, in reminiscences that provide the best sense available of what might have motivated the existential search culminating in his book. In his childhood, during the war, Steiner noted, the persecution of the Jews seemed hypothetical, and he "had less fear of the Gestapo than of the owl my mother used to frighten me when I was bad."

> Of course, I was terrified by the stories I was told; of course, I cried over the martyrdom of my people. But these were a child's tears, and were of the same nature, and fell at the same rate, as those I cried out over the fate of Little Red Riding Hood. . . . In fact, I had more compassion for the [story characters] than for my [Jewish] brothers—famished, emaciated, cankered, and dying though they were—because in my head and in my child's heart, I associated the former with my mother and the latter with the beggars and vagabonds the sight of whom provoked in me a malaise born of fear and disgust.

This conditioning came to be confirmed by the liberation, Steiner continued, during which American soldiers became the "mythical heroes" of the games of his childhood. The Jewish victims did not fit this image. In a sense, he wrote, all Frenchmen should understand his sense of shame; they all had suffered a strange defeat and could not look up to their fathers. "Only I had a double embarrassment as a Frenchman and as a Jew," he wrote.

> "His father died in the deportations," my friends' parents whispered amongst themselves, looking on me with a mixture of pity and commiseration. "He was a Jew, and the Germans came to pick him up one day." Everyone had a story in those days of a Jew taken away. These parades of men who did not have the time to get dressed and women who cried had something indecent about them for me, and my greatest happiness would have been to have an American soldier for a father.

He finished by explaining that his "irritation" at his identity became "revolt" when he learned that his friend's mother had told her son to be especially careful around Steiner because of the tragedy of his father's death. "I found this singularity shameful."[7]

But how to respond as an adult? In the first place, Steiner argued in these pieces, he had had to reject assimilation. It had been tried, Steiner wrote, but it now seemed clear that there were better models of coexistence than the false prospect of complete immersion of Jews in the host populations in which they found themselves. "Isn't it clear now that the lands which received us have not been crucibles in which one could simply let oneself melt away, since our deep will is otherwise and points toward our own sense of self?" he asked.[8] Going further, he dismissed those Jews who were angered by his book, speculating that they were chagrined simply because he had seen through their project to forget themselves. "Many want to be more French than the French, more German than the Germans, in order to live with them. But this path is false. One is French or not. To be Jewish or French is from the outset a contradiction. One must choose."[9] For the same reason, Steiner rejected Sartre's thesis—once shared by many postwar French Jews, as Vidal-Naquet's case makes clear—that without antisemitism, Jewish identity would disappear, a thesis that led many to the limited strategy of targeting their enemies in order to abolish themselves. "The question," Steiner concluded, "is to know whether it is necessary to find an identity outside the presence of and without regard to the enemy."[10] More strikingly, and clearly in the tradition of his father, Steiner added that precisely the acknowledgment of particularity allowed one to forge relations with the other particular groups amidst whom one lived. "Everyone has to be who they are," he testified in the Mandel interview. "I am well in my skin, I am the most authentic man possible, and, therefore, closest to French nationalists."[11]

In these pieces for a Jewish audience, Steiner also explained, more fully than in his mass-circulation pronouncements, why his shame at the recent memory of the Holocaust had not led him, in his father's footsteps, to a Zionist position. "I tried to forget the problem in trying the Israeli experiment," he said in his interview with Mandel, "but failed." As noted earlier, he had spent a year and a half in Israel, which he nevertheless, he wrote, found open to the "fundamental objection" that "it rejects Judaism." "The Israelis imagine themselves as Israelis rather than Jews. But this does not interest me. If the point is to have a country, I prefer France."[12] Explaining why he had come back to France after his year and a half in Israel, he recounted that he had come to see Zionism as simply providing a country rather than the kind of identity he sought: "Condemned to be nothing more than the citizen of a country like all the others . . . , I prefer the more temperate, spiritual, gourmet, and cultivated one. Of course, I wanted badly to search for my obscure destiny, but only on condition that it was at least comfortable."[13] Israel revealed, Steiner wrote, that power and heroism were not enough, because, while alluring, those values had to be allied with an authentic project. Having chosen to live as a Jew in France, he explained, he still needed his own Vercingetorix, Bayard, Chevalier of Assas, Leclerc, and Charles de Gaulle (all French patriotic icons). But in Israel, he testified, "I found heroism, but lost Judaism, and it did not interest me any more to be a hero without Judaism than a Jew without heroism."[14] He clarified in his other confession in *L'Arche* that Israel had risked "losing contact with certain traditional Jewish values," with the result that "just when in the diaspora a specifically Jewish life wants to be reborn . . . , Jewish youth may have to determine themselves, not by their relation to Canaan their homeland, but inside their exile, in order to assure Judaism's survival."[15]

The results were the affirmation of a kind of existential Jewish particularity, not located except in spiritual peoplehood, in which the Jews are separate from all lands they might inhabit, in which neither integral assimilation nor separatist normality are possible. A "Jewish nationalism without a country," as Steiner put it in another interview.[16] The possibility of this identity had, of course, been revealed not in the Warsaw resistance nor even, Steiner clarified once again in these materials for a Jewish audience, among the Zionist and leftist partisans, like Abba Kovner, who during the war as in his own day were "in a position of total rupture with Judaism" rather than epitomizing it. What *Treblinka* showed is that the Jews in the camps "went to their deaths precisely because they refused it." They were not, like Westerners, a people who glamorized death but rejected it. And when it became clear that all would die, that the camp would close and obliterate everyone, only then did they organize a revolt. In doing so, they disclosed the roles of both passivity and activity in Jewish life and therefore in the circumstances of Nazi persecution, and revealed a genuinely Jewish model of heroism. In response to Steiner's musings, Mandel commented, in wondering admiration, "I find, with surprise and approval, that you take what people call metaphysical realities seriously. . . . The religious personality of the Jews, in your book, is primordial. But one doesn't encounter this view anywhere these days."[17] (For his part, Edouard Roditi, an American poet who had lived in Paris for many years, referenced *L'Arche*'s coverage of the Steiner affair in his complaint to an American audience about a strategy of publicity that "assum[es] that any discussion of the Holocaust is 'useful' [and] merely . . . keep[s] its readers in a constant tizzy about being Jews, but without their ever really figuring out all that this may mean in terms of positive beliefs."[18])

No doubt *L'Arche*'s approbation gratified Steiner, but it is not clear how much it mattered to him that his book might offend his elders. After all, they were not his true audience. "I apologize," he confessed, to those "whose hands my book burned because their hearts have already been singed by the flames of the crematoria." (He exempted from his mea culpa "the professionally offended, the doctors in martyrology, the blind polemicists, and the screeching birds of the monument of the holocaust.") But he explained to his Jewish audience in the heat of the controversy that his apology did not amount to a concession of mistake, because youth—only as a youth and to the youth of his day could he have written his book—justifies all. "But I also will tell them that I do not regret anything because I am right, and that I am right because I am twenty-eight years old."[19]

■

Few older Jews, however, welcomed Steiner's project with Mandel's enthusiasm. Among the most significant facts about Steiner's project is that he did not even bother to raise, among the live options for Jewish identity that he surveyed, the by then hallowed figure, particularly powerful in France because of its waves of proletarianized East European immigrants, of the laboring militant. The Yiddish-language dailies (there were still three in Paris at the time, one Bundist and one communist along with one Zionist paper) returned the favor in their contemptuous, but ignored, reactions, pieces that testify to the gap in reception between this audience and those who proved eager to affiliate with Steiner's new project—including not just secular French intellectuals but sectors of the Jewish public as well. The voice of the Yiddish-language newspapers—the voice often originating with and directed at those closest, biographically and sociologically, to the genocidal events—was usually rhetorically irreverent, theoretically simple, and morally bracing.[20] And its response to Steiner was completely unified and uncompromisingly harsh.

In this interregnum era between the events that caused many to lose faith in leftist radicalism and the Six-Day War, which cemented the conversion of many Yiddish-speaking Jews from leftism to Zionism (albeit often of a leftist variety), the Bundist and Communist papers were still dominant. In the issue of *Unzer shtime* (Our Voice) immediately following Steiner's interview with *Le Nouveau Candide*, Borvine Frenkel rose in outrage, in an article with the unsubtle title "A French-Jewish Writer Who Ought to Be Pilloried."[21] Frenkel edited the newspaper, which was associated with the Bundist (East European Jewish socialist) movement.[22] Frenkel began very simply by calling *Treblinka* "the nastiest book that has ever been written about the six million." Frenkel considered it "shameful in the extreme," indeed psychopathic, "to write if you have not yourself been deported." At this stage of the debate, however, Frenkel and others reacted more to the interview Steiner had given than to the book he had written. "If a writer who is ostensibly Jewish can say in an interview that the victims of the camp were the collaborators of the executioners, in Treblinka and in the other camps," Frenkel wrote, "then he is simply a criminal." Frenkel said he could hardly be surprised that *Le Nouveau Candide*, a right-wing publication, had run such an interview, for it had traditionally exploited "the Jewish theme" in order to attract readers. But Steiner's answers had gone far beyond even the norm for the magazine; his replies during the interview were "amazing even to the journalist" who elicited them. "To the already rich and swampy muck of antisemitic and defamatory literature, there has now been added another filthy gutter," Frenkel wrote ruefully. The canard of Jewish passivity had been heard before, Frenkel observed, if never with such "base cynicism." Just as important, the Yiddish-language community was clearly familiar, far more so than the French public, with some of the sources on which Steiner had drawn. By "daring to calumniate" against "the ghetto heroes who, out of fear, chose struggle" in order to be able to die actively rather than passively, and finally against the deceased who died in any manner, Steiner had, Frenkel wrote, put himself "beyond the pale." Frenkel concluded by calling to Jews to "come out publicly" against "this lampoon of a book" in "the sharpest possible way."

In a subsequent number of *Unzer shtime*, Frenkel printed a letter that another of the paper's editorial team, Irène Kanfer, had sent to *Le Nouveau Candide* in response to Steiner's interview (but which it did not print in its extensive later coverage of the controversy it had initiated).[23] Kanfer wrote that the excerpt in *Les Temps modernes*, though a "shocker," at least gave the impression that Steiner's assertions were "based on solid documentation." That, for Kanfer, was what made the allegations Steiner leveled in the interview all the more amazing and reckless. It took a special kind of daring, she noted, for someone so "ignorant" to choose as his theme the greatest mass killings perpetrated in modern history. She noted that when she had edited a recent book of Holocaust poetry—the first such book of its kind in the French language—she had carefully read Betti Ajzensztajn's *Underground*

Activity in the Ghettoes and Camps.[24] Proceeding to recount several of "innumerable" episodes of resistance and heroism catalogued in this source (she also appealed to "the historian Wilhelm Shirer" and his "monumental work," *The Rise and Fall of the Third Reich,* which she said also supported her claims), Kanfer finished: "No, Mr. Steiner! The feeling of shame . . . ought not to be on the Jews' side." Notably, neither Frenkel nor Kanfer acknowledged that Steiner had raised the potential charge of shame as a confused young man and with a claim to have refuted it.

Had the journalistic team at *Unzer shtime* allowed anger at Steiner's interview to get the best of them, causing its members to react too harshly to Steiner's book before they had even had time to digest it? Some readers were willing to make a tolerant distinction between the interview and the book. Not Frenkel. When he returned to the subject at the end of April, he lumped them together as one mass of outrage and insult. In spite of the "song of praise" sung by Simone de Beauvoir in her preface, indeed in spite of the endorsements of major Jewish figures, Frenkel came down unambiguously on the side of the book's critics, including the non-Jew David Rousset. The book, on Frenkel's closer reading, turned out to be "through and through a plagiarism living parasitically at the expense of other books—and victims." It added to their testimonies only an unnecessary dose of "anemic mysticism." Frenkel dismissed *Treblinka* as "inflated kitsch," pumped up by "cheap novelistic tactics, no doubt with a movie in mind." (Indeed, Frenkel added, "one has the impression that the whole book was written to make a spectacular commercial film.")[25] Unlike Mandel, Frenkel refused to countenance the hypothesis that Steiner had come to the materials in the book actually intending to ask and answer the existential questions about his Jewish identity that he had posed so emotionally in his interviews. Frenkel went on, in this no-holds-barred critique, to dismiss the pseudo-metaphysical arguments Steiner offered about the Jews and their need to live. Throughout the text, Frenkel even observed, "You will find many contradictions, exactly as in the personality of the author—half-Jewish and half-Christian. The only thing whole is his arrogance."

A similar, heated response to Steiner's *Treblinka* is to be found in the second of the major Yiddish dailies of the time, *Di naye prese* (The New Press), produced by the communist faction of the Yiddish-speaking Jews, and reflecting a very live ideological option amongst immigrant Jews of the era, though one already in the process of waning.[26] The article appeared under the pen of Georges Kenig, the paper's well-known editor. In his pungent contribution, titled (translated roughly) "The Author of 'Treblinka' Has Gone

Off the Deep End," Kenig acknowledged that Steiner "has talent: he can paint a scene, he can create an atmosphere, he can keep his reader breathless." Unfortunately, as Kenig went on to observe in an almost melancholy reflection, Steiner had put these gifts to dubious ends, so that his book had become "a pamphlet against the martyrs and an alibi for the executioners."[27] Kenig acknowledged that "a small part of this book rests on actual facts," but not much. Kenig could, by this time, cite the reception of *Treblinka* by the radical right as evidence of the uses to which Steiner's ignorant theses could be put. "Whether intentionally or not, Steiner provides evidence for *Rivarol,* which is only too happy to agree that the Jews are hated by those who surround them everywhere and always." With a flourish, Kenig concluded that while Steiner may have found many thousands of buyers for his book, in the process he "lost everything, as a writer, as a Jew and as a human being."

As in *Unzer shtime,* there were no dissenters to these views in *Di naye prese.* These articles were neither ambiguous nor measured in their conclusions. They reflected, one may fairly infer, the natural reaction of the populace closest biographically and sociologically to the subject of Steiner's book. The question one might therefore ask is not why the Yiddish papers responded that way but why the general Jewish public did not, as its members—scandalized by Steiner, fortified by the glowing reception of many Jewish notables, and titillated by the debates of the intellectuals—rushed to celebrate (and buy) the book. For most crucially, unlike practically all the other Jewish respondents, notably Steiner and Levinas, the Yiddish journalists did not see themselves as addressing youth.

Such silence is in itself significant. In his remarkable ethnography on such leftist Yiddish-speaking Jews, researched not too many years after the Treblinka controversy, Jonathan Boyarin titled his poignant chapter on intergenerational transmission "Children and Other Strangers," emphasizing the huge gap—linguistic, political, and attitudinal—between the Yiddish immigrants and their own descendants. "Even while rejecting Jewish law," Boyarin remarks, "the immigrants never had to choose whether or not to be identifiably Jewish." Not so, however, for their children, who normally learned Yiddish only very poorly and, having missed the formative history of their parents, did not share their distinctive Yiddish cultural politics. Boyarin suggests that a "proper answer to the question of what in the children's Jewishness is taken directly from their parents and what borrowed or invented elsewhere" would require attention to "the difference between a chosen identity and a fated identity. The former bears a risk of superficiality corresponding to the latter's risk of ethnocentric nonreflection."[28] No identities are fully fated or fully chosen, of course, but it is true nonetheless that different historical circumstances provide different amounts of room for maneuver in combining fate and choice in forging a self, since different circumstances involve different degrees of external coercion and provide different configurations of existential options. A study of the Treblinka controversy, perhaps, can illustrate the transition from relatively more fate to relatively more choice, in the historical context of the changing of the French-Jewish generations. What is significant, in this regard, is that the leftist Yiddish writers, perhaps aware that their way of life would fall away, that the conditions for its historical emergence and duration had passed, did not even try, or at least did not succeed, in offering it to the young, even as they confirmed it for themselves.

■

Not even the Zionist Yiddish papers, representing the reading of another faction of the older immigrants, affiliated with Steiner's project, relatively closer though they might seem ideologically to his vision of renewed Jewish particularity. This fact is indicated by the elegant responses to the Treblinka controversy by Moshe Szulsztein (1911–1981), the "unofficial Yiddish poet laureate of Paris," as Boyarin described his standing in old age.[29] Szulsztein, born near Lublin and an interwar immigrant to France, then a member of the communist resistance in wartime, had, like many Yiddish speakers, moved during the 1950s from communism to Zionism, after the serial indignities that wiped out a once culturally fruitful relationship between Yiddish speakers and communist politics (indeed, as the earlier surveyed contributions show, a relationship that lasted much longer in France than in the Soviet Union itself).[30] Still, Szulsztein's Zionism, like that of other ex-communists, sounded in a strongly socialist register, and he affiliated with the Israeli political movement Mapam, a left labor Zionism especially solicitous of inherited Yiddish culture.[31] Szulsztein penned his response to *Treblinka* in the main Zionist Yiddish daily *Unzer vort*, in a massive, seven-part article, printed over a week.[32] In these years, before the Six-Day War shifted the attitudes of immigrant Jews completely, *Unzer vort* did not yet have the market dominance it would have later, a distinction that would eventually allow it to last longest of all of the Parisian Yiddish dailies; but Szulsztein's article nonetheless reflects another important category of Jewish identity at the time, a voice emanating from the older generation, like the others surveyed so far, if representative of the newest tendency in it.[33] A month later, Szulsztein published a follow-up analysis on the entire controversy in *Arbeter vort,* another Yiddish newspaper of the era.[34]

Like other commentators, Szulsztein decried the sly and offensive marketing campaign, denouncing Steiner as well as his publisher for the lurid imagery and scandalous allegations with which they had polluted the public square out of the lowly desire for profits. Steiner's public interventions were designed so "that people would talk about him, to create a stir, and to make it easier for him to sell his wares," Szulsztein said. To succeed, he continued, books in Paris needed "either a big prize or a big scandal." Faute de mieux, Steiner had chosen the latter, the easier course since it required "no jury, no exchange of competent opinions, no analyses of the work, only a little immodesty, chutzpah, and frivolity."[35] Such a brashly stated verdict amounted to the commonest theme of the Yiddish reaction to Steiner's book. Unlike the other Yiddish journalists, however, Szulsztein bothered to read all of Steiner's public pronouncements carefully, most especially those in *Le Nouveau Candide* and *L'Arche,* and to respond to them point by point with serious arguments, rather than vituperative screed alone. (He claimed to analyze the book as well, and found it inseparable from the interviews, but cited and discussed only the latter).

Szulsztein also dwelled with anger on the fact that Steiner had in effect surreptitiously relied on sources well known to the Yiddish-speaking community while claiming to have discovered the problem of the death camps all by himself. Noting the existence of many earlier contributions, chiefly (at that time) in Yiddish and whose authors he could simply name since they were already familiar to his audience, Szulsztein borrowed from this argument the overall title of his piece. The well-developed library of Holocaust literature in Yiddish, beginning during the war and accumulating afterward, meant that from Szulsztein's perspective Steiner had simply stood on the shoulders of giants while claiming to walk tall by himself. Szulsztein used a different comparison in ridiculing Steiner as "the Columbus of Treblinka." Likening himself to a Native American surprised to learn that he had now, after so many years, been "discovered," Szulsztein wrote sarcastically: "Suffice it to say that I haven't been waiting twenty years for the heroic navigator Jean-François to wager on setting out over the choppy waves of testimony, to glimpse the dry land, and discover the land of Treblinka."[36] Szulsztein's argument is understandable given the sector of the French-Jewish community from which, like the other Yiddish writers, he spoke. Neglected, however, in such a perspective—one shared by many others—is the fact that his well-known land, though already a home in his own circles and in his own language, had not yet become a shore for larger masses, not least Jews in France, to hit upon and settle in seeking a new foundation for their identities, especially not for youth. Szulsztein did not reflect on the fact that only belatedly, and in the form of what he considered a travesty, had this larger epoch-making event begun to occur, through the displacement of his language and the vulgarization of his sources.

When he came to the substance of Steiner's public claims, one of Szulsztein's most telling responses was that the actual terms of the Treblinka controversy—and above all, the question of Jewish complicity—reflected a culture that had not come to grips with the Holocaust and had not really begun to think about Jews in the way it did the general run of humanity. In a canny analogy that he elaborated at length, Szulsztein raised the case of Oradour-sur-Glane, the French "martyred village" that, as the site of much-publicized Nazi atrocities against (non-Jewish) Frenchmen, had been ritually memorialized as a central element of postwar French culture.[37] But, Szulsztein aptly observed, nobody charged the Oradour residents with passivity or complicity, since it went without saying that there had been no historical alternative to their suffering. The mere fact that they had undergone it implied nothing about their moral fiber. Why would the fact that Jews were targeted and victimized lead to different premises for judgment?[38] The example, Szulsztein said, suggested the larger failure of emphasis in Steiner's book and in the terms of the controversy it set off. The focus on how and why the Jews, innocent victims, had died in fact displaced an alternative focus on how and why the Germans—and their non-German collaborators—had killed them.[39]

Most crucially, and most interestingly, the fact of Szulsztein's metamorphosis from communist to Zionist in the decades since the war did not, to come to Steiner's central project of Jewish reactivation, lead to any sympathy for Steiner's search for Jewish particularity, so heatedly anathematized by Szulsztein's former leftist compatriots. Szulsztein began by defending the Warsaw ghetto uprising against Steiner's calumnies. Far from simply accepting death, of an aggressive rather than passive kind, the Warsaw fighters, in Szulsztein's interpretation, were facing different historical alternatives and emphatically chose the best course available. "The main goal of the ghetto fighters," Szulsztein explained, "was to *take* and to *give:* to take revenge and to give warning to mankind. Of the results of their struggle it is irrelevant to say that it failed, as Steiner does, since they did not aim for a military victory over Nazi Germany. Their desire in engaging in the struggle, put into words, is what remains as their testament: 'To die with honor! Either to survive, and only as free men, and if such is not possible, to die as free men.'"[40] They simply obeyed the same imperative that animated men everywhere, warning humanity as a whole, even if humanity sadly failed to listen.

It followed, Szulsztein wrote, that Steiner's attempt to champion Jewish particularity—in the past and therefore in the future—ran aground, his testimonial voyage to identity leading nowhere. Szulsztein in fact devoted a large part of his article to countering Steiner's views in this regard—admitting that he hesitated to enter into his "labyrinth of scholasticism and pseudo-philosophical speculation"[41] but doing so nonetheless—by repudiating any belief in a particularly Jewish morality or drive. The hypothesis of a "specifically Jewish morality," Szulsztein complained, might actually convince "Steiner's book's non-Jewish readers" (he wrote early enough not to see how many of Steiner's Jewish readers agreed with it as well). In the end, however, it was nothing more than a "bizarre theory."[42] Thus, the Jews in the war were not on any "high mission to be able to bear witness for history," even religious Jews who chose the martyrdom of *kiddush hashem,* whom he interpreted, citing the case of the poet Israel Stern in the Warsaw ghetto, as engaging in acts of spiritual resistance rather than cowardly passivity.[43]

For Szulsztein, the will to life, much as Rousset had argued, rooted itself in "human instinct, absolutely not a Jewish one." Explaining himself, Szulsztein cited Jean de la Fontaine's early modern fable, "Death and the Woodsman," in Yiddish translation (apparently his own), in defense of his position that the supposedly Jewish zest for life over death is simply a human trait:

> Le trépas vient tout guérir;
> Mais ne bougeons d'où nous sommes:
> Plutôt souffrir que mourir,
> C'est la devise des hommes.

> Der toyt heylt oys unz, vos an emes, yedn vey dem harbn,
> Nor glaykher nisht tsu ayln zikh tsu im bikhlal;
> Beser iz tsu laydn eyder shtarbn—
> Dos iz fun lang dem mentshs an alter klal.

> Death ready stands all ills to cure;
> But let us not his cure invite.
> Than die, it's better to endure,—
> Is both a manly maxim and a right.[44]

Szulsztein's Yiddish rejected particularity. As with his reference to Oradour, the choice of a hallowed French classic as proof text is undoubtedly no accident. No Jewish identity, Szulsztein insisted, is required to grasp this truth, only humanity. Whatever his break from his erstwhile communist friends, who rejected Steiner's particularism in the name of universalistic solidarity, Szulsztein's new Zionist allegiances did not keep him from following them on this point.

Szulsztein did not offer any particular plan for the future, for how to remember the Holocaust as a new generation arose. It is true that, unlike the other Yiddish writers, he did face the alleged generational caesura directly. But, coming at the end of his article to the difficulty that so preoccupied many commentators, Szulsztein simply denied that Steiner posed a problem to, for, and about Jewish youth of the period. Though plausibly inveighing against the penchant elsewhere in the Jewish world to overrate Steiner's typicality of youth as a whole, his response went to the opposite extreme by reducing the young author to a complete idiosyncrasy, albeit one with which Jewry would have to suffer, since it was in a way part of the same assault begun on them so many years ago. The Holocaust, Szulsztein concluded, resembled "a bomb with a mechanical time-delay: fragments from it are still falling. They cripple minds and bring about complexes, diseases, and anomalies. And Jean-François Steiner is one of the victims of this heritage."[45]

■

Immigrant journalists of different ideological stripes, then, combined in a common contempt for Steiner's enterprise, whether understood as historical reconstruction or presentist activation. Both within and beyond their newspapers, the most widespread opposition to Steiner's book came, as the last chapter began to suggest, from the Jewish deportation community, whose most engaged members were often close in political ideology and organizational affiliation to the Yiddish-speaking writers (whether of the more traditional leftist or newer Zionist variety). What their activities show is the number of Jews who self-consciously created, and lived according to, a Jewish variant on the deportation identity so central to French postwar life.

To judge from the sources, there were several who, in response to the interview in *Le Nouveau Candide* and then the book itself, were activated into an energetic campaign of organizing the French-Jewish deportation community against Steiner's enterprise. The *amicale* for Jewish survivors of Auschwitz wrote Steiner to implore him to correct the record in *Le Nouveau Candide*, and a Comité de vigilance pour le respect de la déportation et de la résistance mobilized with a campaign of circular letters to other associations of survivors.[46] Of this latter group, a core of figures—Henri Bulawko,[47] Ralph Feigelson,[48] and, perhaps above all, the indefatigable Miriam Novitch—rallied together with special rage against Steiner's book, seeking multiple paths into print and urging the principals in the affair, like Beauvoir and Fourcade, to change their public stances out of respect for the memory of the victims.[49] But it does not seem that this struggle met with much success, as their voices were confined to the publications of their own milieux, and their entreaties beyond essentially ignored. (Novitch, who maintained close ties with Yad Vashem, in fact produced an entire book against Steiner, published the next year, but for next to no readers.)[50]

Similarly hostile to Steiner's enterprise, but certainly winning the competition for most dedication and intensity amongst Jewish sources in their campaign against the young author, were *La Presse Nouvelle* (The New Press) and its editor, the Birkenau survivor Marceau Vilner. Communist in orientation like *Di naye prese,* and sharing the same title in different tongues, *La Presse Nouvelle* provided a weekly French-language edition for readers of similar commitments as those of its sister publication and, like it, greeted Steiner and his book with implacable rejection in its incessant coverage over the months. *La Presse Nouvelle* involved a different team of writers and commentators and provided the way into print for many leftist Jewish activists; the most interesting reason to examine it is not, however, simply to allow more rehearsal of the substance of the often repetitive debate. It permits, rather, a return to the outstanding question: why did this Jewish wing of the deportation community line up so substantially behind Rousset, in spite of his hesitation in acknowledging the particular fate of the Jews during the wartime events?

The answer appears to be, roughly, the historical importance of an underlying, universalist Jewish identity that commited itself to resisting Steiner's project to take such inherited self-understandings in a strongly differentialist or particularist direction. Vilner, who died the year after organizing his campaign of opposition against *Treblinka,* personally composed several attacks, and made sure his paper chronicled the controversy throughout its course. Decrying *Le Nouveau Candide*'s swastika-adorned cover, Vilner began his denunciation by suggesting that the paper, as a right-wing publication, had simply used Steiner, as it had Roger Peyrefitte's earlier book, to return antisemitism to the range of acceptable opinions after the postwar moratorium on the sentiment. The magazine, he wrote, sought "to have confirmed by a

Jewish author Nazi theses on the extermination in the camps, and thereby to 'excuse the inexcusable.'"[51] In a series of articles that followed, Vilner denounced Steiner and praised Rousset to the skies for having debunked the myth of the specificity of the Jewish people (and not simply in the camps). In Vilner's own formula, repeated several times, Steiner had served up a "'Jewish Pétainism' in messianic sauce," misrepresenting the past in order to forge a Jewish variant on integral nationalism. For Steiner's rereading of the resistance in the camps as fundamentally Jewish in inspiration falsified the fact, Vilner insisted, that so many resisters had done so out of their communist allegiances, and he showed particular chagrin over the passage from *Treblinka* in which a communist militant organizing insurrectionary activity is made to say that he does so for ethnic-existential rather than universalist-political reasons. How, Vilner asked in the name of his own interpretation of Jewish identity, could Steiner ignore "the rich past" among Jews "of fighting for liberty and humanism, as well as contributing to progress and to science"?[52]

He could ask such a question, quite obviously, because of what he thought Jews should embrace from their past in his own day. Correspondingly, Vilner could not understand why others on the left found anything of merit in Steiner's enterprise, beginning with Simone de Beauvoir, of course.[53] It was in a similar spirit that Vilner interviewed his fellow communist Pierre Daix, wondering why, as a leftist militant, he could have written such a positive review in his own journal, *Les Lettres françaises*. "To particularize the genocide as [Steiner] did," Vilner complained, "is to forget, as you yourself have observed, that the difficulties of the other deportees were similar." Daix did not disagree, but, having begun his review with the observation that "the time of the sons has arrived," thought Steiner's painful self-consciousness and forgivable immaturity had to excuse him. In any case, he added, "One cannot deny that Treblinka was a camp dedicated to the Jews alone."[54]

What the various kinds of opposition suggest, nevertheless, is that it is clearly improper to speak globally of "silence" about the Holocaust, in France or perhaps anywhere, in the post–World War II years. What is to be found when the sources in the Treblinka affair are fully surveyed, rather, is an older Jewish generation that failed to transmit its memories and its identity to a wider public and a subsequent generation. All the Yiddish writers (Szulsztein most especially) knew and cited the mostly Yiddish sources on which Steiner had relied—notably Dvorjetski on Vilna and Rachel Auerbach on Treblinka—and were evidently confused how anyone could take Steiner's work as new (much less correct).[55] Their inability to see the constitutive limits of their own knowledge base is therefore a striking feature revealed by the Treblinka controversy. It may be that France illustrates this fact especially well since, as the preceding survey suggests, in France leftist Jews created a subculture that, however good its fit with the dominant majority political consensus, and however rich the body of knowledge and even the cadre of public authorities on the genocide it developed, also entailed serious limits on its dissemination. The subculture failed to be heard or failed to convince (or both).[56]

None of the writers surveyed so far—with the possible exception of the communists, as Vilner's question to Daix implies—doubted that the Jews had suffered exceptionally during the war. They thought this fact went without saying, and thus the drift from concentration to extermination elucidated in the previous chapter simply did not concern them. The question was whether to integrate, on solidaristic grounds, Jewish with general victimhood. They sided with Rousset because they felt that no particularizing moral consequences flowed for Jews from Hitler's isolation of them. They did not see in Steiner's particularism much else, accordingly, than the propagation of racism and, thanks to his allegation of complicity, even antisemitism. This fact explains their intially curious sympathy for Rousset in his polemics against Steiner's book. The reason was not just, as Pieter Lagrou persuasively if apologetically argues, that the antifascist universalism that Rousset represented could show some genuine superiority to existing historical alternatives: "There may have been an ideological hegemony assimilating various experiences to some holistic martyrdom, but this was at the same time what many of the Jewish victims who actively adhered to the anti-fascist paradigm needed at this moment. . . . [T]he identification with anti-fascism was a means of overcoming the appallingly arbitrary affliction that had hit them, a way to take possession of their own destiny."[57] There is also the fact that, for all that it often de-emphasized or even obscured relative victimhood (by preempting the competition of victims), antifascism had an aspirational quality that resonated with the leftist politics of many Jews of the time. It served, rather than suppressed, their identities. Hence the irony: the conditions for the wide publicity of Jews' memory of their particular fate in the war were in part provided in spite of the political and moral opposition of many Jews to one of its earliest public vehicles.

■

As noted, the existing Jewish community in France had not only its particular immigrant newspapers and deportee circles, all highly politicized and factionalized, albeit finding common cause for once during the Treblinka controversy,[58] but also an established tradition of historical inquiry about the Holocaust, little disseminated amongst the general public though it certainly was. Nearly every historian of consequence in this tradition, most associated with the important Centre de documentation juive contemporaine (CDJC), engaged in the Treblinka affair, amongst whom two, Michel Borwicz and Léon Poliakov, were most prominent and important. To examine the historical experts is not simply to turn to another aspect of the quarrel of ancients and moderns; it is also to see the historical limits of the early discipline of Holocaust history, as established in close connection with the Jewish community, in raising the profile of the events it studied. Why, when its practitioners had worked so tirelessly since the events themselves to amass evidence, to research monographs, and to pen chronicles, did only the irresponsible young fabulist Jean-François Steiner—as they saw him—find the mass audience the subject truly deserved?

Originally known as Maximilian Boruchowicz, before his emigration to Warsaw and then Paris, Borwicz (1911–1987) had survived the Lvov ghetto and Janowski camp before becoming one the founding members of the immediate postwar Jewish Historical Commission in Poland; after his 1947 emigration, he subsequently established himself as a French scholar of the war (and especially of the camps) before the topic became popular.[59] The author of many works in Yiddish and Polish, notably the three-volume *Arishe papirn* as well as a French state thesis, early monuments of historical research on the Nazi genocide, Borwicz published a work on the Warsaw uprising around the time Steiner's comparatively huge success appeared.[60]

Through the anger—and envy—evinced by Borwicz in his interventions, it is possible to read the significance of the Treblinka affair as the displacement of an earlier literature about the Holocaust, precisely thanks to the widespread credibility of Steiner's claim that nothing before had been said. Borwicz's complaint targeted not so much what Steiner narrated and argued as his authority to speak at all. Borwicz, organizer—as he recounted at the *Combat* debate—of wartime resistance, claimed to have shown in his respected but little-read historical works that there was nothing specifically Jewish about the Jews' conduct in the ghettos and camps. All peoples, he testified, wanted to survive in order to bear witness to their experience, and "I don't see in this fact any mystical or racial trait."[61] In a published review of *Treblinka*, Borwicz handed down the proverbial verdict that what was true in Steiner's work was not new, and what was new not true. For Borwicz, the true question of the Treblinka affair was how such a book had, through promotion by turns sly and offensive, been blessed by the establishment for re-cycling already available but obscure material as it if were itself original. "In reading it," Borwicz wrote, "I thought for a moment of sending him to my own book. . . . He would have learned many things that he deigned to ignore. But then, in looking again at his public declarations, spread under the aus-pices of swastika publicity, I realized that it wasn't worth it. This boy wants not to know. He wants to scandalize."[62] Borwicz made clear his preference for the ancients over the moderns.

Though no doubt, in part, correct, Borwicz's perception, like Szulsztein's, may have been too self-involved to see the paradox that, to judge from the Treblinka affair, it may have been *on condition* of his own generation's super-session as the one that shaped perceptions of the recent past—as well as on condition of the kind of publicity that he despised—that the knowledge of the genocide could have become more generalized. Beauvoir put this point more harshly, no doubt partly with Borwicz in mind, when she said: "One has the impression that [this polemic] is brought about . . . by a group of Jewish writers themselves rather old, who wrote their own books—excellent in themselves—but who have never reached a wide public, and seem to be angry at a young man's success."[63] Even when cast as a confrontation between rival claims to research expertise, everyone stressed that the Treblinka affair set youth against age.

Even more undoubtedly, Beauvoir also referred to Léon Poliakov (1910–1997), who had also assumed a very combative attitude almost a decade ear-lier in the polemics occasioned by the appearance of André Schwarz-Bart's Goncourt prizewinning *The Last of the Just*. Once among the most inter-nationally distinguished historians of the Jewish genocide and of the long his-tory of antisemitism that led up to it, Poliakov, born in Russia, had emigrated to France before the war and contributed to the foundation and early work of the CDJC, the main French research center on the genocide, which dated from wartime. At Nuremberg, he assisted the French prosecution team.[64] Po-liakov's book *Bréviaire de la Haine* (in English as *The Harvest of Hate*) counted as one of the first major histories of the organization and perpetration of the Final Solution; it is worth noting, in light of the discussion of the Christian-ization of the genocide in the previous chapter, that Mauriac also had written the preface to that book.[65] In 1966, by which point two of the four volumes of Poliakov's *History of Antisemitism* had also appeared, he certainly counted as the most well-regarded authority on the period in the France of his day.

Steiner's implacable enemy throughout the dispute, Poliakov had initially submitted a highly critical reader's report to Steiner's publishing house Fayard upon reading the manuscript at the publisher's request. But Fayard, though it took the report seriously at first, eventually allowed Simone de Beauvoir's enthusiasm for the project (and commitment to write a preface) to override Poliakov's scruples.[66] In his various public interventions after the appearance of the book, Poliakov did not hesitate to ridicule Steiner's alleged historical errors, dwelling with special contempt and anger on Steiner's reference to the "great Sabbath knife" used to execute the SS Max Biala, which he considered a fantasy reproducing the antisemitic charge of ritualized sacrificial murder. "Even if there were such a thing," Poliakov wondered in his review, referring to the knife, "how could it have gotten into an extermination camp?"[67] Poliakov focused, too, on Steiner's seeming internalization to his narrative of a racist and stereotypical imagery of the Germans and the Jews, decrying Steiner's portrait of Jews as "close to the archetype imagined and propagated in the past by Édouard Drumont, or even Julius Streicher."[68]

But most combatively, Poliakov singled out Steiner's advocacy of a Jewish particularity, not simply in passivity but also in revolt, by denying any Jewish essence of any sort. "There is no Jewish nature nor Jewish essence," ran the headline in *La Presse Nouvelle* above one interview with him. Jewish specificity, Poliakov commented, "exists in general, in the same way that there exists a Spanish specificity or French Protestant one." But though rooted in a deep history, this specificity could not be elevated (or reduced) to a transhistorical imperative: "transforming it into an 'essence' or a 'nature' is to fall into racism," Poliakov insisted.[69] For Poliakov, the imagery of *Treblinka*'s narrative, and its core thesis of a Jewish essence that underwrote the revolt, ultimately helped to locate Steiner in a tradition of thought about Jewish identity: the tradition of Steiner's father. Poliakov did not name him, but surely alluded to him in saying: "They have often been labeled 'Jewish fascists,' and in fact these intellectuals are characterized by an exaggerated cult of violence, and also most often by a hateful distortion of the pacifist tradition of the ghettos. And if there is a point on which they converge with antisemites, it is that of 'Jewish passivity.' I believe that it is to this spiritual family, today in the process of disappearance, that it is best to link M. Steiner." But then Poliakov went even further: "Confused though [his philosophy of Jewish identity] is," he wrote, "it seems to me to echo the biological mysticism dear to the racists (above all, German racists) of the beginning of this century."[70] It is clear that Poliakov did not respond to Steiner's "mystico-nationalist" thesis simply as a historian.

In response to Poliakov's allegation, which extended Rousset's, Steiner demurred, in one of the public fora: "The charge of racism is absurd," he claimed. "I do not speak of a Jewish race, just as I do not speak of a German race. I do speak of the Jewish people and, even more specifically, of the Jewish people of Poland. I do not speak of Frenchmen, nor American Jews, or assimilated Russians. I only spoke of Polish Jews who had no attachment to their country since, aside from a minority that constituted an emancipation movement after 1917, the majority lived closed in on itself [*repliée sur elle-même*]. . . . They were a nation apart, a state within a state, in a sense."[71] Needless to say, it remained difficult to discern such a distinction in the book itself, and few came to grasp it as a result of Steiner's interventions in the course of the dispute.

■

In debates about the realities of history, then, an equally serious debate about the future of identity is there to be read, even amongst the historical experts. It was in fact in public conversation with Borwicz and Poliakov, on the brink of his own massive scholarly engagement in Jewish and Holocaust history, that Vidal-Naquet boldly endorsed, against these reigning and presumably authoritative experts, Steiner's argument for the commitment to existential particularity that must have driven the Jews in their insurrection. Against these and other critics of the book assembled by *Combat*, Vidal-Naquet continued to insist on what he called "a Jewish specificity in the revolt." "I believe, contrary to David Rousset," Vidal-Naquet concluded, "that Steiner is right when he describes the dramatic solitude of the Jews and especially of the Polish Jews who formed a relatively homogeneous community." What could have driven such a perception?

In a striking and thought-provoking comment, in light of his prior engagements during the Algerian war, Vidal-Naquet likened his discovery of the Jewish specificity supposedly at work in the Treblinka revolt to his startling realization that Arab nationalism rather than Enlightenment universalism had driven the anticolonial insurrection he had famously advocated a few years before.

After the war in Algeria, and especially when [Ahmed] Ben Bella arrived at the aerodrome of Tunis crying out, "We are Arabs! Arabs! Arabs!" . . . , I understood that the Algerian insurrection had in large part had the character of a religious revival of Islam. And you know the notorious *mot d'ordre:* "Arabic is my language, Algeria is my motherland, and Islam is my religion." . . . All this made me understand a number of things, notably some traits that the Jews in the ghettos and camps of Poland possessed, whether these Jews had been "de-Judaized" or not. . . . Personally, and in spite of everything else, I am grateful to Steiner for having made me understand the existence of a certain Jewish specificity. I certainly wouldn't justify it as he does, but, in the end, even an atheist like myself can feel its presence.[72]

While Vidal-Naquet did not develop this tantalizing connection, it is surely crucial in grasping his conversion to Steiner's point of view.

The interpretation of *Treblinka* as illustrating the power of ethnic solidarity against racist oppression did, however, receive some elaboration in the reflections of the survivor and eventually famous contributor to Holocaust literature Jean Améry (1912–1978), living in Belgium and reporting on the controversy to German readers. He recalled that when, as an Auschwitz inmate, he heard the news of the Treblinka uprising, it seemed as if "there had really taken place an event of historical-metaphysical redemption, just as Steiner describes it." For Améry, Rousset erred in damning Steiner as a racist because, as recent anticolonialism confirmed, solidaristic revolt from below differed morally from racist subordination from above. Rousset's error had been to conflate them as if they were equivalent. In a rather striking comment, Améry opined that "Steiner developed on the example of Treblinka a theology without God, one similar to that Franz Fanon in *The Wretched of the Earth* has already made known; out of the depths of humiliation man develops a self-salvation through *violence*. Revolt and violent actions have a redemptive character in such instances, where before man was nothing but a suffering object of historical events."[73] The unanticipated power of communal identity in recent nationalist liberationism, expressed in bloody revolt, over the presumptive force of universalistic commitment—as Améry's comment suggests, a frequent though often perplexing discovery in this era—played a role in Vidal-Naquet's initial sense of what had must have motivated Jews further back and what, apparently reflected in and promoted by Steiner's démarche, could come to drive them again. Vidal-Naquet even, briefly, felt its charms himself.[74]

■

Not alone. For balancing, and apparently outweighing, the attempts by the Yiddish newspapers, the larger leftist deportation community, and the academic experts to beat back Steiner's enterprise in the Jewish community, were the affirmative endorsements of his book, notably by the masses of youthful enthusiasts for his work. Of course, like Mandel, many other senior Jewish literary figures publicly celebrated *Treblinka*'s accomplishment. Wladimir Rabi, one of French Jewry's most important men of letters at the time, provides a case in point. When the controversy broke out, Rabi wrote Steiner's mother to reassure her that Poliakov, though an "excellent" historian, "knows nothing about literature," and was not to be feared. Later Rabi, who had known Kadmi Cohen, wrote a favorable review of *Treblinka* in *L'Arche*, where he chronicled literary affairs, noting that he "found in the son the same enthusiasm and the same power of affirmation, whatever his lack of experience, [and] the humor of Kadmi Cohen, for those who remember it."[75]

Nicolas Baudy, the French-Jewish intellectual who gained fame early in the postwar period for editing the Jewish intellectual organ *Évidences* and ran, in 1966, the Alliance Israélite Universelle's *Nouveaux cahiers*, followed suit in his more reflective and essayistic journal. For Baudy, Steiner's project, however marred in its execution and by his reckless public statements, had to be understood empathetically. "What does it subjectively represent for the author," he asked about the text in his introduction to the symposium that he organized in which Steiner and Levinas squared off, "this Jew, son of a deportee, who did not know the events, whose consequences he nevertheless felt and which continue to concern him, except through the intermediation of his elders?" A book by a youth with such a past had to be read differently, Baudy said. And did not its success, with a large non-Jewish as well as Jewish public, reveal the limitations of the community's prior memorialization of its losses? For more than twenty years," Baudy wrote, "we have vainly counted up our dead, vainly because the tallies are only a poor indication of what occurred, and a whole apparatus of conventions, keywords, taboos, and euphemisms has been forged in order to speak of this history whose details have accumulated—all without succeeding in making the grand lines of what happened appear to our contemporaries. . . . [Steiner] has obviously upended all the conventions of mourning and it is good that he has done so."[76] Where the Yiddish writers sometimes exploited Steiner's mixed parentage to place him beyond the pale, Baudy willingly located him in the community and reflecting its dilemmas.

Just as strikingly, prominent notables of the French community likewise endorsed the book, though little information remains about the terms in which they did so. The president of the Jewish Consistory, Admiral Louis

Kahn, as well as Rabbi Josy Eisenberg did so, in a radio appearance, and Steiner gave a lecture in the great synagogue on the Rue de la Victoire (later, however, the famous and long-serving French grand rabbi, Jacob Kaplan, condemned the book).[77] The Consistory, organizing a radio broadcast to memorialize the Warsaw uprising, asked Steiner to participate (perhaps ill advisedly, given Steiner's views on that revolt); and Steiner appeared in a televised dialogue with Eisenberg on April 17, and apparently turned in a performance deft and sympathetic enough that some initially troubled by his print interviews were placated. One viewer commented: "An apparent cynicism is often only, for the young, a mask for deep sensitivity."[78] Of course, others were straightforwardly in favor of Steiner's notion of Jewish specificity—for example, Dr. Charles Merzbach, an important spokesperson for Orthodox Judaism who intervened in the public debate at the Théâtre des Ambassadeurs to lend his support to such a notion (one not, he insisted, assimilable to the racism of antisemites).[79]

Though no doubt the forgiving and empathetic reception Steiner garnered from Jewish notables mattered, even their responses tended to make clear that they were not his true audience. And while it is, of course, difficult to quantify as such the response of "the next generation" (the title that Baudy used to sum up his reflections), the anecdotal evidence in favor of the generational interpretation is powerful. By now it is clear that if the Treblinka affair did not pose one generation against another, it was at least perceived as doing so. Steiner certainly understood matters that way at the time, noting in a letter to his American publisher that while only "most of the spiritual, religious, and intellectual elites of the Jewish people" took his side in the acrimonious disputes, the "totality of Jewish youth" had done so.[80]

Le Nouveau Candide printed several such expressions of youthful admiration as part of its letters section, one praising the interview for announcing "what a whole generation of Jews has been waiting for now for too long" and another hoping that the book would "liberate me from the annoyance and malaise that I unconsciously felt in reading testimonies."[81] Another emblematic letter that Steiner received from a young Jewish woman—he received many from avid young admirers—recounts the absorbing days of reading *Treblinka* she had lived. "The little world in which I live," she wrote, "faded into the background, and I lived with my brothers at Treblinka. But I still pose myself the question: Why did the Jews let it happen? Why?"[82] That letter—is it moving or maudlin?—matched the general perception that Steiner had raised a genuine problem, if not of intellectual substance, then of intergenerational continuity. In *Le Nouvel Observateur*, Beauvoir, who suspected that "a great many young Jews asked the same question" that Steiner posed, recounted that she had herself received a note from a young girl saying, "It is difficult to be Jewish, but now it is less difficult, because I understand many things now that I never grasped, thanks to this book."[83] The generational perplexity appeared with even more prominence in the intra-Jewish publications, whether they were generous or grudging in acknowledging it. "It is symptomatic," an editorial in *L'Arche* had it, "that Jewish youth, by a majority, passionately defend this book that, leaving the facts it recounts aside, reveals their doubts, their thinking, and, in a certain sense, their hopes."[84] In fact, Steiner would make appearances before various Jewish youth groups for almost a year thereafter to speak about the subject.[85] Finally, even *La Presse Nouvelle*, unremittingly antagonistic to Steiner's book, acknowledged in its reporting that, after the panel of Jewish historical experts spoke out against Steiner at the Salle Lancry, it was the young people in the audience who defended him.[86]

■

Finally, there is Levinas, who responded to the Treblinka affair with one of his most personal, and most affecting, pieces of writing. His response is interesting in itself, but it ratifies a generational interpretation of the affair and allows something to be said, in conclusion to this chapter, about the need for a renovated Jewish identity for which the Treblinka affair provided the occasion. I shall argue that Levinas's response is actually quite close to Steiner's own project; though it did not speak to Jewish youth, it did offer an identity— an opposite but perhaps equally constructed identity—for them.

Now titled "Nameless" (Levinas later reprinted it under this heading in a collection called *Proper Names*, in which all the other essays were dedicated to commentary on a specific person), Levinas's short but intellectually and rhetorically overpowering essay originally appeared in a debate organized in *Les Nouveaux cahiers*, in the same issue in which Steiner's piece addressing his generation also saw its way into print. And it is in many critical ways—so far unknown to Levinas scholarship, often uninterested in the historicity of the texts it addresses—an answer to Steiner's project.[87] Indeed, though Levinas's work generally shunned any self-contextualizing gestures, this essay, while a response to the Holocaust and in that sense firmly anchored in time, reflects Levinas's belief that specific circumstances of writing matter only for the chance they allow to transcend circumstance.[88] And yet, I will suggest, it matters a great deal that Levinas produced his first—and arguably most direct—piece of writing about how to remember the Holocaust in the circumstances of the Treblinka affair. It matters not just because these circumstances offer an irreplaceable key to the meaning of the essay but also because they may force a more skeptical point of view on what the essay proposes. Levinas's response reveals how much, in directing his energies against Steiner, he may have ended up sharing with a figure the flaws in whose thinking may seem more immediately evident.

The essay is an unusually accessible example of Levinas's philosophy, though replete as usual in his prose with manifold allusions to traditional Jewish sources and energized by evident, albeit exquisitely controlled, passion about the topic. Levinas begins by explaining his point of view on the problem of the new generation that Steiner, whom he nevertheless does not name, raised with his book and in the debate. For those who lived through Holocaust years as adults, including Levinas, the distinctive relationship to the past had consisted of painful and guilt-ridden memory. "Twenty years can do nothing to change it," Levinas writes in a heartrending expression of the guilt of the survivor. "Soon death will no doubt cancel the unjustified privilege of having survived six million deaths. But if, during this stay of grace, life's occupations and diversions are filling life once more, . . . nothing has been able to fill, or even cover over, the gaping pit. We still turn back to it from our daily occupations almost as frequently, and the vertigo that grips us at the edge is always the same."

This "vertigo" is the knowledge, Levinas says, that ethical norms can entirely lose their usual role in the workings (no matter how imperfect) of public institutions and in the slogans (no matter how opportunistic) of political rhetoric. In the postwar period, such institutions and rhetoric have returned—partial and unsatisfactory in their success and believability, to be sure, but conditioned by the universal agreement that right and wrong matter. "Racism, imperialism, and exploitation remain ruthless," Levinas acknowledges, even in postwar circumstances. But "[w]hat was unique between 1940 and 1945 was the abandonment [of the terms of good and evil]. People always die alone, and everywhere the hapless know despair. And among the hapless and forlorn, the victims of injustice are always the most hapless and forlorn. But what words can describe the loneliness of the victims who died in a world put in question by Hitler's triumphs, in which lies were not even necessary to Evil, certain of its excellence?" That vice has been forced again to pay tribute to virtue, in other words, is little satisfaction, but it means that victims of injustice today can appeal to the conventional wisdom that humanity should live justly, because they are victims of a failure to live up to the norms of ethics rather than an attack on ethics as such. For the victims of the Holocaust, however, justice lost any foothold in the external world; it was forced to retreat into the inner life alone, or to depart the world entirely. "How to put into words the loneliness of those who thought themselves dying at the same time as Justice," Levinas asks, "at a time when judgments between good and evil found no criterion but in the hidden recesses of subjective conscience, no sign answering from without?" Likening the situation of the Jews in the Holocaust to a biblical punishment (and test), Levinas writes: "[T]hese were the 'straits' of the first chapter of Lamentations: 'None to comfort her!'"

But unless Steiner and other young people were to be left to their own devices, the hardships and lessons of these straits, not experienced and then remembered daily after the resumption of normalcy, would have to be communicated. Steiner provoked Levinas, for the first time in his writing, to reflect on whether those who had missed the events, and needed an interpretation of it, should be taught.[89] "Should we insist on bringing into this vertigo a portion of humanity whose memory is not sick from its own memories?" he asks. But Levinas does not dwell on this question; he must have concluded that, since Steiner had forced the issue, the dangers of virtual (rather than lived) memory had to be courted. Significant in this opening is that Levinas's essay does not address the young—does not address Steiner—but rather the problem for those who had experienced the Holocaust posed by those who had not. "What of our children?" Levinas asks. "Will they be able to understand that feeling of chaos and emptiness?"

In spite of the difficulty and the hazards, Levinas responded to the Treblinka affair with, in effect, a curriculum to teach: the content of what those who had survived "should or can transmit in the form of a lesson twenty years later" to the Jews who followed them. It is this lesson plan, a kind of alternative to the activist, even martial, appropriation of the Holocaust that Steiner had offered, that occupies the bulk of Levinas's reflections. It consists of three lessons.

The first lesson that Holocaust memory imposes is that Jewish assimilation is both adventitious and superficial. The assimilation of modern times, so unceremoniously interrupted by persecution, never redefined who Jews are in essence, Levinas contends; stripping them bare, the Nazi years also exposed this fact. Of course, it bears noting that this lesson begins where Steiner himself did: combating the "illusion" of assimilation in order to define the truth of Jewish particularity. For Levinas, the Nazi years showed, at the price of a grim test, that the blessings of assimilation are, whatever their worth, dispensable gifts. "In that world at war, forgetful even of the laws of war," Levinas explains, "the relativity of all that seemed necessary since we entered the city suddenly became apparent." The expulsion from the society into which Jews had integrated demonstrated that their identity as Jews not simply preexisted but could outlive it. It made clear that Jews remained Jews even when the cities and civilizations that had allowed them to join in modernity cast them out.

In a sense, the Jews during the war, Levinas suggests, in a metaphor at once brilliant and disturbing, were returned to their primal narrative, set apart from the nations in an arid climate and forced to live without comfort, stripped of all except their essential relation to the divine. "One can do without meals and rest," Levinas notes, "smiles, personal effects, decency, and the right to turn the key to one's own room, pictures, friends, countrysides and sick leave, daily introspection and confession." The enforced austerity of expulsion did, however, have one positive consequence. During the wartime, the bare problem of existence mooted the desires possible only on the basis of the secure existence that modernity and integration allowed, but by the same token it also revealed what Jews had known more clearly before their age of advancements and comforts. "We returned to the desert," Levinas claims, "a space without countryside, or to a space made to measure—like a tomb—to contain us; we returned to a space receptacle. The ghetto is this, too, and not just a separation away from the world."[90]

This first lesson creates the conditions for seeing a second. It is not simply that Jews have an essence that assimilation can disguise but not abolish and that this essence is more necessary than the civilization that can temporarily obscure it. For such an argument does not explain what that essence is. Ironically, Levinas agrees with Steiner that the camps, the depredations, and even the death reminded Jews who they had always been—perhaps even, in a sense, created optimal and irreplaceable conditions for learning it. Now that his commentary has reached the core of Jewish identity that the war revealed (the discovery of such a core is also the subject of Steiner's narrative), Levinas's writing most undeniably proffers an alternative. For what the Jews found in themselves at the heart of the war on them was ethics rather than violence and passivity rather than action. Steiner had erred, then, in allowing the last word to the Treblinka victors who responded to the lamentable straits of the Jewish people. That had to be reserved for the victims, who,

Levinas says, remembered "[t]he highest duty, when 'everything is permitted,' [which] consists in feeling oneself responsible with regard to [the] values of peace." And here Levinas offers his most direct reversal of Steiner's ethic of vitalist liberation: this highest duty, he writes, consists "[i]n *not concluding, in a universe at war, that warlike virtues are the only sure ones; in not taking pleasure, during the tragic situation, in the virile virtues of death and desperate murder; in not living dangerously only in order to remove dangers and to return to the shade of one's own vine and fig tree.*"[91] For "in crucial times, when the perishability of so many values is revealed, all human dignity consists in believing in their return."

This study of the Treblinka affair has not been intended simply as a massive historical contextualization of a few lines by a master; but it is, one might argue, that too. I would submit that these sentences in Levinas's essay gain their fullest meaning and significance only when they are understood for what they implicitly and most immediately are—a repudiation of Steiner's moral project in his book *Treblinka* and of the position about what lesson the next generation of Jews should draw from the Holocaust that he purveyed in the controversy surrounding it. If the Nazis were death, declaring war against the Jews' life, as Steiner supposed, the Jews did not live up to their principle by fighting back in the camp—adopting an ethic that Levinas clearly associated with a Nietzschean program of living dangerously that he anathematized. Instead, the Jews' highest duty lay precisely in submission and abjection, that is, in the refusal of the virile and warlike hero-ethic that Steiner prized, in the name of the return of true ethics in the future. The Jews were called to be witnesses, not winners. For this reason, in its original publication in *Les Nouveaux cahiers*, Levinas titled his piece not "Sans nom" but "Honneur sans drapeau" (Honor without a Flag). The Jews worked for the cause of morality, rather than conscripting themselves, like other nations, into armies, marching under patriotic flags into battle.

Levinas was not the only figure in the Treblinka affair to respond to Steiner's proposed morality of self-assertion with a defense of the passive abjection that Steiner had found shameful enough to write a whole book against. Richard Marienstras, who promoted in these years an ideology of left-wing Jewish diasporism that gained traction only in the 1970s, at the same moment that numerous French Jews were discovering the power of Zionism for the first time, argued similarly. Born in Warsaw in 1928, a Shakespeare scholar by profession, Marienstras participated in *Le Nouvel Observateur*'s roundtable on *Treblinka*, in which Beauvoir defended her preface to Steiner's book under critical questioning. Unlike Levinas, Marienstras would take his endorsement of the virtues of passivity in a direction critical of the Zionist project and state; but they shared a similar set of premises in repudiating violence and insurrection in the cause of ethics and community. One reason some Jews rejected Steiner's book, Marienstras commented in the transcribed discussion, was that "they would like to project a bellicose and glorious image of the Jews to the non-Jewish world: 'We too know how to defend ourselves by force of arms.'" Steiner, of course, had the same official mission, advertising Jewish passivity in order to unearth true sources of Jewish activism. "But I find this attitude deplorable," Marienstras commented. "Even if in certain circumstances heroism and the virtues of war are good and necessary things, I think that it is dangerous to generalize and to make them absolute values." Steiner thus had made two errors: he presented the Jews' passivity as "shameful" and offered virile self-assertion as the only alternative.

For Marienstras, this "aberrant" depiction foreclosed the option of seeing that Jews might have adopted a passive approach in politics and shied away from resistance for an excellent reason.

> [F]or hundreds of years [Jews] were systematically kept from responding to violence with violence. It followed, for certain Jewish communities of Europe, that nonviolence took on a value: it is not simply that members of these communities were afraid of the violence with which they were threatened—and I say afraid without a hint of embarrassment—but also afraid of the violence they could exact against others. But this attitude is not cowardice. It is even, in my opinion, something admirable to a certain extent. . . . Passivity was not a lack reflecting the absence of a virtue but, in a sense, a virtue in its own right.

No doubt Marienstras differed from Levinas on the reason why passive non-violence is (or became) an integral part of Jewish identity to be prized, but they agreed that the possibility had eluded the young opponent they both rejected. The result, for Marienstras, was the same: focusing on the heroism of the Treblinka insurrectionaries, Steiner "distanced himself excessively" from the victims, unable to see in their deaths anything other than a moral failing.[92]

As for Levinas, in drafting his essay in response to Steiner, he must have felt that the self-evidence and depth of Steiner's moral error made not the problem Steiner had intended to pose but the problem he had biographically and personally become the real topic for thoughtful intervention. Steiner had enacted rather than resolved the problem of teaching the young Jews of the future what to make of their past. Levinas concludes that the third and final lesson, directed at the generational problem that Steiner had performed rather than portrayed, is the necessity of rescuing a permanent—and transmissible—directive about how to conduct one's life from the maelstrom of the temporary (but elemental) situation that the Holocaust had brought about. For civilization can resume, and its pleasures and distractions can reinstitute modern Jews' former forgetfulness, distancing them from the truths revealed in their hardship. "In the inevitable resumption of civilization and assimilation," Levinas insists "we must henceforth . . . teach the new generation the strength necessary to be strong in isolation, and all that a fragile consciousness is called upon to contain at such times. We must . . . revive the memory of those non-Jews and Jews who without even knowing or seeing one another, found a way to behave amidst total chaos as if the world had not fallen apart."

Though it is difficult, in turn, to understand the specificity of his response to Steiner without some knowledge of his more general philosophical project, Levinas's essay makes this much clear: the true heroism of the Jews, if they are to be understood as heroes, is their preservation in thought and action of a moral code ultimately separate enough from institutions and society to survive their breakdown (and in that case to be cherished until their resumption). It is a mission in which, Levinas acknowledges, non-Jews can participate since, after all, morality is relevant to them too. But, as it is the Jews' special task, it defines who they are in a wholly distinctive manner.[93] The Jews' appointed role of preserving rather than betraying morality, even when the social anchor for it is gone, implies their responsibility, in Levinas's vision, for a set of truths "on the near side of civilizations," truths in the name of which civilizations are "made possible, called for, brought about, hailed and blessed," but which civilizations do not themselves create. Put anachronistically, but accurately, Jewish identity and the morality for which it stands are not, for Levinas, socially and historically constructed. "The Jews are a people like all other peoples," Levinas admits, "they, too, desire to know that the voice of their conscience is recorded in an imperishable civilization." But "by a strange election, they are a people conditioned and situated among the nations in such a way (is this metaphysics or sociology?) that they are liable to find themselves, overnight and without forewarning, in the wretchedness of its exile, its desert, its ghetto or concentration camp—all the splendors of life swept away like tinsel, the Temple in flames, the prophets without vision, reduced to an inner morality that is belied by the universe." It is then, at that most crucial moment, that the Jews must preserve rather than betray this "inner morality." Levinas concludes: "election is indeed a hardship."

■

Largely unknown, outside French-Jewish circles, at the time he wrote, Levinas and his philosophy have since become impressively influential in recent years, in France and across the world, within the Jewish world and beyond it, because of their awe-inspiring moral commitment. When one bears in mind, as one should, that it was a young and impetuous journalist whom Levinas roused himself to answer in this essay—doing so with the authority of personal experience of the war years, the rhetorical virtuosity of an accomplished moralist, out of deep familiarity with Judaic sources, relying on the developed philosophy of a master thinker at the height of his powers—it is tempting to conclude that the abilities of these two figures (and therefore the achievements of their respective texts) are simply beyond compare. Aside from their common occasion, *Treblinka* and "Nameless" are simply not parallel. Many may also conclude, without hesitation, that Levinas's response offers a preferable ethical vision, one more durable, inspiring, and moving, than Steiner's putatively callow admiration for Jewish heroism and existential vitality. And yet if it is, from one perspective, an answer—perhaps a conclusive answer—to Steiner, if from that perspective it seems a devastating repudiation of his project, Levinas's essay from another perspective occupies much of the same ground. This is not surprising, since—though only contextualization of the essay makes this clear—both Steiner and Levinas saw themselves facing the same historical challenge. Both of them were writing in response to the problem of what meaning the Holocaust should acquire for the new generation who had not lived through it. Facing the same problem, their solutions shared a few crucial—and contestable—features.

As already noted, Steiner and Levinas implicitly agreed, first, on the premise—on reflection, the suspect premise—that the Holocaust created a privileged occasion for the revelation of Judaism's most fundamental existential core. In Steiner's case, only the syndrome whereby passivity led to activity brought the Jews' principle of life into the open. As for Levinas, expulsion from civilization, while no one would wish for it, can provide for Jews a reminder of their God-given role in the preservation of basic moral values. In this regard, Levinas's analogy between the primal encounter of the Israelites with their God and their encounter with Hitler during the war, while scintillating, is also troubling. The idea that a wholly external threat—rather than an act of faith in response to God's call and of obedience to his commandments—could create even a roughly parallel situation, because they both strip away comforts and restore an elemental sense of identity, may grant excessive pathos to the situation such a threat creates. The community in extremis is not necessarily the community most primally in touch with its most essential definition.

Steiner's and Levinas's definitions of Jewish identity, to come to a second similarity, were perhaps closer together substantively than may at first appear to be the case. After all, Steiner, though prizing the vitalistic heroism that Levinas rejected, partly overlapped with him in endorsing a monitory and testimonial role for the Jews, the one that Vidal-Naquet accurately summarized in his article in *Le Monde* as the Treblinka Jews' recognition of "their function as *witnesses*, the role in which the medieval church had thought to imprison them[: it was] only in wanting to make themselves witnesses of horror in the world and to play Israel's role among the nations that the Jews of Treblinka found the strength to survive."[94] Levinas did not explain whether, to return to the problem of such concern to Steiner, some Jews would nonetheless have to survive, and therefore fight, in order for them to play their monitory and testimonial role in history. However, he did single out—in passing and somewhat disconcertingly—the French partisan maquis as an example of the solicitude for morality undertaken when humane values fail, suggesting that the preservation of ethics might, in spite of his praise of passivity and abjection, require strength and activity in their name. These comments do not close the distance between these after all two very different figures, but they may seriously diminish it.

Both of these similarities, of course, highlight most of all the third, most fundamental, and perhaps most dubious supposition that Steiner and Levinas each adopted—the one rejected most forcefully by Rousset and Poliakov in the midst of the affair—that there is a core Jewish identity to speak of at all, to be disclosed not simply in the straits of a criminal maelstrom, and out of an interest in witnessing, but at any time or in any place and for any reason. In contemporary jargon, Steiner and Levinas shared the "essentialist" premise that Jews have a stable identity immune to history, a communal self not subject to revision by cultural shifts. In this sense, both authors, in their proposals for the Holocaust's meaning for later generations, reduced Judaism—the Judaism espoused by the variety of kinds of Jews in prewar Europe, the plethora of ways they might have (must have) interpreted its meaning during their plight in the war, and the diverse fashions for them to articulate and rearticulate it afterward, the cacophany of reality this chapter has tried to recover—to a singular vision that each, for his own reasons, preferred. In this sense, it is perhaps less interesting than at first glance that the singular vision of each one seems to rule out the singular vision of the other. To put the suggestion in perhaps too challenging a form, where Steiner ventriloquized the voices of triumphant survivors according to his interpretation of the meaning of Jewish existence, Levinas channeled his rival but equally reductive philosophical position into the silence of disappeared victims. But both spoke.

∎

It is true, then, that the Treblinka affair offered to the new generation diametrically opposed views of the nature and future of Jewish identity. But is the difference or the similarity in such positions more striking? Such essentialist visions of identity, Jewish or otherwise, ironically emerge, often enough, precisely when the models proposed are mostly willed rather than assumed, chosen rather than inherited, invented rather than discovered, made rather than found, even when the models are presented as revived from the distant or recent past. This verdict may even apply to those in the debate who, against Steiner, wanted to deny the reality or the importance of Jewish particularity, since their affirmation of the continuity of Jewish identity with universal humanity often interpreted the latter as if it were simply another name for the left-wing militancy they assumed coincided with the interests of all. Poliakov alone clearly repudiated the association between Jews and any necessary identity. The participants in the controversy stood on the brink of an era in which particularist difference, once unpopular, came to be prized, not simply by Jews and not simply in France. Such a fact makes it yet more important to see in the Treblinka affair, near the very origins of such a return to the claims of identity, that the identities affirmed—power and weakness, most obviously, assertion in the name of life and abjection in the service of morality—were perhaps closer together than their advocates believed at the time.

5

The Revolt of the Witnesses

Also part and parcel of controversies, defining them as essentially as other factors, are the voices excluded from them and drowned out by the polemical fury—either entirely, or until impressions have already been formed, and the controversy closed, by a public too fickle to wait to learn everything or hear everyone: who, in other words, is *not* heard. The unheard voices, in the case of the Treblinka controversy, were those of the camp's survivors, nine of whom Steiner had interviewed in preparing his book, and others of whom learned of and read his book after the fact. The publicity of Steiner's oral history in *Paris-Match*,[1] his allusion to it in his book, and his citation of it in the controversy must have been taken by most, during the vitriolic public battle, as guaranteeing, at the very least, that *Treblinka* authentically reflected the particular sources and testimonies on which he and his publisher advertised it as relying. But this premise turned out to be fundamentally contentious and, outside France, came to be tenaciously disputed.

The fact that Steiner claimed at all to ventriloquize the voices of the living witnesses—to serve as their amplifying mouthpiece and to accomplish the mission he attributed to them of bearing a message to the world—is, of course, interesting in itself. It not only afforded the book an irreplaceable "reality effect" but suggested a new vision of the wartime, and of the Holocaust more particularly, available only through victim testimony.[2] In the midst of his own controversy exactly thirty years later, Daniel Jonah Goldhagen took special care to note, rather plausibly, that "[o]ne of the serious omissions of much of the historiography of the perpetration of the Holocaust" had been its failure to draw on the accounts and testimonies of the victims. Slaves and victims of violence and repression are indispensable witnesses to the actions of their oppressors and tormentors. They can tell us whether their victimizers acted with gusto or reluctantly, with relish or with restraint, whether they abused their victims verbally or performed their tasks with detached taciturnity. No historian would dare write of the conduct of American slave masters without drawing on the available accounts of slaves. Yet many historians of the Holocaust and of Nazism—as can be seen in their writings, including those of many of my critics, including [Christopher] Browning and [Raul] Hilberg—rarely, if ever, listen to the voices of the dead Jews speaking to us through their surviving diaries or to the voices of Jewish survivors recounting the manner of their treatment at the hands of the ordinary German practitioners of the Holocaust.[3]

It is, in this light, striking that, very early in the construction of the genocide, Steiner made it a principle of research to base his account not on the historical and administrative sources that illuminate Nazi terror from the point of view of its organization and perpetration—Raul Hilberg's strategy—but instead almost purely on testimonial sources that explained what it was like to experience that terror from the point of view of the victim. (Ironically, Steiner nevertheless came close to Hilberg's result both in his portrait of Nazi "technique" and in his remarks about the passivity of the victims.)

In a letter written at the time, Steiner explained himself on this point more fully. "I only cite four Germans in my book [and] I did not interview any German in order to write it," he explained to a correspondent. "In fact, it is not the Nazis but the Jews in whom I found myself interested. I wanted to write about the ordeal of the Jewish people and not an objective history. The book is authentic, but not objective."[4] Although he did not claim it to be as true as a purely factual account, he did want the book to reflect the different and putatively deeper truths of Jewish identity in the straits of the genocide, and reliance on Jewish witnesses seemed the likeliest way to achieve this effect. Attending to the survivors' voices, then, could serve very different ends in Holocaust representation, to which one must also add that the survivors' voices themselves, as time passed, did not necessarily fall silent.

Steiner's ongoing relationship with his sources, indeed, vividly illustrates the ambiguous status of testimonial voices in historical reconstruction, since they often offer the appeal of straightforward objectivity—and authenticity—but also belong to living individuals who continue to speak of their near death even as they evolve in life. This chapter listens to some of them—not so much, however, to document the truth about Treblinka and its revolt as to attend to the postwar vicissitudes of witnessing, with the voices so frequently available, as in Steiner's book, only in a ventriloquized (both amplified and distorted) version. This aspect of the controversy, international in its scope like the dispersion of the survivors and the diffusion of Steiner's text after its French apotheosis, rarely broke out of private correspondence. Yet there is no denying that it is an essential part of the reception story.

In his relationship with the witnesses after the publication of his book, Steiner faced more than the predictable difficulties of the contemporary story-teller whose sources can still talk back. Not surprisingly, some of those authors whose writings Steiner had unceremoniously instrumentalized to his own ends, and the survivors who thought their interviews were similarly treated, were angered by the uses to which their written and oral testimonies had been put (without, however, always having read the book). And they organized, or were organized, into a campaign against Steiner's work. Though too late, as a result of the delay in their response, to affect the French controversy in the slightest, it is remarkable that their work proved almost entirely ineffective in affecting foreign translations and notably Steiner's great American success. Indeed, it is not too much to suggest that this last reception history—the reception of Steiner's book by Treblinka survivors and their spokespersons—illustrates yet another important feature of the origins and career of post-Holocaust consciousness generally. It helps understand how what Annette Wieviorka has called "the age of the witness" came about.[5]

■

In composing *Treblinka*, as already noted, Steiner drew on multiple kinds of sources: the published accounts of a number of figures, as well as testimonies collected by the Polish historical commission in 1945 and later, in greater number and depth, by Yad Vashem, and—finally and most important for this chapter—on new interviews of his own with nine survivors on a research trip to Israel in 1965. The published narratives had, before his text appeared, remained obscure, just as most of the prior interviews recounting horror and survival had lived only the life of the archival file. But Steiner's process of popularization and vulgarization did not simply lead from Jewish into other languages, from a small audience to a large one, or from pained and tentative self-expression to dramatized and accessible prose. Though sometimes indicted for simply plagiarizing his sources, Steiner in fact filtered their experience through a unifying narrative and ideological purpose that superimposed his own message on their different and more disparate meanings.

Among Steiner's testimonial sources, two above all responded to the book: Marc Dvorjetski (1908–1975), whose Vilna account Steiner had used for the initial parts of his book, and Rachel Auerbach (1903–1976), a Yad Vashem archivist, director of the testimony unit, whose historical investigations and interviews Steiner had borrowed as the basis for his own generalizations.[6] Steiner relied largely on Dvorjetski's narrative for the story of Pessia Aranovich and the discovery in Vilna of the beginnings of the Nazi extermination. A Vilna physician acknowledged by name in the original edition of Steiner's narrative, Dvorjetski had lived in France after the war but had moved to Israel by the time Steiner's book appeared. Dvorjetski's work, like many testimonies that appeared before widespread interest in their subject matter, went largely unread on its original appearance.[7] But Steiner dramatized Dvorjetski's story by twisting some facts: in Steiner's narrative, Dvorjetski only slowly comes to believe Aranovich's report of the shootings and, for this reason, eventually is said to feel complicit with the murderous project of which the shootings are a part.

When he received and read *Treblinka,* Dvorjetski wrote Steiner—though only once the controversy had to all intents and purposes ended—and protested the perversion of his account in no uncertain terms. "In many passages," he wrote, "you attribute sentences and words to me that I never said or wrote and which contradict my sentiments and my actions as well as my past in the ghetto." Aside from the several factual errors and wholesale inventions he pointed out, Dvorjetski complained about his wholly fictional insertion into the syndrome Steiner hoped to attribute to the Jews in the book. Thus, for example, Steiner had written that Dvorjetski "felt beaten by a monstrous system in which the victims inadvertently made themselves accomplices of the executioners."[8] Dvorjetski replied: "Unfortunately, these imaginary passages are an insult to the truth of my whole past. . . . All of these passages are shameful to me and I reject them with indignation."

This "dramatization" of his role, Dvorjetski complained, exaggerated the shock caused by the discovery of the program of intentional genocide. "You apparently wanted to make me a 'dramatic figure,' a naïf whose eyes are opened by Pessia Aranovich's arrival. [But] I had had the sad opportunity of knowing the Nazi system since 1939," he wrote to Steiner. He noted—and pointed out many passages from his testimony to support—the fact that he had refused in 1941 to become part of the Vilna *Judenrat* in order to avoid complicity in the persecution. In light of Steiner's narrative malfeasance, Dvorjetski closed by demanding that all reference to his name and book as well as the specific passages of dialogue and sentiment that Steiner had superimposed on his accounts be entirely suppressed from future editions of the book.[9]

■

Not the angry Dvorjetski but the energetic and redoubtable personality of Rachel Auerbach became Steiner's main antagonist, representing the unified group of Israeli survivors. Not herself an inmate of Treblinka, Auerbach had been a collaborator of the historian Emmanuel Ringelblum in the Warsaw ghetto, and worked with Michel Borwicz on the immediate postwar Polish investigative commission before her own emigration, allowing Ringelblum's hidden archives to be unearthed.[10] As part of these duties, Auerbach had collected many testimonies of Treblinka during and after the war, which she published herself in connection with the early work of the commission.[11] A founding member of Yad Vashem, the Israeli Holocaust memorial and museum, and the director of its testimony collection, Auerbach brought her recorded testimonies with her to the archives of the new center; it was at Yad Vashem that she met Steiner in 1965 where he had come to study the testimonies during the preparation of his book—and where she provided substantial and unwitting aid to his project.[12] A letter from Steiner to her makes clear that they were on excellent terms up to the time that *Treblinka* actually appeared.[13]

Auerbach felt Steiner had agreed to allow her to vet the text of the book before publication; but he did not submit it for her inspection. Upon reading *Treblinka* in early 1966, Auerbach could hardly believe what the friendly and courteous young man she had met a year earlier had done with her painstakingly collected testimonies and immediately began a campaign to have the text altered. It is only fair to note that, in her organization of the survivors, she spoke for a number who did not speak or read French and who thus probably never had any direct acquaintance with *Treblinka*'s text.[14] Steiner clearly felt, during this whole period, much like Hannah Arendt did in facing what she called "the Jewish establishment," an orthodoxy that did not bother to take new ideas seriously (or read the books that contained them) before denouncing them.[15] Auerbach likely familiarized some of the survivors with whom she had put Steiner in touch during his research with the contents of the text—or at least her interpretation of it. For it is clear that, offended by the charge of Jewish complicity, she did not fathom Steiner's overall message. As a result, none of the witnesses understood that Steiner's official intent in the book had been to make good on the will he attributed to their revolt to testify to their experience.

Whatever their means of learning of the book's contents, and whatever interpretation of his project they acquired, several of Steiner's early interlocutors came to be enormously disappointed with him, indeed, in some sense were retraumatized by the experience of the Treblinka affair. In the original acknowledgments to his book, Steiner gratefully listed the names of the nine Treblinka survivors whom he had reinterviewed in Israel and wrote that his conversations with them had been "sometimes pathetic, and while I am anxious to thank [these witnesses] for all their help, I also want to ask their forgiveness for coming to their homes and breaking the spell of their new lives, plunging them once again into the hell which they are trying so desperately to forget."[16] They did not, however, grant this request for absolution.

One of the survivors, Eliyahu Rosenberg, whom Steiner claimed during the controversy in France had since thanked him for publicizing his testimony, wrote him to protest, in very pained terms, the manipulation to which he felt he had been subject, both as a source betrayed by Steiner and, later, as a photographic subject during Steiner's brief trip to Israel—before the contents of his text became generally known—in March 1966.[17] Evidently, Rosenberg had spent more than thirty hours with Steiner, an experience that severely tested him. It was Rosenberg who recounted to Steiner that he had hoped to become a witness through the revolt, the desire that Steiner had made so central to the mystical forces driving it and that he thought his book would in effect gratify. But Rosenberg, who like many of the others did not have access to Steiner's text in the French language, came to judge his enterprise based on the complicity thesis that the publicity made so prominent. "Do you not remember," he wrote Steiner, "that last day when I fell ill in your car, so exhausted that you had to take me home, all a result of the powerful emotions I felt in telling you what I lived through at the camp? Is it because I was forced to remove dead bodies from the gas chambers and burn them that you deemed me a murderer? I did not deserve that those who will read your book throughout the world will say of Eliyahu, who testified against Eichmann and at the Düsseldorf trial: 'He is the assassin.'" Like at least one other survivor, Rosenberg wrote directly to Steiner to ask for the suppression of his name from the book.[18]

In the months that followed, Auerbach worked to represent Dvorjetski, Rosenberg, and the other Israeli survivors. "We responded to your requests in the most generous and loyal manner," she wrote Steiner as soon as she had an opportunity to read the book. "I personally cut no corners in familiarizing you, in the course of our discussions, with the totality of the problems of the death camps, as they had become clear in the course of research." She complained,

> I went so far in my confidence in you, that I did not hesitate to give you the description of Treblinka that I wrote based on the testimony that I had collected already at the end of 1942 from the mouth of an escapee from the camp. I also gave you my historical report *From the Fields of Treblinka,* published in book form after I participated in November 1945 in the inspection of the camp, on the actual scene with the Judicial Commission, in the presence of a group of survivors. I had hoped to make known to the world, through the intermediation of the French language, both the horrors experienced by the Jews and the acts of vengeance and revolt that occurred in the deepest hell that Treblinka was. But now I ask myself if I had the right to do what I did for you, unfamiliar as I was with your views on the Jews' eradication.[19]

Auerbach reserved her main criticisms for the superimposed message Steiner had foisted on his materials, for, in her opinion, there was "a bizarre difference between what you describe and the conclusions that you draw from it."

> On the one hand you show the moral strength of the Jewish conspirators at Treblinka, who succeed in winning over the whole mass of the internees to the insurrectionary cause. But, on the other hand, you call them throughout traitors and murderers of their own brothers. On this point, I would underline the fact—which is contained in your own description of the camp—that if the Jews, menaced by the German whips and revolvers did all kinds of accessory jobs such as carrying away gassed bodies and separating their goods, they did not participate in the act of extermination itself.[20]

But since Steiner had not restricted himself to this point, Auerbach did not restrict herself to criticizing it. "And as if the contradictions of meaninglessness of your moralizing digressions on the subject of the Jewish people were not enough," she continued, "[o]n the one hand, you glorify the general acceptance by the Jews of their own death when they did not try to save their lives by becoming traitorous accomplices and, on the other, you so repetitiously criticize the Jews for going like lambs to the slaughter, accelerating and magnifying the extent of the extermination. Thus, you add to this confusion that you create in your novel through your historiosophical considerations."

Even in light of these aspects of the book, however, Auerbach concluded by mentioning her hesitancy to lump Steiner together with "Anna Arendt, to the point where you become a collaborator of the contemporary successors of the Nazis who, not happy with having exterminated six million, want to perpetrate a further, moral murder on the Jews in robbing them of their human and national dignity." As such remarks make clear, from the beginning Auerbach did not understand herself as speaking simply for the Treblinka survivors she had known or whom she conscripted into a campaign against Steiner's book; rather, she felt she represented all survivors and, through them, the Jewish people as a whole. But Auerbach did not yet, at this point, want to impute to Steiner the "coldly calculated" intention either of insulting the Jews or of "creating a public scandal in order to raise the interest in your book in order to make it a sensational best-seller." Accordingly, she suggested several ways in which the book, in future printings, might be saved from what she hoped were the author's inadvertent mistakes. "This is the reason," she concluded, "that I have written to you in order to offer you my help for the last time." In fact she offered him an ultimatum: either change all the names in the book, expunge the "bizarre and malevolent accusations" against the Treblinka inmates as well as the "retrograde 'pseudo-historiosophy' of the Jews, shot through as it is with exotic and anti-Jewish mysticism," and finally publicly disavow his conclusions as the "result of an overhasty analysis of material unfamiliar for you," or else she and her colleagues would organize a campaign of denunciation of the book and the author.[21] In the event, a letter of protest by Treblinka survivors appeared in the Israeli newspaper *Ma'ariv* in late May 1966.[22] But this letter had no echo in France itself.

■

In many respects, the interventions by Dvorjetski and Auerbach came too late. In his reply to her, Steiner reported to her on the controversy already in full swing. He cited to her all the praise, both Jewish and non-Jewish, that he had received. She had focused—and continued to focus—all her energies on Steiner's apparent charge that the Jews were complicit in their own death, and clearly had not understood its role in Steiner's larger argument about the relationship between complicity and revolt. He wrote to her of "sadness that I have felt in seeing that practically the only attacks against *Treblinka* have come from my Jewish brethren."[23]

There was the question of how to respond to her ultimatum. Steiner had already decided, and recommended to his American editor, to change all the names of survivors still living to avoid any threat of legal liability.[24] He stopped the presses of the French reprint then in course, a response also advised by lawyers, in order to change these names as well as to suppress those of the witnesses he had interviewed and listed in concluding the original edition with acknowledgments. (This action pained him, he explained to Auerbach, because "in describing their participation in the revolt . . . I thought I had paid homage to their heroism.") He likewise agreed to correct the factual mistakes in future editions and foreign translations, once the line between facts and interpretations had been fixed. He wanted in particular to respond to Dvorjetski's complaint, and did so by changing his name; for, as he explained in a letter, "[t]he respect that is owed to this hero means that one does not debate his demands even when he seems to be mistaken."[25] Accordingly, he most fully edited the section about Dvorjetski to remove the implication that the Vilna doctor had felt powerless facing down the Nazis and experienced the guilt of a collaborator.

To be sure, Steiner remained unrepentant about the validity of his text. As regards the interpretive matters Dvorjetski and Auerbach had presented as serious calumnies, Steiner complained to the latter that "ripped from their context, they give a completely false and distorted picture of my book." He went on: "You say in your letter that I 'call [the Jews] throughout traitors and murderers of their own brothers.' I would never bring myself with enough vigor against this interpretation: I never formulated and will never formulate an allegation so atrocious and so contrary to my deepest convictions." He finished by asking: "And if this had been the meaning of my book, do you really think that General de Gaulle, François Mauriac, Edmond Michelet, Marie-Madeleine Fourcade (president of the Action Committee of the Resistance), Professor [Jacques] Madaule (president of Amitié judéo-chrétienne), Professor [Henri] Baruck [sic], Michel Salmon, Nicolas Baudy, Arnold Mandel, Admiral [Louis] Kahn (president of the Jewish Consistory) would have enjoyed, esteemed, and defended my book?"[26] The parade of names that Steiner could cite is not inaccurate, as already shown, but it makes clear that the reception of *Treblinka* took place independently of the revolt of the witnesses. By this point approximately eighty thousand copies of Steiner's book had already been sold; the controversy had proceeded on the basis of the original text.

■

Though, like the initial revolt of the sources, irrelevant to the unfolding of the controversy, it is worth pursuing the dynamics of the revision of the text for the further light it casts on the responses of the living witnesses to the broadcast of their voices. For alterations in the text—in both French and other languages—indeed occurred, in direct response to Auerbach's interventions, though in a manner that completely failed to satisfy her demands.

Initially, Steiner responded bravely in a letter intended to reassure his American editor, Michael Korda, whose firm Simon and Schuster had just bought the translation rights: "If Yad Vashem were so foolish to file a lawsuit it would provoke an international scandal which could only redound to *Treblinka*'s favor and demonstrate the historical and moral accuracy of its arguments."[27] But Hachette (the company that owned Fayard, the book's actual imprint) nevertheless reacted quickly to Auerbach's complaints, sending a lawyer, Jacques Mercier, to Israel in late May to attempt to find a compromise that would allow the book to be reprinted and translated with as little alteration as possible. Though some of the survivors also threatened individual lawsuits, Mercier warned Auerbach that any such action would backfire, forsaking the immediate chance to influence the book's text and possibly adding more fuel to the scandal's fire.[28] According to a stenographic record of his visit to Yad Vashem, Mercier attempted to soothe tensions by explaining the achievements of the book, emphasizing that not Steiner's collaboration thesis but a new perception of the "horror at what the Nazis did to the Jewish people" had been the main fruit of *Treblinka*'s publication. But he said he empathized with the understandable complaints of Yad Vashem's officials, agreeing to attempt to influence Steiner to suppress the most inflammatory passages that Auerbach had identified.[29]

But though, as noted, all the names of living survivors were changed, even for French editions of the book reprinted after May 1966, Steiner resisted further alterations as soon as he understood the legal dimensions of the situation his book had created. Nonetheless, pursuant to his lawyer's agreement with Yad Vashem, Auerbach traveled to Paris in July 1966 to "assist" Steiner in the further correction of his book. In exchange, she wrote, Yad Vashem would not divulge its role in the revision and Steiner could present any changes as his own decision (she held out the hope the publisher would send an errata sheet for the one hundred thousand French copies already sold by summer). Apparently, Auerbach and Steiner worked together for several days, meeting five times to discuss the text of the book in painstaking detail.[30] As she later reported, however, Steiner budged very little under her tutelary supervision. As she explained in an article written for the Zionist Yiddish daily *Unzer vort* in early 1967, "When I began to work with the author, he argued over every word and every expression and became more and more stubborn each day.

I tried to use every means to influence him, as did the lawyer and the direc-tor of the Hachette publishing house." But, she explained, Steiner largely re-fused her interventions, a fact she attributed to the malevolent influence of Constantin Melnik, his sensationalizing editor.[31]

Eventually, the relationship between Auerbach and Steiner completely broke down, and she pursued her agenda through the lawyer. They inter-acted through the summer and into the fall of 1966, as the foreign editions were in process.[32] According to Mercier, it was Auerbach's independent at-tempt to interfere with the American translation—on which more below—that led Steiner to break off all negotiations aimed at consensual alterations.[33] For her part, Auerbach came to feel that Steiner and Melnik had abused her good intentions (as well as those of Mercier and Hachette officials) to post-pone her public objections and to win time for the book's grand success.[34] But it seems clear, in retrospect, that there never was really any hope for compromise, since Auerbach understandably rejected Steiner's starting point, in studying the Treblinka *Sonderkommando,* in the charge that Jews had been in some sense complicit in the death of their own brethren.

Some changes were made. In later printings of the book, as well as in the foreign-language versions of the text, there were, in addition to the name changes of May 1966, many other kinds of alterations: notably, corrections of factual mistakes and purgation of some offensive passages.[35] In the actual text, Dvorjetski's name becomes David Ginsberg just as Kovner is now Dan Ariel.[36] One of Kovner's most famous partisan associates, Ruzka Korczak, is not only renamed but also regendered as David Rosen. (There is, in later French reprints and in the first American edition, this seemingly disingen-uous note, though one apparently agreed upon in the summer negotiations, as to the reasons for the edits: "The events described in this book are so ex-traordinary in their nature that the author has chosen to change the names of the survivors in order to protect the privacy of these heroes and mar-tyrs.") But though all the names in the text proper of *Treblinka* were changed, not all of Steiner's critics had their names expunged from the orig-inal acknowledgments. Dvorjetski succeeded in having his name deleted, but others, including Olga Imbert and Léon Czertok of the Paris Centre de documentation juive contemporaine, did not.[37] Indeed, Auerbach herself, in all French editions, continued to receive Steiner's thanks. In her letter to *Unzer vort,* she suggested that the reason that their names had been left in the postscript of the book (while other changes took place) must have been a desire "to continue to fool the public."[38]

Otherwise, the factual corrections were the most substantial edits, because many of them Steiner himself must have accepted as incontrovertible. In general, the factual corrections were made in subsequent French printings as well as in the translations. Most were the result of Steiner's imperfect knowledge of the geography of Eastern Europe, mistakes in Yiddish phrases, stereotypical understandings of religious Jewish practices, historical errors about the factual unfolding of the genocide, and the like. Some examples were his reference to the town of Metzrich as near Smolensk, his depiction of religious Jews as blowing the ram's horn on the sabbath, and his exaggeration of the number of Jews in the Warsaw ghetto.[39] In the context of the overall book, these mistakes were generally slight, though for those who were informed about the period (or Jewish culture generally) they were no doubt especially revealing or offensive.[40] Of the main alleged errors that actually figured in the French controversy, Steiner changed one and left the other. He clarified that at Treblinka fifteen thousand Jews did not die every day (which would have led to an erroneously large total), only on those days at the height of the killing. As for the "great Sabbath knife" that one of the inmates is said to have used to kill a guard, and which Poliakov interpreted as a sacrificial instrument of antisemitic legend, it appears in every French edition (it is changed in the English translation).[41]

Then there were the passages "prejudicial to the Jewish people" that Auerbach demanded suppressed. They were a more delicate matter, since Steiner felt they involved interpretive matters and were to be understood differently when restored to their original and overall context.[42] The vast majority of the sections that Auerbach wanted expunged, speaking on behalf of Yad Vashem and many of the Israeli survivors, were those implying Jewish guilt and complicity, a theme that wends its way throughout the book from beginning to end as an essential part of the syndrome Steiner narrated. Though all such passages imputing perceptions of personal complicity by Dr. Dvorjetski were erased from the sections about him, in the rest of the book, aside from a few cosmetic changes, Steiner's claims to this effect remained essentially intact.[43] He could not have changed many of these sections, he must have thought, without utterly destroying the message he intended for the book. Surprisingly, with an occasional exception, Auerbach did not complain about those passages, prominently cited during the controversy, which suggested to some that Steiner had identified on some level with the perpetrators, who were frequently defined as blond and handsome, against the victims, who were occasionally described as revolting and weak. Some of these passages, however, were expurgated from the original text, and did not make it into the English edition, for example.[44]

■

That in any case Steiner's revisions in this regard were not sufficient to suit Auerbach and the Treblinka survivors she organized and for whom she claimed to speak is shown by her campaign to intervene with the American publisher as negotiations over the English translation proceeded. If Steiner would not budge, perhaps his American publisher would. She also put herself in touch with his German, Italian, and Spanish publishers; but the battle over the American edition took on special importance for all sides, because of the expectation of high sales in the large market.

Michael Korda, the managing editor of Simon and Schuster as well as the editor for the *Treblinka* project (and later bestselling popular novelist in his own right), enthused by the book and the prospect of its popular success, had sought readers' reports or blurbs praising the book not only from such luminaries as Senator Jacob Javits but also from the major American historian of the genocide Raul Hilberg; these figures—and everyone else he asked in the United States—greeted the book enthusiastically.[45] (See figure 10). Korda had already concluded, in response to the earliest complaints, that, aside from changes needed to insulate the book from legal attack, it should stand as the author desired it. "[E]ditorial suggestions from an organization that just doesn't happen to like the book, for whatever reason, can be ignored," he wrote Steiner early in the controversy after first hearing of Yad Vashem's opposition. "They don't like your opinions? *Tant pis pour eux.*"[46] As Helen Weaver, the American translator, finished her work, Korda solicited any self-imposed revisions from Steiner, taking denunciations of the text and threats of suit especially seriously only when Walter Eytan, Israel's ambassador to Paris, passed him Auerbach's list of deficiencies.[47]

But when Auerbach wrote Korda to lodge a protest regarding the forthcoming English-language version of the book, and asked him to make the alterations Steiner and his editor had already refused, Korda rejected her entreaties. "I must point out, very strongly," he wrote, "that I do not think *Treblinka* contains any 'calumnies' or 'insults' towards the survivors." Indeed, as he explained, Javits, Hilberg, and others "have been full of praise for the book. None has felt that there is any slur on the victims." In any case, Steiner's right to reinterpret the materials in his sources seemed to Korda like an important matter of principle. Auerbach's passionate defense of the victims notwith-

10. Advertisement for *Treblinka*, American edition. *New York Times*, 11 July 1967. (Reprinted by permission of Simon & Schuster, N.Y.)

standing, Korda declared himself to be "profoundly opposed to the very notion of 'purging' a book, as you suggest, to meet the opinions of any person or group of persons. An author has the right to say what he wants to say, and this is the very foundation of a free press and a free society. It is your right to attack Mr. Steiner's opinions once they are published. It is *not* your right to censor them before publication." Writing to this Israeli survivor of the Warsaw ghetto, who wrote as representative of the Treblinka witnesses Steiner had interviewed, the American editor concluded, "It is, above all, the question of an author's right to speak his mind, which I regard as a central—perhaps *the* central—object of the [U.S.] Constitution."[48] As a result, only Auerbach's serial request for suppression of her name from the acknowledgments to the American edition met with success.

In reply, Auerbach insisted that her views, as a representative of the actual protagonists of the book, who were after all Steiner's interviewed sources, were presumably entitled to deference beyond that Korda accorded to "any person or group of persons."

> While caressing the Treblinka prisoners, the author does not stop spitting in their faces and repeating like a maniac, his heinous insults, calling them the murderers of their own brothers, and the hangmen's helpers. . . . [H]ow can you, a man so close to literature, be astonished that all the survivors feel mortally hurt by the invectives of an author emerging from nowhere, and assuming the vest of their judge? . . . Why are you insisting on the word freedom in a free society, when the author simply spits on all those anguished persons, so cruelly hit by fate?

But in spite of Auerbach's further concerns about the number of Holocaust survivors in the United States whom Steiner's accusations would offend, Korda repeated that she could not force the revision of "statements of opinion" as opposed to errors of fact.[49] As Korda concluded, anticipating enormous American sales for the book, "I obviously cannot accept demands for changes from any other source [than the author] whatsoever, especially when I do not feel they are necessary. I have read *Treblinka* many, many times, in numerous versions, and now that the corrected English text is ready, I feel it is a work of brilliance, truth, and power. . . . [H]e and his book deserve the success he will undoubtedly get in this country."[50] As it happened, his prediction would prove correct. As the publication date of May 15, 1967, neared, Simon and Schuster arranged an author tour, beginning with a major luncheon at Lutèce, a series of press opportunities and radio interviews, and a multicity tour. Eventually, the book would sell as many as two hundred thousand copies.

What the attempt of the victims and survivors (if Auerbach is taken as their representative) to reject and correct *Treblinka* documents above all is not so much the irrelevance of what Holocaust survivors find defamatory to what publishers find profitable as an important historical fact about the emergence of Holocaust consciousness: that the victims of the genocide were not destined, often enough, to be either the initiators or the audience for the memory of it as formed by larger publics. (As already seen in the Yiddish press, this observation applies not simply to these particular survivors but to older Jews closest to the experience of the Holocaust quite generally.) The survivors' testimonies were not popular but popularized, which is to say that only their vulgarized processing succeeded, at least until a much later date, if then. It is ironic, then, but historically crucial, that the American advertising for the book presented Steiner as having "borne witness" to the courageous heroism of the Treblinka Jews, whom the process of publication had, for Steiner to speak, involved silencing.

■

As Steiner had interviewed in Israel only nine of the survivors of the Treblinka revolt, fewer than half of the total even in that country, there were others whose memories were not directly used as sources for the book but who read it, in some version, after its publication. Of those in this category, the response of one, the Prague engineer Richard Glazar (1920–1997), is especially noteworthy and affecting. Glazar obtained and read *Treblinka* only in 1968, in French, and immediately upon reading it wrote an open letter to Steiner, addressing him by his first name though they had never communicated (the letter, however, never to my knowledge appeared in print).[51] Glazar's own testimony—redacted over the years, published in small part in 1967 in the Czech monthly *Mezinárodní politika* (International Politics)— appeared as a whole only in the 1990s in German, years after Glazar's emigration to Switzerland following the Prague Spring, before his post-communist return to his home.[52]

"A quarter of a century is slowly piling up on Treblinka," Glazar began his letter. "Of the authentic statements made by the few unfortunates who were able to and did give testimony immediately after the liberation, none received such publicity that 'the world got to know about it.' On the other hand, twenty-eight year-old French journalist, Jean-François Steiner, succeeded." Glazar reported that he had read *Treblinka* the moment he obtained it, "in a single day and night, and a very bad night it was for me." But he empathized with, or at least understood, the personal situation out of which Steiner had written the book, as the son of a victim and a youth who could not come to grips emotionally with what had transpired. Still, Glazar recounted, there was a yawning gap between the eyewitness and the narrator.

At the end of his letter, which details this deviation, Glazar offered a hypothesis about what had actually occurred in the redaction of *Treblinka* and how and why the book had come to depart from the complexity of the evidence. Since it is a strongly plausible theory, it is worth citing at length, along with Glazar's other measured reflections on *Treblinka*'s significance. "I think I have an explanation as to how it happened," Glazar wrote.

> At very first acquaintance and with the first stories you gathered, you discovered a sensational pattern and thesis: They sank to the lowest depths of cowardice, became collaborators with the "technicians of death," fellow-criminals; each of them, so as to survive one day of Treblinka, paid, figuratively speaking, the daily sum of the lives of fifteen others, of fifteen of his brothers and sisters—all this in the interests of the Jewish philosophy of life and the courage to survive at any price. Finally they rose in the famous uprising, which proved to be a kind of sacred rectification of their initial lamentable actions, and this entire philosophy; some, mainly the leading figures of the uprising, had relinquished their sense of humanity to such a degree, that they could only acquire it again by giving their own lives and sacrificing themselves—they knew that for them there was no road away from Treblinka.

Unlike some of the other survivors, Glazar clearly understood Steiner's thesis in its full elaboration. He still found it wanting.

> This immense literary concoction took hold of you, you no longer wished to hear any more about the reality of Treblinka, and you no longer took in any more details. You reconciled all the time factors and, in fact, rearranged, invented, added things and "produced" the story, so that it would fit into your own preconceived pattern, which was probably instilled into you not only by Treblinka, but by the mixture of mysticism, nationalism, and the fashionable dry cynicism. . . . You no doubt have a right to your own elaboration, to your own "produced narration," but in that case it should not have been called the story of Treblinka, but a tale "about an extermination camp."

Glazar went so far as to propose a disconcerting "test," one that would force Jean-François to imagine himself actually arriving at Treblinka and experiencing, as a result of his separation from his companions, the new moral categories that the camp created—ones that decisively mooted all the terms of Steiner's analysis since, Glazar said, in Treblinka complicity, like choice itself, no longer made sense. "You would be standing there with the others, naked," Glazar wrote in a passage chilling in its scenario and devastating in its implications, with his rhetoric at the point of breaking down into the stream of consciousness of his memories,

> suddenly in the confusion they would tell you to dress again—quickly, quickly . . . . Then they would lead you over to us, the 'slaves.' "Look sharp now, here's your foreman, you'll work here!" You'd look round perplexed, dazed. While running past you with our packs on our backs—we're not allowed to stop for a moment—we would take a peep at you curiously, cast understanding glances at one another. Meanwhile we've been telling you three or four times, shouted it at you feverishly—that the others are dead already— and you don't, you just can't believe it—you look just the way we did then, like everyone else . . . . . . you're just like us, no different—and we're no different from you—all people are like that. And that's how you become one of the more dead-than-alive slaves of Treblinka. Cowardice, shame, bravery? These concepts had different content in Treblinka and "out there in real life." The older ones of us often spoke about this—that it was this very difference that the world would never comprehend. Yes, I also sometimes have the unpleasant feeling that I let those dear to me go to the slaughter "just like that." But that is how I feel today, when I can choose coffee or tea for breakfast, jam or marmalade, rolls or bread. . . . And as for you, today, Jean, I know of another type of terrible human cowardice and weakness, namely when a person is unable to admit that his ideas fail to stand up to reality.

Finally:

> My friend, you made an attempt to "write yourself out" of your own shame, to find yourself an answer as to how it could possibly have happened. If you did in fact rid yourself in this way of one shame, you certainly burdened yourself with another, of which—in the eyes of those that survived Treblinka—you will never be free. . . . One day, when more thorough, truthful people than you will immerse themselves in the story of Treblinka, they will not let themselves be carried away by a tale in which the suffering of the time prior to, during, and

after Treblinka is somehow discounted, when they will separate out the legend
from the truth and suppress the eruptions welling up from individual fantasy,
it will probably turn out that you—I'm sure unconsciously—have contributed
more to the forces of evil than of good. You know what I refer to;—"There you
are, how exaggerated it all is, it was really nothing like that . . . . ." Meanwhile,
by a strange reversal of values, it is right to attribute one good thing to you,
namely that you at least drew attention of part of the world—a world in a hurry,
and wearied by all the great goings-on—to an almost forgotten Treblinka.

Glazar, the last remaining survivor of the Treblinka uprising Steiner had, at
least, made known to the world, died in December 1997 when he threw himself out a window of a Prague senior center, shortly after his wife passed away.[53]

■

Thus the origins of the "age of the witness," as Wieviorka has labeled the
most recent phase of Holocaust memory, often in a sense came to be bound
up with the displacement of the witness. (Of course, such displacement did
not always occur, or rather took place through the framing activities of very
different interpreters: Glazar, for example, later served as a source for Claude
Lanzmann and Gitta Sereny in the years after the Treblinka affair.) Just as revealing as the fact that the witnesses did not successfully intervene in the
French controversy over *Treblinka* is that, in the American case, their marginalization occurred not only when they were too late but also when they
were in time. As Melnik wrote to Steiner at the time, "On reflection, Israel
cannot really ruin us: they were too late for France, and too early for America."[54] After Steiner's initial interviews, which he used in ways the survivors
were unable to find acceptable, no one listened to them at any point during
the process. The revisions of the text may have slightly affected the reception
of the book in the United States; but there as in France, where the public had
tens of thousands of copies of the unvarnished original to read, the central
theses of Steiner's book remained to cause commotion—and win allegiance.

In any case, by summertime, the French public, presumably exhausted by
the Treblinka affair, had moved on. Public discourse, however, had been
changed ineradicably. And when they returned from vacation, they had a
new Holocaust controversy in which to be caught up. They were entering an
age in which Holocaust controversies, for better or worse, were becoming a
permanent feature of public life, not only in their society but in the global
community, too.

6

The Aftermath of the Controversy

The Treblinka affair occurred before the next stage in the so-called Vichy syndrome, when Robert Paxton's epoch-making masterpiece about the French national revolution of the war years, along with Marcel Ophuls's film *The Sorrow and the Pity* in a more popular mode, would cause the mirror to crack, and the French people to fall into a period of painful introspection about their own role in the Jewish genocide.[1] But if, as the historian Donald Reid has recently suggested, the Vichy syndrome had two partly independent elements, the replacement of a narrative of deportation with a narrative of genocide and the new perception of French culpability in it, in this book I have suggested that their trajectories were only partly linked. The myth of French innocence in the war need not have entered crisis for the patriotic memory of resistance to be significantly challenged in public.[2]

Put differently, the perceptual isolation of the Jewish genocide from Nazi criminality more generally, along with the reassertion of Jewish identity occurring in tandem, were well under way when the new interpretation of Vichy emerged half a decade later; more radically, one might suggest that the former may have been required for the latter to be so strenuously debated and politically challenging. More signs of the Holocaust's emergence in French culture were, in any case, available even in the short period following the Treblinka affair, beginning with the subsequent Holocaust controversy, which occurred a few months later, establishing trends confirmed by the Six-Day War of 1967 and the rise of Holocaust consciousness in France after the May 1968 events.

Jean-François Steiner's moment of notoriety and controversy was brief. And yet it came at a critical moment in the evolution of Holocaust consciousness, and provided a preliminary indication of what the future would hold.

■

Hannah Arendt's *Eichmann in Jerusalem* appeared in France in late 1966, practically introducing its author to that country. Arendt's book had been published several years before in the United States and the United Kingdom and shortly after in Germany (though it did not appear in Israel until 2000).[3] The comparative delay of publication in France meant that the polemical energies and memorial debates of the Treblinka affair had barely subsided when a tempest around the excerpts from Arendt's book occurred. Its prepublication publicity adhered to the formula likewise followed by Steiner's *Treblinka* a season before, with the book heralded by excerpts placed in the highbrow *Les Temps modernes* and in successive numbers of the mass-circulation *Le Nouvel Observateur*.[4] (See figure 11.) Whereas Sartre's journal printed Arendt's factual survey of deportations in Western and Eastern Europe, as they were depicted at the trial, *Le Nouvel Observateur*'s selections were, as Arendt herself observed, "chosen from a sensationalist viewpoint," condensing much of the book into a few pages and highlighting her most scandalous remarks about the Jewish councils.[5]

Like Steiner's own sensational interview, the excerpt run by *Le Nouvel Observateur* and, above all, the highly stigmatizing headline "Is Hannah Arendt a Nazi?" under which it printed some angry letters a few issues later, bespeak both local French scripts for publicizing books and the career of public controversy to which Holocaust reception from the 1960s came to be inextricably linked.[6] In this case, it was Pierre Nora, then near the beginning of a spectacular career as an editor (and of course as a historian in his own right), who included the translation of Arendt's book as one of the first volumes in his Gallimard "Témoins" (Witnesses) series. (The publisher's blurb, likely written by Nora, a Jewish intellectual from a *grand bourgeois* family, read: "Here is the accused, Adolf Eichmann: a monster or—which is worse?—an excellent functionary? And here is our witness, Ms. Hannah Arendt. Yesterday his potential victim, today his witness.") Since, by this point, Arendt's book had been the subject of a fierce international dispute, Nora decided, following a warning from Léon Poliakov, to publish a brief editor's note together with the book itself familiarizing French readers with the dimensions of the controversy so far (summarizing, in particular, the already-published exchanges between Arendt

11. "A Disturbing Document." Cover of *Le Nouvel Observateur*, 5 October 1966. (© *Le Nouvel Observateur*.)

and her critics Walter Laqueur, Jacob Robinson, and Gershom Scholem).[7] Finally, Nora organized the publicity for the French version of *Eichmann in Jerusalem,* which ensured its success but angered his author. He felt, he wrote in a contemporary letter, that he had arranged it so skillfully that he might have gone too far, "intoxicating the press to the point of incurring the risk that not enough debate will occur to raise the sales of the book!"[8]

Nonetheless, Arendt and her publisher, Denver Lindley of the Viking Press, initially responded angrily to Gallimard's publicity strategy ("Whoever submitted *Eichmann* to *L'Observateur* was very much lacking in common sense," Lindley wrote Michel Mohrt of Gallimard in early December), but Nora defended the campaign.[9] Nora explained that, while he shared the indignation of Arendt and her publisher at *Le Nouvel Observateur'*s shameless trivialization of the issues, the excerpt had sold books and paved the way for the numerous more intellectually serious reviews Nora had organized (by his childhood friend Pierre Vidal-Naquet among others). While apologizing for the headline, Gallimard press agent (and Pierre Nora's sister-in-law) Léone Nora assured Arendt that "no members of the editorial staff of the journal really thought you were a 'Nazi,' since if they did, they would never have considered a prepublication excerpt from the book and presentation of it."[10]

Most important, for the present purposes, Pierre Nora explained "the error of judgment" that Arendt might easily make because of her "distance" from the French scene—a distance that, he insisted, "may not allow an exact enough understanding of the French intellectual atmosphere of the moment." It was *Eichmann in Jerusalem'*s fate, he told her, to

> arrive in France in the same year that . . . Steiner's *Treblinka* also appeared. . . .
> Of a very poor quality, [*Treblinka*] unleashed an intense polemic which saturated public opinion and gave one the general feeling of a sacrilegious and blasphemous "revisionism" that reveled in attacking the best causes. Our essential task had to be to make it clear that Ms. Arendt's book, preceded in France by hearsay about foreign polemics, could not be confounded with these vulgar productions. For before a public that reads poorly and judges hastily, the work risked being monopolized by a sector of opinion only too happy to be able, without having read it, to mine it for "antisemitic" positions. We ran the risk therefore that . . . the book would succeed marvelously thanks to a public reception that missed its content.[11]

It may be, however, that *Le Nouvel Observateur'*s introductory coverage, which Nora arranged, exacerbated rather than defused this risk. To a significant extent, Arendt's book came to be conflated with—and oversimplified by—the terms of the controversy that had immediately preceded it.

Of course, Arendt's charge that the heads of the *Judenräte* were "collaborators" may well have received the most attention in any case. Yet, in a point many French readers must have missed, Arendt—unlike Raul Hilberg and, more frontally, Jean-François Steiner—confined her explosive allegations to the Jews' leaders, refusing to extend the claim to her people as a whole. By and large, a failure to make this crucial distinction made the Eichmann controversy seem, at times, like a recycled version of the Treblinka affair.[12]

In her text, Arendt duly recorded the prosecution's "contrast between Israeli heroism and the submissive meekness with which Jews went to their death—arriving on time at the transportation points, walking on their own feet to the places of execution, digging their own graves, undressing and making neat piles of their clothing, and lying down side by side to be shot." In her own voice, she indicted the collaboration of the Jewish leadership, recklessly speculating that more Jews would have survived if their spokesmen had not been so compliant. "The moral problem," Arendt wrote in a few notorious lines, "lay in the amount of truth there was in Eichmann's description of Jewish cooperation, even under conditions of the Final Solution. . . . Wherever Jews lived, there were recognized Jewish leaders, and this leadership, almost without exception, cooperated in one way or another, for one reason or another, with the Nazis. . . . [T]his chapter of the story . . . offers the most striking insight into the totality of the moral collapse the Nazis caused in respectable European society—not only in Germany but in almost all countries, not only among the persecutors but also among the victims."[13] As already ought to be obvious, such an uncomfortable suggestion appeared in more places than in Eichmann's trial (and Arendt's reflection on it) in the pivotal period of the 1960s; it also came to be aired in France, out of the moral anguish of Abba Kovner, in his essay translated in the period, and then—spectacularly—through its repetition by Jean-François Steiner from a second-generation point of view. And as Nora predicted, reviewers had been primed by the sensationalism of the prior year to respond to Arendt's charge of complicity as if it were the sole moral lesson of the book, except that they often generalized it to include all Jews rather than the leadership Arendt had specifically indicted. In an exemplary review, not surprisingly by the same Pierre Démeron whose interview with Steiner had set off the Treblinka affair, and published in the same magazine, it was stated that the most violent criticism of Arendt's book had been occasioned because "the author argues (but she is not the first and *Treblinka* by Jean-François Steiner recently showed how passionately this question has been debated) that the Jews collaborated in their own extermination." No wonder, given the ease of reducing Arendt's book to Steiner's charge, that, in the same piece, Démeron recorded Nora as saying as he publicized his author: "Beware, this book is dynamite!"[14]

By late 1966, Arendt had come to see such sensationalizations of her work, not as a predictable extrapolation of her own text's candor, but as a perversion of it by scandalmongers and the "Jewish establishment" interested in avoiding her hard questions by attributing to her views she did not hold. Not placated by Nora's assurances that he had her book's best interests in mind in publicizing it the way he did, Arendt wrote with particular outrage about his reported description of the book as "dynamite." "To tell the truth," she remarked ruefully, "it is nothing of the sort. . . . To say that this book contains 'dynamite' means already to fall in with the protestation of the book from interested Jewish quarters. By announcing the book as 'dynamite' I fear that the publisher has, certainly without being completely aware of what he was doing, opened the doors to this regrettable sensationalist reaction."[15] Nora explained, again, that his intent had been the reverse, to save Arendt from appearing in the French context as an ally of antisemites, and that he had intervened with his old classmate Démeron to provide him with an alternative spin.[16]

Nevertheless, the vast majority of the contemporary reviews identified Arendt with the collaboration thesis. And so the initial French debate began with the mistaken premise that she alleged roughly what Steiner had. The notable reviews by Ernest Mandel,[17] Albert Memmi,[18] and Manès Sperber[19] were critical of Arendt for her putative assertions about specifically Jewish behavior or for her reckless manner of writing that lent itself to misinterpretation. (Among major reviews, only one piece of entirely unalloyed enthusiasm, by Roger Paret, appeared.)[20] Just as they had in the Treblinka affair, the most important historians of the genocide then operating in France, Borwicz and Poliakov, cited the scruples that anyone who wanted to speak about this past seriously must impose on herself, ones that Arendt, depicting Jewish collusion, clearly lacked. Referring not just to Arendt but no doubt also to Steiner, Poliakov, who had denounced his erstwhile foe as a racist, wrote: "A certain way of describing the victims' behavior, or even the insistence on their imaginary complicity, risks devolving into the perspective [that] if the Jews were massacred, their conduct, *or their singularity*, must have had something to do with it."[21] The point, however, is that most reviews took as a point of departure that Arendt had made a grand case about Jewish collusion (a view that would not survive much contact with the actual text). Dissenters—for example, Vidal-Naquet insisting that what Arendt had offered "is not really a study of the Jews' attitude facing down Nazism, though Jewish 'collaboration' is treated in a few pages"—did not win the day in framing the discussion.[22]

In the end, Arendt differed from Steiner, not because she did not also stress the passivity and "collaboration" of the Jews, but because she singled out their leaders, thus avoiding the depiction of a general syndrome that Steiner had offered. As she repeatedly insisted in the course of the international controversy, she had merely *reported* the Eichmann prosecutor Gideon Hausner's question to many witnesses of how the Jews could have gone so willingly to their deaths—and dismissed this question as "a fine point" and even as "cruel and silly."[23] Going in exactly the opposite direction from *Treblinka,* Arendt, when she briefly considered the topic, averred without qualification that "the well-known fact that the actual work of killing in the extermination centers was usually in the hands of Jewish commandos," while "horrible," was "no moral problem." More important, like Beauvoir and Rousset, in the French context, Arendt dismissed the perception of Jewish particularity in camp behavior on the grounds that groups of any and all nationalities were made to play such roles in the Nazi system.[24] As we have seen, she learned this lesson, illustrated in *The Origins of Totalitarianism,* from Rousset; and his influence on her is confirmed again in light of her direct citation of him, once more, in the Eichmann book:

> But the sad truth of the matter is that the [emphasis on general Jewish passivity at the Jerusalem trial] was ill taken, for no non-Jewish group or people had behaved differently. Sixteen years ago, while still under the direct impact of the events, David Rousset, a former inmate of Buchenwald, described what we know happened in all concentration camps: "The triumph of the S.S. demands that the tortured victim allow himself to be led to the noose without protesting, that he renounce and abandon himself to the point of ceasing to affirm his identity. And it is not for nothing. It is not gratuitously, out of sheer sadism, that the S.S. men desire his defeat. They know that the system which succeeds in destroying its victim before he mounts the scaffold . . . is incomparably the best for keeping a whole people in slavery. In submission. Nothing is more terrible than these processions of human beings going like dummies to their deaths." (*Les Jours de notre mort,* 1947)[25]

Rousset's insight that the "collaboration" of the Jews in the camps had occurred according to laws that made everyone collaborators was precisely what made

Hausner's question "cruel and silly." But it appears that Rousset's thought, after the Treblinka affair, no longer set the terms of debate in France, and discussion of Arendt proceeded without this crucial passage of her text in mind.

Vidal-Naquet's reflections were, as noted, an exception. But they also suggested that the attention to Jewish singularity introduced by Steiner in studies of camp behavior, and extrapolated by him outside it, had found in Vidal-Naquet only a temporary advocate. In his review in *Le Monde*, Vidal-Naquet argued more in the spirit of Rousset, and now Arendt, noting that the problem of elite "complicity" did not "have anything specific to this case about it; one could easily find analogous behavior in studying, for instance, the reactions of the Armenians to the Turks both before and during the massacres." As if, only a few months after his remarkable intervention in the Treblinka affair, he were now reflecting on his embroilment in it, Vidal-Naquet went on to wonder about the cultural conditions for and ideological function of the thesis of Jewish singularity. "Yet no one outside the Armenian community would raise such issues. *Why then* are they always raised when it comes to Jews, and to them alone? Is it because the Jews 'sell' well? Undoubtedly, but also because the 'election' of the Jewish people comports with many different, and often contradictory, sets of values—the Jews' values and the Christian West's values. And it is in this sense—and in this sense only for an atheist—that Jewish election is so deeply rooted in this West's history."[26] It is easy to read these lines as commentary on the Treblinka affair, since Vidal-Naquet had seen not just Steiner but other particularists—Christians and antisemites—find Steiner's singularity thesis of use. To understand them, and the whole history of the West, one had to come to grips with the belief in singularity; but, Vidal-Naquet now suggested, it had no other meaning or reality beyond its function as an identity-reinforcing belief often at variance with the facts. Only as a belief, serving diverse and sometimes conflicting ideological projects, mostly theological or nationalist, could he explain why it so preoccupied the public, first in the Steiner episode and now with the reception of Arendt's text in French life. He had already begun to take a critical distance, then, on an idea so seductive to him only a few months earlier.

For her part, in response to the French debates, Arendt repeated the restriction of her charge to the leadership, almost tired of her own self-defense; the French edition of *Eichmann in Jerusalem* contained her 1964 postscript underlining the distinction, and she emphasized it in her correspondence with the Noras, her publishers.[27] No matter. Thanks to the sensationalizing designs of her French editors and the French press, and—I am suggesting—

thanks to the immediate precedent of the Treblinka affair and the way it confirmed old identities and shaped new ones, French readers ignored these technicalities, since much discussed, of Arendt's position.[28] Arendt's thesis, as one respondent to *Le Nouvel Observateur* coverage wrote, "is the same as that J.-F. Steiner defends in *Treblinka:* the Jews made themselves accomplices in their own extermination."[29]

■

The original French reception of *Eichmann in Jerusalem* thus took place in the trivializing wake of the Treblinka controversy. But it also has to be understood—like the Treblinka controversy itself—in the activating run-up to the Six-Day War of 1967, which occurred in the following summer. For the other major difference between Arendt and Steiner is that what passivity she found she did not see as part of a progressive syndrome leading to the uplifting conclusion of empowering revolt and breathtaking victory against impossible odds. For her, Jewish resistance groups were "pitifully small," "incredibly weak," and "essentially harmless." While their existence "dissipated the haunting specter of universal cooperation, the stifling, poisoned atmosphere which had surrounded the Final Solution," they were by no means the full-scale antidote that Steiner had hoped to find in them.[30]

A season later, the search for activation, having led to Treblinka in the past, returned Steiner, and many others, to Israel in the future. While (as this book suggests) Joan Wolf surely exaggerates when she says that "[t]he Six-Day War marked the first widespread Jewish presentation of the Holocaust in French national debate, Jews' first sustained public discussion of the Nazi genocide outside of the Jewish community," she is certainly right that it proved a turning point, to which one must add, as a second catalyzing factor, the disaffection after 1968 with radical politics and the rediscovery of ethnic identities amongst elites.[31] The war, of course, prompted Charles de Gaulle's disconcerting prejudicial comment against the Jewish people, a remark that, as much as the war itself, reactivated in France the Jewish identity of many (Raymond Aron not least). Jean Daniel, writing in *Le Nouvel Observateur,* confirmed the effect of these events on the process of the perceptual separation of the Holocaust from the war: "The will to exterminate the Jews appears to him," Daniel criticized the French leader, "only as one among the abominable acts of a horrible war." As Paige Arthur has noted, the controversy took place around the same time as an international tribunal convened by Bertrand Russell, in which Sartre participated, adjudicated claims of

American genocide in Vietnam, a trial that also contributed to the currency of the genocide concept and served to activate memories of the Jewish genocide.[32] The distinctions amongst different crimes of war were quickly becoming unavoidable. In some way, Steiner's self-reactivation, and his attempt through it to reactivate the Jews of his time and age, anticipated and prepared for the global effect on Jewish self-understandings of the Six-Day War a year later, and the centrality of the Holocaust to contemporary Jewish identity that many historians have traced to this event.

As noted above, Steiner actually had a period of disappointment with the Zionist enterprise, up to and including the period of the drafting and reception of *Treblinka* in the mid-1960s. But when hostilities broke out the next year, Steiner flew immediately to the region and testified in an interview that "the young Israelis adopted the same combat that I described at Treblinka. The victory of Israel today is just as extraordinary as, but not more so than, the victory of the Treblinka insurgents, who succeeded in horrific circumstances in destroying the camp. These are all in fact the same men." The courage of the young soldiers who had achieved a thrilling victory, Steiner testified revealingly, they felt as "a duty in the true sense, in the deep sense, not a duty for the country, but something else, an internal exigency." This internal compulsion, Steiner explained, involved a return to the same quest for life that had animated these "same men" in Steiner's book.

> They were fighting at the same time against Hitler, against the Nazis; when they fought, they did not have the Egyptians in front of them, but all the executioners of the Jewish people for two thousand years; and this combat, it responded to the question: how is it possible that the Jewish people allowed themselves to be massacred in this way? There was a response to this question, the response of the young Israeli soldiers: "This will never happen again." It was a way for them of overcoming the whole history of the dialectic of the Jewish people. And it gave them an unimaginable force that they don't understand themselves today; they are a little astounded and shocked. They themselves were not conscious of the terrible will that drove them. . . . If the Arabs had been ten times more numerous, Israel still would have won. [33]

In a sense, Steiner affiliated with the war victory without leaving the ground he had staked out before. For him, the Zionist enterprise, hitherto in rupture with Judaism, came back to it in the difficult circumstances of geopolitical encirclement, existential challenge, and unexpected triumph by force of arms and the victory of life over death.

■

The year 1967, of course, also saw the foreign publication of *Treblinka,* notably in the English-speaking world, where by all accounts, after serialization in the *Saturday Evening Post,* it sold phenomenally, in a much larger market than the one it had originally conquered, thanks to widespread publicity and national book club selections.[34] "At first in France, and now in Britain, Germany, and the United States, the signs of a best seller have appeared," Neal Ascherson announced in the *New York Review of Books.* "Jean-François Steiner's documentary novel will from now on become the general reference for 'the camps,' as *The Diary of Anne Frank* and its dramatizations became ten years ago the general reference for the tragedy of the innocent individual under the Thousand-Year Reich."[35] Its reception in the public press left little to be desired, with many intellectuals—most notably George Steiner—also praising its achievements, and most of the other initial reviews expressing attitudes between complimentary enthusiasm and fawning prostration before the book's narrative success. While national papers usually referenced the terms of the controversy about the book, the many reviews in local papers simply enthused about it as a harrowing and thrilling read.[36] Rachel Auerbach, Jean-François Steiner's nemesis, had only slightly more effect on the American reception than she had had on the American text, and it was not for a lack of trying.[37] Only in the Yiddish press, not surprisingly, which featured a number of articles penned by the well-known journalist S. L. Shneiderman critical of the English version of Steiner's book, did her views have much public airing, and then only in evidently restricted precincts.[38]

In later years, Jean-François Steiner essentially disappeared from the public stage. His most significant reappearance in the following decades (his other, far less successful books aside) may come as a surprise.[39] In 1997, more than thirty years after the Treblinka affair, Steiner took the stand to testify in favor of Maurice Papon at his Bordeaux trial for crimes against humanity. Steiner continued, as he had earlier, to resist the image of the Holocaust that he felt had since come to dominate French (and world) culture, notably after the reversal of the Yom Kippur War of 1973 encouraged a move away from the heroic appropriation of the Holocaust that his book exemplified. Steiner, now, interpreted Holocaust memory as an ersatz and profoundly un-Jewish religion, a morbid cult that alone explained the legal entanglements from which Papon suffered. Arno Klarsfeld, one of the prosecutors and son of the famous Nazi hunters Serge and Beate Klarsfeld, asked Steiner in his cross-examination if he was the "token Jew" (*juif-caution*) of the Papon crowd. To which Steiner responded, "I am nobody's Jew" (*le Juif de personne*).[40]

Understandably, some critics have attempted to re-read *Treblinka* using the "key" provided, after the fact, by Steiner's later actions. It is an interpretation of his initial reception, rather than of his later trajectory, that this book has tried to accomplish; but it bears noting that such a retrospective reading strategy will not allow a thorough understanding of how the book could possibly have resonated as it did at the time, including, as I hope I have shown, how *Treblinka* succeeded in "centering" the Holocaust in French culture rather than in initiating its revisionist denial.[41] *Le Juif de personne:* and yet in his youth, before Steiner became a comparative cipher once again, he had affected a great many. It is not the least of the ironies of the Treblinka affair, then, that Steiner, in setting it off, helped bring about the conditions for the Jewish memory that he claimed was already dominant to become the common sense of French culture.

■

Although Steiner has essentially disappeared from the public stage, the debates he instigated in the Treblinka affair, mostly inadvertently, have far from died down, either in France or in the other countries in which the Holocaust has become a moral touchstone and constant theme of political interrogation. In this sense, the Treblinka affair is still operative. There is first of all the problem of the successor generation to those victimized by the Holocaust, and of this second generation's "postmemorial" interpretation and reenactment of experiences that define it deeply. Then there is overlapping problem and persisting controversy, like the others occasionally spilling over into a wide public, about the validity of renarrating or "reexperiencing" life events not one's own, not as a familial descendant but as a later historian or fictionmaker, drawing on documentary sources and recasting them in some new form. Next there is the debate, this one especially French in its most interesting and intense renditions, over whether to focus on concentration or extermination in interpreting the nature of Nazi criminality, a debate of great consequence for the overall meaning of the war in defining collective identity and moral engagement. Finally, there is the question of the implications of the Holocaust—of its intentional public uses—in articulating collective identities for the future, and especially Jewish identities.

Jean-François Steiner introduced to a broad public a very early example of "second-generation" consciousness, a phrase coined by Helen Epstein only in the late 1970s. As a child of a father he barely knew, who had been deported to Auschwitz when he was five years old, Steiner attempted to reimagine the Holocaust that had consumed his parent but that otherwise—as he emphasized during the controversy—remained hypothetical and remote for him. The "second generation" of the Holocaust has since been studied and categorized in much detail, with different authors preferring to discuss those biographically related to victims or survivors alone, and others grouping them together with those who, though unrelated to the experience of the Holocaust through close family, have tried nonetheless anchor their identity to it. Since Epstein's work, the notion of "second generation" has given rise to a host of other concepts such as "postmemory," "secondary traumatization," and "vicarious witnessing."[42]

The establishment of such belated relationships to prior events, which the Treblinka affair early put on display, has in recent years been subject to criticism, as various writers have dismissed the second generation's quest for meaning through the Holocaust as narcissistic and presumptuous.[43] What the Trebinka controversy makes utterly clear is that there has been no single psychological course for the second generation to follow, and that different members of the second generation may develop antithetical identities based on their attempts to reinvigorate the same traumatic past at different historical moments. The contrast, noted earlier, between Steiner and Henri Raczymow's Esther—one of whom relives Treblinka in order to create a life-affirming vision of escape, the other to fantasize about dying there—makes this fact clear enough. And though one could easily elaborate a typology of the psychic aftereffects of parental or cultural trauma and loss (a typology that would involve commitment to some psychological theory), it is just as important to emphasize the political and historical contexts in which memory formation occurs. Of the survivors themselves, Annette Wieviorka makes the obvious but important point that even for those touched personally by remembered events, memory

> also expresses the discourse or discourses current at the time through which a given society grasps the events the witness has endured. In principle, testimony expresses the irreducible singularity of each individual, each life, and each experience of the Shoah. But it expresses it in the words of the period during which the testimony is given, based on preconceptions and expectations of the time, which instrumentalize the testimony to political or ideological ends, and contribute to the creation of one or more collective memories, diverse in their content, form, function, and purpose, whether these are explicit or not.[44]

The point is doubly true of the children of the second generation, who did not even have the "original" contact with the remembered events, and some part of the idiosyncrasy of Jean-François Steiner's identity in 1966 is no doubt the result of shifts in personal needs and collective perceptions occurring over the four-decade evolution of second-generation consciousness since his intervention. As noted in chapter 2, neither the psychological nor the political interpretation of posttraumatic identity formation and cultural production is totally adequate, and no one has yet achieved a satisfactory account of their interrelation. As the "second generation" continues its evolution, it is precisely such a theory that demands to be found.

■

But this necessary, and ongoing, membership of the second generation in more general collectivities, the mutual implication of biography and history, overlaps with another quandary, continuing since the Treblinka affair, about how much authority to give to historical sources in one's attempts, as a member of the second generation or not, to reanimate the past in some newly processed representation. In light of the revolt of Steiner's sources, and his free mixture of fact and fiction, one may want to seek refuge in the position that the witnesses' testimony is authentic simply by virtue of what it is and should control all later representations. This "documentary" intuition, of course, is not restricted to this early case but has recurred constantly in the history of the genocide's reception, up to and including the present day.

In the main, responses to this quandary, both in the philosophy of history in general and in the domain of Holocaust representation in particular, have taken the form of a polarized opposition between irreconcilable positions: between utter and unbending faith in the witnesses and transfer of authority, grudging or enthusiastic, to the narrator. The standoff between these two positions, at least in the Anglo-American world, is best exemplified by the collision of the famous historians Carlo Ginzburg and Hayden White. Whereas Ginzburg appealed to "just one witness" to safeguard against the relativism implied in the empowerment of the narrator, White's well-known position involved privileging the narrator, who is forced—sometimes by the fragmentariness of the evidence or sometimes by its overabundance, above all by the refusal of the story to tell itself without his aesthetic and ideological intervention—to award himself form-giving primacy in the process of reconstructing past events.[45]

These positions, though taken to an impressive level of theoretical sophistication in recent debates, are the poles between which Holocaust representation has been vacillating since long before White and Ginzburg squared off. The powerful belief in the priority of witnesses came to be voiced in France as a result of the Treblinka affair. A pioneering and still frequently cited article in *Le Monde* of 1972, written by Cynthia Haft, then a young American professor of French literature (and later an archivist at Yad Vashem), is especially insistent on it. Alluding to the many important—but obscure—books published by French internees in Nazi camps since the war and, especially, just in the aftermath of it, Haft attacked a newer trend that had begun to displace these narratives. "Beginning recently," she wrote, "books have begun to appear on the market—sometimes along with publicity of questionable taste (everyone has seen, in the metro corridors, posters emblazoned with swastikas hawking *Treblinka*)—books that hope to reach the public by taking advantage of our worst tendencies: sadism, rape, violence, torture, murder, in the style of horror films." Denouncing this sensationalization of the deportation that *Treblinka* represented, Haft admitted that Steiner "did not plagiarize." But he nonetheless, she protested, "invented a formula" followed by others: gather together and renarrate "the testimonies of the survivors without bothering with accuracy too much—after all, everyone knows how unreliable memory is anyway—and without worrying about exploiting the emotions of the reader by resorting to a popular style."[46]

Haft's early position—especially in light of the fictionalizing excesses of Steiner's work—has a kind of intuitive justice, but before immediately accepting it one should consider another view. Ruth Franklin, in her interesting recent study of the German writer Wolfgang Koeppen, has drawn an opposite conclusion from the fact that both the original and recycled narratives are just that—narratives. The fact that there is no such thing as pure witnessing, Franklin argues, suggests that no one has a proprietary claim even on his own experience, for

> [i]t is becoming increasingly clear that to consider any text "pure testimony," completely free from aestheticizing influences, is naïve. In fact, every canonical Holocaust text involves some graying of the line between fiction and reality. Of course there is an important difference between the "editing" that our minds do instinctively (it could also be called "forgetting") and the deliberate, goaldriven work that an editor performs on a literary text, fact or fiction. But the end result is still the same: a text, whether written or contained within the mind, that is a faithful and yet inevitably incomplete representation of actual events.

In Franklin's view, if a difference persists between the witness and the writer who recycles testimony, it is a mistake to elevate the mere fact of the difference into the decisive criterion of evaluation; it matters not primarily which is closer to the truth but also whether the ends, ideological, moral, or aesthetic, to which the truth is put are defensible and how successfully the ends are achieved.[47] If Franklin's representative post-positivist perspective were accepted, Steiner's moral departure from the point of view of his sources, while important to record, would count at best as a preliminary to judging him (at least after he had changed the names in his texts to acknowledge the reconstructive nature of his text more honestly).

I have no solution of my own to offer to this quandary except to note the existence of and difficulties with the solution proffered by the most thoughtful current commentator on Holocaust representation: Dominick LaCapra. Often seen as White's *compagnon de route* in the renovation of historical thinking, from the beginning LaCapra sensed a danger in his ally's approach. "The record," LaCapra remarked in a 1978 review of White's work, "is presented [in it] as an inert object to be animated by the shaping mind of the historian. This gesture, however, simply reverses the positivist mythology of the mimetic consciousness and substitutes for it an idealist mythology which converts the formerly meaningful plenum of 'the record' into dead matter or even a void."[48] This reversal posed a particularly severe threat insofar as the record consisted of human testimonial sources. In response to this danger, and throughout his career, LaCapra has advocated a strategy of compromise between the passive reception of "reality" by the self-effacing factologist and the activist, even demiurgic creativity of the empowered narrator, called to assign meaning through the selection of the facts and their emplotment. But LaCapra's model of compromise has varied widely over the years with his own evolution, so that deconstructive reading, psychoanalytic transference, and interpersonal dialogue have all been called on to provide a model or theory of mediation.

The extent to which this search has been simply terminological rather than theoretical is beyond the scope of these reflections. But in his most recent discussions, LaCapra has offered yet another term for the mediation he advocates, recommending an ideal of "empathy" between the narrator and his sources, most especially when those sources are traumatized witnesses, as in the Treblinka affair. Continuing to stress that his commendable quest for mediation "should not be confused with the radically constructivist positions taken by Hayden White," LaCapra presents "empathy" as a mode of historical understanding that can find the right blend between passivity and activity, affectivity and analysis, identification and hostility, and victimization and heroism.[49] With respect to the representation of traumatic episodes, including Steiner's use of his sources in creating his book, the last dichotomy is especially noteworthy; for narrators must avoid, LaCapra argues, the Scylla of repeating the traumatized self-understanding of victims just as they must steer clear of the Charybdis of any "attempt to derive reassurance or benefit (for example, unearned confidence about the ability of the human spirit to endure any adversity with dignity and nobility)."[50]

The pressing question is: what precisely is empathy? After all, on the answer to it hangs the hope for mediation, and thus the interest in avoiding the extremes of passive objectivism and activist fabrication. In perhaps his clearest formulation, LaCapra writes: "Empathy, as I have construed the term, is to be disengaged from its traditional insertion in a binary logic of identity and difference. In terms of this questionable logic, empathy is mistakenly conflated with identification or fusion with the other; it is opposed to sympathy implying difference from the discrete other who is the object of pity, charity, or condescension. In contradistinction to this entire frame of reference, empathy should rather be understood in terms of an affective relation, rapport, or bond with the other recognized and respected as other."[51] But these are precisely Emmanuel Levinas's terms—ironically so, I think, in light of this study of the Treblinka affair. The language and substance of this conclusion, that is, appear to suggest that, because of its groundbreaking contribution to a philosophy of recognizing and respecting the "other as other," Levinas's thought is a place to look for the advancement of LaCapra's search for mediation through empathy. After all, one way to understand Levinas's thought is as a renovation of his teacher Edmund Husserl's presentation of a theory of *Einfühlung* or empathy in the early years of the twentieth century—in those years, when Levinas began his thinking, a new word and concept both in German and (through translation) in English.[52]

But whether as a matter of personal failing or theoretical insufficiency, Levinas, I tried to show, renarrated the Holocaust in his essay "Nameless" in just as much a message- or theory-driven manner as Jean-François Steiner did. (Of course, as I noted, Levinas narrated through the silence of the dead rather than, as in Steiner's case, ventriloquizing for those still living.) This is not to point out the futility of the quest for a workable theory of empathy by narrators toward their sources, particularly with respect to traumatic events. It is rather to suggest how easily such a quest may defeat itself, providing an apology for overriding plurality and diversity in the name of some preferred set of values—a risk courted even by those who insist, at times ritualistically, on the importance of treating "the other as other." Here again, the Treblinka controversy is, in a sense, still ongoing.

■

The debate over the nature of Nazi criminality, the controversy over whether to understand it through Rousset's paradigm of *univers concentrationnaire* or through Steiner's paradigm of Jewish genocide, likewise rages still. For many years, the embattled emphasis on the centrality of the Jewish genocide in the overall repertory of Nazi crimes had still to win its way; then, in many countries, it came to enjoy a kind of orthodoxy, scholarly and public, that only now, if even now, shows signs of stress. The year after the Six-Day War and its galvanizing effect, in France as elsewhere, on Holocaust consciousness would see the publication of Olga Wormser-Migot's state thesis, *Le Système concentrationnaire nazi, 1933–1945;* though its title might suggest otherwise, it effectively pursued the insistence on the distinction between concentration and extermination beginning its slow emergence during the Treblinka affair. In fact, Wormser-Migot's book would insist on the distinction in too categorical a manner later in need of nuance; but as a sober historical work based on documentary sources, it contributed decisively in France to the career of the distinction between concentration and extermination.[53] In later years, with the rise of French Holocaust consciousness, the distinction would become much more prominent, thanks to Vidal-Naquet's work, along with that of an increasing number of respected academic experts on the Jewish genocide whose voices have become ever more trendsetting.

Ironically, however, in recent years—a period of David Rousset's belated return and perhaps posthumous revenge—the viability of the distinction between concentration and extermination has been revisited once again, especially in French circles. Numerous factors contributed to this tendency, expressed by many authors of different ideological stripes. Indeed, after a brief interregnum, a group of European (and especially French) intellectuals has begun an attempted—no doubt qualified and far more theoretically sophisticated—return to the immediate postwar perception of a universe of camps and the present-day engagement on behalf of humanity that traditionally followed from it. Many tendencies nourished this challenge to the perception of the singularity and differentiation of extermination that grew slowly but powerfully beginning in the 1960s, not least the revived penchant for comparing Nazi and Stalinist horror, a comparison evidently facilitated by a shift in emphasis to their common camp universe—a commonality Rousset, after all, stressed early on.[54] Sometimes, as in the controversial work of Alain Brossat, the Israeli treatment of the Palestinians is also at issue, an example in which an indiscriminate usage of a generalized notion of "camps" can run disparate phenomena together.[55] But even Vidal-Naquet, so influential in propagating the distinction in the years after the Treblinka affair, has written in his recent memoirs that "the two systems, that of concentration and that of extermination, . . . are, I now think, closer cousins of one another than it is sometimes thought. Why do I say this? Not at all in order to deny that Treblinka and Dachau had distinct ends: killing on the one hand, isolating from the world and, possibly, extinguishing, on the other. But one must add that the machine for killing was born in proximity to the machine for extinguishing and that at Auschwitz and Majdanek the two systems were combined."[56] The very fact of the potent European renaissance of Rousset's ideology of the *univers concentrationnaire*, which has touched even one like Vidal-Naquet who forcefully opposed it, should put one on guard against its easy dismissal, even in its updated form, as a superannuated and disproved relic of deportation consciousness.

For Omer Bartov this contemporary renewal reflects more or less simply a "peculiar French manner" of relating to the past involving a "reluctance of French intellectuals to focus on the Holocaust as an event in its own right," motivated by an interest in occluding the collaboration of France and its intellectuals "in that very specific event" coupled with a desire to assert France's "status as the center of European civilization and the conscience of humanity."[57] For Bartov, the unmastered French past implies that the right to moralize about others' crimes, and return to Rousset's activist denunciation of new camplike formations, has not yet been earned. But surely this reductive and pathologizing explanation of the return of the vision of a contemporary *univers concentrationnaire*, in an age in which events have spread camps even further, is too quick and easy. It cannot historically explain the reemergence of the discourse or normatively preempt all of its possible uses, and in any case the idea of a *univers concentrationnaire* has not returned in France alone. More important, as Bartov has himself acknowledged, "the universalization of victimhood, despite its particularist-apologetic potential, can also serve the cause of combating genocide," not to mention rouse vigilance against other crimes.[58] Nevertheless, in insisting on the continuing recognition and preservation of the difference between concentration and extermination, as Steiner and Vidal-Naquet did in 1966, Bartov surely has a point.

The power—and difficulties—of a generalized rather than particularized image of Nazi criminality is nowhere on more serious and sophisticated display than in the compelling and influential but occasionally troubling work of Giorgio Agamben, a contemporary Italian philosopher and, one might argue, Rousset's most significant if unwitting disciple today. Agamben began developing his views with an article in the French newspaper *Libération* titled "What Is a Camp?" Subsequently, he has elevated the camp, following Arendt (though not mentioning Rousset), to be the centerpiece of his philosophy of modernity, in a series of writings culminating in his *Remnants of Auschwitz: The Witness and the Archive*.[59]

In that book, the full contribution of which is beyond the scope of the present reflections, Agamben focuses on the figure from survivor accounts of the *Muselmann,* the one, driven for many witnesses beyond the boundaries of humanity, whose life could no longer be distinguished from death. According to Agamben, whose book is presented as a commentary on Primo Levi's writings and interviews, the *Muselmann* is "only now, almost fifty years later, . . . becoming visible."[60] Though Rousset did not dwell on the *Muselmann,* to enumerate some of the elements of the camp on which Agamben lays stress is nevertheless to see in his work a revival, and renovation, of Rousset's old paradigm.

In fact Agamben cites Rousset twice, albeit through other sources. One citation tells of the erasure of the distinction between *bourreau* and *victime* and the universality of abjection in the camps: "Victim and executioner are equally ignoble; the lesson of the camps is brotherhood in abjection."[61] The other citation, taken from Rousset unknowingly through Arendt's use of it, suggests that the camps showed that "everything is possible," inaugurating a new era in which an analysis of the camp, which confused rule and exception, can cast meaningful light on ongoing politics since.[62] But Agamben owes more than he realizes to Rousset's founding vision of the concentration camps, beginning with the general premise, which Rousset introduced, that it is possible and useful to speak and write about "the camps" as a unitary phenomenon, following through to specific themes revealing their true essence—from the evaporation of the divides between criminal and victim and normality and exception to the existential nudity of what Agamben calls "bare life"—and finishing in the apparent meaninglessness of the distinction between living and dying. For Agamben, as for Rousset, dying and death are (in Agamben's word) "indistinguishable."[63] More important, aside from the other continuities, is the renewed strain of activism: the analysis of the camp as an unprecedented new formation is supposed to serve as a warning today, for significant features of it are ongoing though civilized life has supposedly resumed.[64]

But above all, there is the shared claim between them that an analysis of a concentration camp or some element of it explains in a significant sense the extermination of the Jews in the death camps. Of course, Rousset's analysis did not feature the *Muselmann,* but the continuities are not in the emblematic figure in which Agamben sees the camps epitomized but in the substantive content of the epitome. For Agamben, since the *Muselmann* appeared in many concentration camps that were not, like Treblinka, devoted to exterminating Jews (the titular though not constant subject of Agamben's work, Auschwitz, blended aspects, as Vidal-Naquet says, of both institutions), it turns out that an analysis of the concentration camp figure of the *Muselmann* is a key to understanding the exterminatory project directed at the Jews alone, at Treblinka and elsewhere. For Agamben, then, citing testimonies from many different camps throughout the long period of Nazi rule, the *Muselmann* is "the perfect cipher of the camp," precisely because he "touched bottom," and reveals the "core" of the camps that "no one wants to see at any cost."[65]

An alternative interpretation of Nazi criminality might place the immediately exterminated, rather than the interned and still living *Muselmann,* at the center, but that choice would force more emphasis on where, precisely, such immediate extermination occurred and who, precisely, suffered it. In other words, it would require the heterogeneous vision of "the camps" so intensely contested in recent years, beginning in Jean-François Steiner's time. It is something like this alternative that Steiner, along with Olga Wormser-Migot and many others later, opposed to the once ubiquitous rhetoric of the *univers concentrationnaire.* For Agamben, however, the *Muselmann* is the central figure, and he goes so far as to say that "the Jews knew that they would not die at Auschwitz as Jews," but rather as *Muselmänner,* figures to whom in principle anyone, Jews or non-Jews, could find themselves reduced.[66] As with Rousset, the effect of Agamben's comparatively homogenizing interpretation of Nazi criminality is to displace analysis from the immediate death that most Jews suffered upon entry into death camps to the terrible but real survival those allowed to live in concentration camps were granted—even if such survival was no more real or lasting than the pathetic *Muselmann* could claim.[67]

In the most striking statement of his thesis, Agamben claims that the new visibility of the *Muselmann*—occurring only today—suggests "that the paradigm of extermination, which has until now exclusively oriented interpretations of the concentration camps, is not replaced by, but rather accompanied by, another paradigm, a paradigm that casts new light on the extermination itself, making it in some way even more atrocious. Before being a death camp, Auschwitz is the site of an experiment that remains unthought today, an experiment beyond life and death in which the Jew is transformed into a *Muselmann* and the human being into a non-human."[68] Agamben's statement that "the paradigm of extermination . . . has until now exclusively oriented interpretations of the concentration camps" is curious. If it means a paradigm that has placed intentional mass death of the Jews at the center, then the statement is, of course, demonstrably false. But the likelier interpretation of Agamben's argument—according to which concentration and extermination are actually versions of one another with their emphasis on the boundary between life and death, while Agamben's new paradigm is one stressing the boundary between humanity and inhumanity—is itself not totally beyond the choice between concentration and extermination. For an emphasis on the blurring in the Nazi camps of the distinction between human and inhuman involves a prior assumption, as in Rousset's work, that analysis of "bare life" in such generalized camps can serve by proxy for an analysis of immediate extermination in the killing centers that targeted Jews specifically.[69] And so it must be remarked that Agamben's new paradigm shares much with one version of the paradigm it supposedly is introduced to accompany (but not replace).

Far from moving to a new theory, one might well then argue, Agamben is renovating an old one: precisely the paradigm of the *univers concentrationnaire*, the oldest and most durable optic in the history of understanding Nazi criminality. As with Rousset, and Arendt who drew on him (Arendt is an important, albeit selectively used, source for Agamben in some texts), there is a generous interpretation according to which, as all these authors urge, there is a continuity, not a caesura, between concentration and extermination, such that understanding the former provides the key to understanding the latter. It is something along these lines that Agamben means when he says that "the camps in the system of Nazi biopolitics" are "not merely the place of death and extermination; they are also, and above all, the site of the production of the *Muselmann*. . . . Beyond the *Muselmann* lies only the gas chamber."[70] Above all: the former does not displace the latter, but it does provide its true meaning. The question—a historical and theoretical question—is whether it matters that many *Muselmänner* were produced, living corpses though they might have been, in concentration camps that involved no intentional exterminatory project (indeed in some cases before the "Final Solution" ever began) and whether it matters that most Jews died, gunned down on sight or gassed in extermination camps, without ever becoming *Muselmänner.* The question, more generally put, is whether the assumption of easy continuity between concentration and extermination, old-fashioned or newfangled, obscures more about the past that it reveals. These are the dangers of an image of generalized victimhood: though girding the reader to be vigilant against present and future crimes, it should not come at the price of ignoring the particularities of past deaths.[71] In the vexatious and continuing alternative it posed between concentration and extermination, too, the Treblinka affair continues.

■

The debate about how to conceptualize the camps is also, as Rousset's career and Agamben's writing make obvious, equally a debate about how to frame moral identities through present appeals to the past, about the validity of public uses of history and memory, debates that numerous studies indicating the significant sensationalization and commercialization of the Holocaust have helped illuminate (and occasionally obfuscate).[72] It is in this final sense that the Treblinka affair, in which sensationalization and commercializaton were already obvious factors, again endures to this day.

Of course, the particular generation of French Jews at issue in the Treblinka affair—whose identity was publicly perceived to be a new quandary thanks to Steiner's intervention—moved on from his book in many different directions. Evidently, in these few concluding pages, there is no hope of studying the evolution and fecund pluralization of French-Jewish identity in the years since Steiner wrote. Suffice it to say that Steiner's call to youth augured a major, and ongoing, crisis in republican-integrationist French Judaism, created by a number of overlapping developments.

First, of course, there occurred the fearful then triumphant moment of the Six-Day War itself, which for the first time allowed Zionism widespread headway in French life. "Our Youth Rediscovers Its Soul," one chronicler reported in *L'Arche* in a special issue of 1967 titled "Israel Shall Live!" "The young Jews of France, now that Israel has been driven to its destiny, are giving birth to a purified Judaism, rid of its unseemly controversies and stylistic quarrels," the author explained.[73] In terms of historical reflection on the Second World War, the theme of Jewish resistance, so prominent in France thanks to the Treblinka affair, would become a major subject of study and publication around the time of the 1967 war, not simply in France but there too.[74] Other processes promoting a new search for particularity, in the longer term, included the crisis of the left and the return of many student activists to Jewish identities in the 1970s, and of course the challenge of the newly arrived Algerian community—still a wholly hypothetical challenge at the time Steiner wrote—to the cultural hegemony of the standard French-Jewish integrationism and republicanism.[75] The content of the particularity, however, has remained subject to extreme lability. Over the long term, once the drive toward a heroic articulation of the genocide passed, it is the redefinition of Judaism as ethical insight that has marked post-Holocaust French Jewry with the most impressive power—a transformation in self-understanding that Emmanuel Levinas's "consecration," as Pierre Nora in an important recent analysis of his community has called it, symbolizes most conveniently.[76] Thus Steiner's attempt to reimagine the Jewish past heroically won out only briefly, but in the longer term it is Levinas's proposal for the reclamation and reinvention of Jewish identity as post-Holocaust morality that has taken hold.

Having dwelt sufficiently, in the prior chapter, on the functions and perils of the construction of particularizing identities that call on the past, at times demanding its reliving to properly frame one's beliefs in the present, it may be best to observe in conclusion that the answer is not simply to revert to the universalizing identities so under challenge in the course of the Treblinka affair. (As shown, of course, appeals to the particularity of Judaism need not rule out putatively universal values, as the cases of the Christian response to the Holocaust, and Levinas's ethical view in a different way, make clear.) Indeed, in spite of their inspirational power and though often an antidote to morally problematic and historically fictitious claims about specific cultural essences, universalistic identities often share many of the same ethical difficulties and traffic in the same creative fictionality as the particularist identities they present themselves as overcoming. In all cases, the past is under significant threat of instrumentalizing distortion as memories for the future are revived.

In recent years it is the contemporary thinker Tzvetan Todorov, returning more self-consciously to David Rousset's perspective than Agamben has, who provides a fitting argument to interrogate about the proper uses of past memories in the construction and furtherance of present identities.[77] Todorov's basic claim is that memory—of the Holocaust, for example—is subject to ethical use and problematic abuse. He acknowledges that traumatized individuals have every right to their personal memories; his concern is with (in Jürgen Habermas's phrase) the public uses of history. (Evidently, implicit in this perspective, which sides strongly with what I have called the political rather than the psychological theory of memory, is that a person's or a culture's relation to its past is fundamentally under his or its control.)

Since the Treblinka affair, the singularity of the Holocaust in the past has been much discussed. And it is clear that, as in that controversy, the notion that Jewish victimhood stands out from other wartime events has played a profound role in authorizing or confirming particularistic Jewish identities. Figuring as part of a cohort of French intellectuals in this regard, Todorov dedicates much of his writing on the subject to the argument, not always frontally offered but usually directly implied, that the Jewish Holocaust memory looms too large, and leads to the wrong identities, in the contemporary world. A "sanctifying" approach taken to the Holocaust, Todorov says, "automatically prevent[s] us from learning any lessons from the event and would close off all 'application.' It would be paradoxical, to say the least, if we asserted that the past should be a lesson for the present, and at the same time that it has no connection with the present. Things that are sanctified in this way are not much use to us in our real lives."[78] For this reason, he indicts a "cult of memory" that, he says, ritualistically commemorates the Holocaust but does not mobilize in the present against roughly comparable disasters, including contemporary examples of genocide and ethnic cleansing.[79] The key, then, is, Todorov says, to "mov[e] on from your own misfortunes and those of your close relatives to the misfortunes of others." This manner of response, Todorov says, is more dignified because it involves recognition of the proper uses of the past.[80]

Not surprisingly, Todorov has been among the principal advocates of a revival of David Rousset's life and thought, to which he most recently devoted a compelling vignette.[81] For Todorov, Rousset is important because he exemplified the proper use of memory. He did not stand by silently when news of Soviet camps became known in the West, or excuse communist crimes, like his fellow leftists, as a slander purveyed by capitalists or the price to be paid for utopia. Living through the era of totalitarian wrongs, which Jews would (Todorov suggests) later jealously interpret as the forum of their exclusive and climactic suffering, Rousset did not fetishize the particularity of his own experience, denying to other victims the right to complain. Instead, Rousset insisted on the commonalities between Nazism and communism without recklesslessly assimilating them together.[82] Earlier than most, he denounced

Stalinist camps and mobilized against them, calling former inmates of Nazi camps to his aid, while other Parisian intellectuals turned a blind eye.

The difficulties with Todorov's position are twofold. The first is the danger that his present-minded universalism poses to truth about the past. For Todorov sometimes writes as if the endeavors of gaining historical clarity about the differences among past crimes and taking moral action against present and future crimes are somehow mutually exclusive. And the spirit of comparability can lead to just as serious problems as the "cult of uniqueness" that Todorov decries. Thus, one can easily agree with Todorov that these aspects of Rousset's career are quite inspirational. And yet, as the Treblinka affair illustrates, Rousset refused to acknowledge that the extermination camps for Jews were different in nature and purpose from the concentration camps that had interned common-law prisoners and political enemies like himself, because this fact interfered with his mobilization of the memory of the past for the sake of the present. For the same reason, he wanted to remember Jews in wartime, in part falsely, as if, though perhaps subjected to their own special fate, they were coequal members of the antifascist resistance that defined his own prewar and postwar activity. Todorov's hagiographic treatment of Rousset omits these facts. It points to the danger that the "proper use" of memory that Todorov advocates, and not simply the "wrongful abuse" that he condemns, can also lead to the distortion and instrumentalization of the past. Beyond Todorov, the right hope is perhaps for a culture in which accuracy about the past is not too easily perverted in the quest for contemporary relevance—by *either* the spirit of comparison *or* the "cult of uniqueness."

Second, without gainsaying the occasional uses of universalistic identities rooted in awareness of past crimes, it is to be noted, especially today, that tethering oneself to the past in such a spirit also may *interfere* with moral action in the present, and not simply promote vigilance and provide energy for it. Notice, after all, the kind of reasoning that follows from Todorov's proposal to base reflection on current events in awareness of the possibility that past crimes (like the Holocaust) may recur. Ironically, this universalism shares with the syndrome of "sanctification" that Todorov rejects the erection of those crimes into the standard against which everything afterward is judged. He simply wants to ground their appropriation in humanist solicitude for everyone rather than one's particular people or kind. In this way of thinking, moral and political analysis begins with the single question of how close a given event is to the past crimes that everyone repudiates. Todorov's project of universalistic vigilance presents moral reasoning as if it were a simple question of fact: whether a given event is "close enough" to some past crime to demand intervention.

How rare it is, however, that a commitment to a proper reckoning with extraordinary crimes of the past disposes of the question of what course to pursue in the more ordinary present! Thus, for example, while Todorov rejects the contemporary "war on terror" as close to the ideologies animating past crimes, other figures, such as Paul Berman, summon up the memory of the same historical events precisely in that war's defense.[83] How to decide who is right? The chief problem, then, is that judging contemporary alternatives against the standard of past horror may rule out too little with self-evident assurance and provide no way of selecting among the options that remain. Moreover, it may distract from the search for better means with which to face alternatives, as charges multiply from all sides that *everyone else* has failed to learn the lessons of the past and respond in the correct moral direction.

The Treblinka affair continues in this sense, too. Jean-François Steiner's project of particularistic identity-formation through history may seem more straightforwardly dubious today, though it may have its benign and even beneficent uses too, if Avishai Margalit's recent philosophical articulation of an "ethics of memory" is correct.[84] But the universalistic alternative solves few problems, notably in collective politics, in the contemporary world. And the pretense that it does is often just as troubling, for it encourages the deceptive presentation of what are in fact maximal and controversial stands on current affairs as if they simply and necessarily followed from a minimalist and consensual rejection of past crimes against humanity. Whether particularistic or universalistic, identities presented as closely tethered to some animating past reference point, then, overcome fewer quandaries than one may have initially hoped. This result may seem disappointing, but it is perhaps safer than the pretense that the past exempts the present from the difficulties of political reasoning and the necessity of ideological conflict. And so it is possible that the memory of the past should, very often, lead to the conclusion that humanity must see itself, in the present, on its own, faced with new and difficult choices it has never faced before. Sometimes, the present needs to be haunted only by its own novelty.

But not always. No one can decree an easy end to Holocaust memory, or to the disputes that have formed it with an astonishing regularity itself worthy of reflection. There is therefore no simple balance sheet to this book, or to the larger phenomenon it attempts, through a case study, to illuminate. The need to repeat the Holocaust controversy, apparently compulsive but no doubt with its potential benefits, suggests that there may come times when the past needs to be summoned up to help find moral direction and to create or reinforce identities, whether particular or universal in nature. How to know when, and which, is the problem. The Treblinka affair ended. But the age of the Holocaust controversy is ongoing. For the foreseeable future, for better or worse, it is never-ending.

Notes

Preface

1. "From *l'Univers Concentrationnaire* to the Jewish Genocide: Pierre Vidal-Naquet and the Treblinka Controversy," in Julian Bourg, ed., *After the Deluge: New Perspectives on the Intellectual and Cultural History of Postwar France* (Lanham, Md.: Lexington Books, 2004). Thanks to the publisher for permission to reprint numerous passages from my essay in *After the Deluge,* as well as to the Carnegie Council on Ethics and International Affairs to use some material from my article "The Ghosts of Totalitarianism," *Ethics and International Affairs* 8, 2 (Fall 2004): 99–104. Finally, I am grateful for authorization from the rights holders to reproduce the images I use in this book.

1. The Interview

1. Pierre Démeron and Jean-François Steiner, "Les Juifs: Ce qu'on n'a jamais osé dire," *Le Nouveau Candide,* 14–20 March 1966; part of this interview is available in English as "The Steiner View," *Atlas* 12, 2 (August 1966): 42. The book is Steiner, *Treblinka: La révolte d'un camp d'extermination* (Paris: Fayard, 1966); the English translation (New York: Simon and Schuster, 1967; paperback, New York: Signet, 1968) is by Helen Weaver. The book has continued to be republished; more recent editions bear forewords by Gilles Perrault (Paris: Fayard, 1995) and the late Terrence Des Pres (New York: New American Library, 1979; New York: Meridian Books, 1994). It also quickly appeared in German, Portuguese, Spanish, Italian, and Japanese.
2. Steiner, "Treblinka," *Les Temps modernes* 21, 237 (February 1966): 1406–60; Steiner, "Le chemin du Ciel," *Le Nouvel Observateur,* 16–22 March 1966. The deportee paper *La Voix de la Résistance* likewise printed an excerpt: *La Voix de la Résistance,* 3rd ser., 110 (April 1966): 6–7. Since its publication, *Treblinka* has

sold 175,000 copies in France alone, and been reprinted seventeen times; close to 150,000 of those sales occurred upon its publication. For the overall figure, see Ruth Valentini, "La terrible gloire de Steiner," *Le Nouvel Observateur,* 20 March 2003.

3. David Rousset, *L'univers concentrationnaire* (Paris: Editions du Pavois, 1946); a parallel antifascist venture, though only slightly more familiar in the United States, is Eugen Kogon's *Der SS-Staat: das System der nationalsozialistischen Konzentrationslager* (Berlin: Tempelhof, 1947). Both were soon translated into English: Rousset's book in two different versions, *The Other Kingdom,* tr. Ramon Guthrie (New York: Reynal and Hitchcock, 1947), and *A World Apart,* tr. Yvonne Moyse and Roger Senhouse (London: Secker and Warburg, 1951); Kogon, *The Theory and Practice of Hell: The German Concentration Camps and the System behind Them,* tr. Heinz Norden (London: Secker and Warburg, 1950).

4. Samuel Moyn, "Two Regimes of Memory," *American Historical Review* 103, 4 (October 1998): 1182–86.

5. Henry Rousso, *The Vichy Syndrome: History and Memory in France since 1944,* tr. Arthur Goldhammer (Cambridge, Mass.: Harvard University Press, 1991), 164; cf. 139.

6. Élie [Elie] Wiesel, "Plaidoyer pour les morts," in *Le Chant des morts: nouvelles* (Paris: Seuil, 1966), 195, 197, 199, in English as "A Plea for the Dead," in *Legends of Our Time* (New York: Holt, Rinehart, and Winston, 1968), 178–79, 181.

7. Raul Hilberg, *The Destruction of the European Jews* (Chicago: Quadrangle Books, 1961), in French as *La Destruction des juifs d'Europe,* tr. Marie-France de Palomera and André Charpentier (Paris: Fayard, 1988).

8. I base this (hazardous but plausible) generalization on the press clippings by the librarians at the Institut d'études politiques in Paris, who have compiled press dossiers for several decades on important events like the Eichmann trial.

9. Hanna [*sic*] Arendt, "La banalité du mal," *Les Temps modernes* 21, 238 (March 1966): 1569–1602; Arendt, *Eichmann à Jérusalem: Rapport sur la banalité du mal,* tr. Anne Guérin (Paris: Gallimard, 1966); on Arendt's reception in France, see chapter 6 below. In a letter to the author, Pierre Nora, who edited the Gallimard series in which Arendt's book appeared, doubts the significance of the delay of several years in the appearance of Arendt's work in France ("Peut-on parler de retard?"), but it is, for reasons I will examine, crucial. The British edition, obviously, appeared simultaneously with the American version, and the German translation came out the following year.

10. Anson Rabinbach, "Eichmann in New York: The New York Intellectuals and the Hannah Arendt Controversy," *October* 108 (Spring 2004): 97–111 at 103.

11. Steiner explained in a later interview that the Warsaw insurrectionaries—as he said the contemporary report of SS General Jürgen Stroop, charged with putting them down, revealed—were simply gnats against a Nazi enemy that treated

their revolt as laughable. "Of course, the men who fought in Warsaw were heroes, but for me, Warsaw was a defeat. The Jews who revolted there played into the hands [*fait le jeu*] of the Germans who wanted to kill Jews, and that's all there is to it." Arnold Mandel and Steiner, "Mourir à Treblinka," *L'Arche* 110 (April 1966): 29.

12. David Halberstam, "Nazi-Camp Book Arouses France: 'Treblinka' Stirs Debate on Role of Jewish Victims," *New York Times*, 17 April 1966.

13. "Jean-François Steiner, auteur de 'Treblinka': un jeune à la recherche de la vérité," *La Voix de la Résistance*, 3rd ser., 111 (April 1966): 12.

14. Neil Ascherson, "Chronicles of the Holocaust," *New York Review of Books*, 1 July 1967.

15. Steven Shapin and Simon Schaffer, *Leviathan and the Air-Pump: Hobbes, Boyle, and the Experimental Life* (Princeton, N.J.: Princeton University Press, 1985), 7. On the notion of writing the *histoire totale* of a book, see another work on early modern science, Ann M. Blair, *The Theater of Nature: Jean Bodin and Renaissance Science* (Princeton, N.J.: Princeton University Press, 1997). The innovative premises of early modern studies, recently the more methodologically exciting field, have rarely been applied to modern events and texts.

16. On the first French Holocaust controversy, set off by André Schwarz-Bart's *The Last of the Just* in 1959, see Francine Kaufmann, "Les enjeux de la polémique autour du premier best-seller français de la littérature de la Shoah," *Revue d'histoire de la Shoah* 176 (September–December 2002): 68–96; on later ones, see Joan B. Wolf, *Harnessing the Holocaust: The Politics of Memory in France* (Stanford, Calif.: Stanford University Press, 2004). For a general overview, see Annette Wieviorka, "La construction de la mémoire du génocide en France," *Le Monde juif* 149 (September–December 1993): 23–37.

17. George Steiner, "Postscript to a Tragedy," *Encounter* 38, 2 (February 1967): 33–39.

18. Pierre Vidal-Naquet, *Mémoires,* vol. 2, *Le trouble et la lumière* (Paris: Le Seuil, 1998), 196.

19. I owe a few such quotations from Steiner used in this book, as well as much otherwise unattributed biographical information, to a series of personal communications with him.

20. Michel Borwicz, in Jan-Claude Kerbourc'h, "'Treblinka,' de Jean-François Steiner," *Combat*, 10 June 1966, and Borwicz, " . . . Mais Michel Borwicz n'est pas d'accord," *L'Arche* 110 (April 1966): 30.

21. On the controversy in America, see recently Peter Novick, *The Holocaust in American Life* (New York: Houghton Mifflin, 1999), chap. 7, esp. 137–39; Rabinbach, "Eichmann in New York"; and Jennifer Ring, *The Political Consequences of Thinking* (Albany: SUNY Press, 1997).

22. Novick, "Holocaust Memory in America," in James E. Young, ed., *The Art of*

Memory: Holocaust Memorials in History (New York: The Jewish Museum, 1994), 161; Hilberg, *The Destruction of the European Jews,* 681; Daniel Jonah Goldhagen, *Hitler's Willing Executioners: Ordinary Germans and the Holocaust* (New York: A. A. Knopf, 1996), 330.

2. Author and Text

1. See Kadmi-Cohen, *Introduction à l'histoire des institutions sociales et politiques chez les Sémites: essai philosophique* (Paris: Giard, 1922).

2. Cohen, *Nomades: essai sur l'âme juive,* pref. Anatole de Monzie (Paris: Alcan, 1929), 8–9.

3. Cohen, "La Faillite sioniste," *Mercure de France* 204, 719 (1 June 1928): 257–90; "Principes de politique sioniste," *Mercure de France* 207, 727 (1 October 1928): 5–35 at 15–16; and "Principes de politique sioniste (fin)," *Mercure de France* 207, 728 (15 October 1928): 332–60.

4. On the French allergy to Zionism, see Marcel Abitbol, *Les Deux Terres promises: Les Juifs de France et le sionisme, 1897–1945* (Paris: O. Orban, 1989), and Catherine Nicault, *La France et le sionisme, 1897–1948* (Paris: Calmann-Lévy, 1991).

5. See Cohen, *L'abomination américaine: essai politique* (Paris: Flammarion, 1930); cf. Simon Schama, "The Unloved American," *New Yorker,* 10 March 2003, or Philippe Roger, *L'ennemi américain: généalogie de l'antiaméricanisme français* (Paris: Seuil, 2003), in both of which he is discussed.

6. Cohen, *L'État d'Israël* (Paris: Kra, 1930). See, later in the decade, *Esquisse d'un sionisme nouveau: Les idées reçues en 1897 ne suffisent plus en 1932* (Paris: Kra, 1932), which appeared simultaneously in Yiddish, English, and German editions, and *Apologie pour Israël par un juif* (Paris: Librairie Lipschutz, 1937).

7. Cohen, *L'État d'Israël,* 19, 39, 45–48, 48–49, 90, 57.

8. Pierre Vidal-Naquet, *Assassins of Memory: Essays on the Denial of the Holocaust,* tr. Jeffrey Mehlman (New York: Columbia University Press, 1992), 33, discussing the kinds of sources invoked after the war by the "father of revisionism," Paul Rassinier.

9. These were later printed and circulated as an anonymous pamphlet, with the text retaining the lecture format and camp setting: [Cohen], *Massada: Discours des camps de concentration,* YIVO Archives, Record Group 116, Territorial Collection (France II, folder 40). This booklet also includes the movement's founding Declaration of December 28, 1941.

10. Ibid., Lecture 11.

11. Ibid., Lecture 2.

12. Ibid., Lectures 5, 7, and 11.

13. Ibid., Lectures 1 and 2.

14. See ibid., Lectures 4, 5, and 10.

15. Ibid., Lecture 6. According to Yael Zerubavel, the Masada story went through an international process of rediscovery from the 1920s through the 1940s, providing the name for many different Zionist organizations and publications, and during the Holocaust served as a frequent model in the Yishuv for activist resistance to persecution (in contrast to the passive acceptance associated with exile). Zerubavel, *Recovered Roots: Collective Memory and the Making of Israeli National Tradition* (Chicago: University of Chicago Press, 1995), 63, 70.

16. [Cohen], *Massada*, Lecture 12.

17. Ibid., Lecture 1.

18. Vallat wrote in his memoirs, in a passage very likely referring to Cohen: "I had long conversations with an integral Zionist. He agreed with my general conception of the Jewish problem. He not only avowed that the Jew is an unassimilable stranger, but went further: he declared that the Jew, if he desires to remain loyal to his law, must refuse assimilation!" Vallat, *Le Nez de Cléopâtre: Souvenirs d'un Homme de droite (1919–1944)*, pref. Charles Maurras (Paris: Les Quatre Fils Aymon, 1957), 267.

19. These phrases are cited from Michael R. Marrus and Robert O. Paxton, *Vichy France and the Jews* (New York: Basic Books, 1983), 310–15 at 312, where this curious episode is described in some detail. See also Simon Schwarzfuchs, *Aux prises avec Vichy: Histoire politique des Juifs de France (1940–1944)* (Paris: Calmann-Lévy, 1998), 313–20, and the brief entry in the *Encyclopedia Judaica* (New York: Macmillan, 1972), s.v. "Isaac (Kadmi) Cohen."

20. Marrus and Paxton, *Vichy France and the Jews*, 312, citing Cohen's letter to one Dr. Klassen of the German Foreign Office.

21. Serge Klarsfeld, *Memorial to the Jews Deported from France, 1942–1944: Documentation of the Deportation of the Victims of the Final Solution in France* (New York: B. Klarsfeld Foundation, 1983), 528. He is listed as "Kadimi" Cohen on Convoy 70.

22. Dominick LaCapra, *History in Transit: Experience, Identity, Critical Theory* (Ithaca, N.Y.: Cornell University Press, 2004), 93. He criticizes Peter Novick, whose *The Holocaust in American Life* (Boston: Houghton Mifflin, 1998) sides strongly with a political interpretation of the events he studies.

23. Cohen, *L'État d'Israël*, 56.

24. See chapter 4, below.

25. Tom Segev, *The Seventh Million: The Israelis and the Holocaust*, tr. Haim Watzman (New York: Hill and Wang, 1993), 108–10 at 109; cf. 179.

26. Jean-François Steiner, "Fabrication d'un parachutiste," *Les Temps modernes* 17, 188 (January 1962): 939–51. On the cultural significance of the *parachutistes* in

French culture of the 1960s, see recently Kristin Ross, *May '68 and Its Afterlives* (Chicago: University of Chicago Press, 2002), 36–38.

27. Steiner, "Fabrication d'un parachutiste," 940, 941, 943, 944, 945.

28. See, for example, Steiner, "Qu'est-ce que ça vous fait d'être indépendant?" *Le Nouveau Candide,* 3–10 January 1963; "Ceux qui attendent les automitrailleuses," *Le Nouveau Candide,* 11–18 April 1963; "J'ai vu naître la révolte contre Ben Bella," *Le Nouveau Candide,* 3–10 October 1963; "J'ai vu l'Algérie devenir folle," *Le Nouveau Candide,* 24–31 October 1963; "Ces Français qui servent Ben Bella," *Le Nouveau Candide,* 31 October–7 November 1963; "Ceux qui ont dit adieu aux armes," *Le Nouveau Candide,* 12–19 December 1963; "La dernière révolte d'Algérie," *Le Nouveau Candide,* 18–23 January 1964.

29. On Melnik's role during the Algerian war, see Constantin Melnik, *Mille jours à Matignon: raisons d'État sous de Gaulle, guerre d'Algérie, 1959–1962* (Paris: B. Grasset, 1988); for his memoirs, see Melnik, *Un espion dans le siècle* (Paris: Plon, 1994).

30. See Gilles Perrault, *Les secrets du jour J* (Paris: Fayard, 1964), and *L'orchestre rouge* (Paris: Fayard, 1967), in English as *The Secret of D-Day,* tr. Len Ortzen (Boston: Little, Brown, 1965), and *The Red Orchestra,* tr. Peter Wiles (New York: Simon and Schuster, 1969). For his earlier account of the paratrooper experience, see Perrault, *Les parachutistes* (Paris: Seuil, 1961). In fact, Perrault, at Melnik's request, helped Steiner prepare the manuscript of *Treblinka,* assisting him in rewriting the final chapter to add length and drama. But, contrary to one published source, it was not Perrault who scripted the death of the sadistic guard Ivan the Terrible—a narrative choice that figured in the immense controversy around the capture and trials of John Demjanjuk two decades later—but Steiner who did so, basing the episode on the testimony of Eliyahu Rosenberg among other survivors. Perrault only embellished how it occurred. See Jean-Michel Fournier, "'J'ai fait mourir Ivan le Terrible,'" *Le Journal du Dimanche,* 30 March 1986. For a trace of this debate, see Yoram Sheftel, *The Demjanjuk Affair: The Rise and Fall of a Show Trial,* tr. Haim Watzman (London: Victor Gollancz, 1994).

31. Aba Kovner, "Le miracle dans l'abdication," *Amif* (revue mensuelle de l'Association des Médecins Israélites de France) 13, 123 (March 1964): 221–49. This essay, originating in an October 1945 lecture, first appeared in print as "The Miracle in Abdication" (in Hebrew), *Mishmar,* 7, 14, and 21 December 1945, and is reprinted in Kovner, *On the Narrow Bridge: Spoken Essays* (in Hebrew) (Tel Aviv: Sifriat Poalim, 1981).

32. On Kovner's wartime activities, which were characterized by many moral ambiguities in an atmosphere that made heroism difficult, see, for example, Dina Porat, "The Vilna Declaration of January 1, 1942, in Historical Perspective," *Yad Vashem Studies* 25 (1996): 99–136, and Porat, *Beyond the Reaches of Our Souls:*

The Life and Times of Abba Kovner (in Hebrew) (Tel Aviv: Am Oved, 2000). More accessibly, see the film *Partisans of Vilna*, dir. Aviva Kempner (1987). Rich Cohen's popular *The Avengers: A Jewish War Story* (New York: A. A. Knopf, 2000), in which Kovner takes center stage, suggests that some the assumptions that animated Steiner persist.

33. Kovner, "Le miracle dans l'abdication," 233, 234. At a conference in 1975, Kovner stated: "One personal note: it was I who wrote the famous phrase 'like sheep to the slaughter'—a phrase that haunts me now wherever I go. . . . The phrase that I used then must not be taken out of context. For thirty years I have never repeated it . . . and I have never thought that the sheep had anything to be ashamed of." Kovner, intervention in Henry L. Feingold et al., "Discussion: The *Judenrat* and the Jewish Response," in Yehuda Bauer and Nathan Rotenstreich, eds., *The Holocaust as Historical Experience: Essays and a Discussion* (New York: Holmes and Meier, 1981), 252.

34. Kovner, "Le miracle dans l'abdication," 234, 249.

35. Ibid., 238–39, 241, 243.

36. Steiner, "J'ai retrouvé en Israël quatre rescapés; Ils m'ont raconté leur cauchemar," *Paris-Match*, 9 April 1966.

37. Roger Peyrefitte, *Les Juifs* (Paris: Flammarion, 1966), in English as *The Jews: A Fictional Venture into the Follies of Antisemitism*, tr. Bruce Lowery (Indianapolis: Bobbs, Merrill, 1967). For the advance publicity, see Peyrefitte, "Pourquoi j'écris 'Les Juifs,'" *Le Nouveau Candide*, 7–14 January 1965, and "Le fantastique bluff d'Israël," *Le Nouveau Candide*, 14–21 January 1965. On the book's publication, see Pierre Démeron and Peyrefitte, "Les Juifs et moi," *Le Nouveau Candide*, 28 June–4 July 1965. And see such responses as Bernard Frank, "La réponse d'un Juif: 'C'est un monstrueux cocktail donné dans un camp de concentration,'" *Le Nouveau Candide*, 19–25 July 1965, and Jean Cau, "La vérité sur 'Les Juifs,'" *Le Nouveau Candide*, 2–8 August 1965. The book also had wide resonance in other sectors of the press.

38. Renée Winegarten, "French Culture and the Jews," *Commentary* 45, 1 (January 1968): 27–35 at 27, 28. The most controversial aspect of Peyrefitte's book was its use of a theory of the history of surnames to "unmask" numerous French notables, including Charles de Gaulle, as descended from Jewish origins.

39. Ibid., 30.

40. Jean-Paul Sartre, "Pour la vérité," *Les Temps modernes* 22, 253 bis (1967) (Dossier: Le conflit israélo-arabe): 9–10; Claude Lévy and Paul Tillard, *La grande rafle du Vél d'Hiv (16 juillet 1942)* (Paris: Robert Laffont, 1967), in English as *Betrayal at the Vel d'Hiv*, tr. Inea Bushnaq (New York: Hill and Wang, 1969).

41. Winegarten, "French Culture and the Jews," 30–31.

42. "Ces amoureux: J.-F. Steiner ('Treblinka') et sa femme la petite-fille du maréchal

von Brauchitsch," *France-Soir,* 13 December 1967; see also "Son of Nazi's Victim Weds Marshal's Daughter," *New York Times,* 19 December 1967. This bit of gossip even made Walter Scott's column in *Parade* magazine, distributed in many American newspapers in the Sunday edition (I could not locate the date). One Henry Kitzakowski of Milwaukee, Wisconsin, wrote in to ask if Steiner had "recently married a Nazi." In reply, Scott set the record straight: "Steiner, whose father died at Auschwitz, was secretly married several months ago to Grit von Brauchitsch, granddaughter of Field Marshal von Brauchitsch who commanded the Wehrmacht in Poland, France, and Russia from 1939 to 1941, but was later fired by Hitler. Steiner and his bride first met at the Sorbonne several years ago and fell in love. Miss von Brauchitsch was never a Nazi."

43. Steiner, "Notre destin collectif," *Les Nouveaux cahiers* 2, 6 (Summer 1966): 4.

44. Henri Raczymow, *Un Cri sans voix* (Paris: Gallimard, 1985), 13–14; *Writing the Book of Esther,* tr. Dori Katz (New York: Holmes and Meier, 1995), 3–4.

45. Steiner, *Treblinka: La révolte d'un camp d'extermination* (Paris: Fayard, 1966), 11; Steiner, *Treblinka: The Revolt of an Extermination Camp,* tr. Helen Weaver (New York: Simon and Schuster, 1967), 17.

46. Ibid., 31–32; English ed., 38.

47. Ibid., 41–42; English ed., 47–48. Similarly, as the sentiment of resistance grows in the Vilna ghetto, Steiner remarks that it is the kind of resistance that does not defeat fate but only wins a different version of it. "They were not fighting either to win or to survive, but to send a message to the future, to history, to mankind, or to God, each according to his convictions" (ibid., 47; English ed., 54).

48. Ibid., 85, 87; English ed., 93, 96.

49. Ibid., 19; English ed., 26.

50. Ibid., 283 (not in the English edition, which deletes the entire section).

51. Ibid., 27, also 31; cf. later French reprints and the English edition, 34 and 38, for important changes described in the subsequent chapter.

52. See ibid., 70, 93, 108, 135, 136, 172, 268, 272, 276, 313; English ed., 79, 102, 118, 147, 148, 187, 287, 291, 295–96, 332. The first two quotations are from ibid., 108; the later French reprints and the English edition, 118, omit the phrase "monstrous complicity" but otherwise leave the passage as is. The third quotation is from ibid., 70; the English ed., 78, changes the sentence from an assertion into a question ("Was there an element of cowardice . . . ?") and leaves out the clarification that the cowardice is more apparent than real.

53. Ibid., 100; English ed., 110.

54. Ibid., 122–23; cf. English ed., 133, where it is described as an ordinary knife.

55. Ibid., 134–35; English ed., 147.

56. The most famous invocation of this line is in S. Ansky's well-known play *The Dybbuk* (it had appeared in French in the interwar years and then in an internationally successful film version of 1937 of the same name); but Steiner's use of the

idea as an explanation for the Holocaust (or the Jewish relationship to political authority more generally) extrapolates far from its original meaning in the Hasidic mythology on which Ansky drew, which posited a relationship between salvation and transgression: "redemption through sin." The other epigraph Steiner used is from Heinrich Himmler's notorious Posen speech of October 1943.

57. Steiner, *Treblinka,* 172–73; English ed., 186–87.
58. Ibid., 250–51, 254; English ed., 268–69, 272.
59. Ibid., 167; English ed., 181.
60. Ibid., 277; English ed., 296.
61. Ibid., 16; English ed., 22.
62. Ibid., 312; English ed., 331.
63. Ibid., 70; English ed., 78.
64. See ibid., 55, 78–79; English ed., 62, 86–87.
65. Ibid., 69–70; English ed., 77–78. Steiner's likely source on Nissenbaum is Yad Vashem scholar Nathan Eck's *Wandering on the Roads of Death: Life and Thoughts in the Days of Destruction* (in Hebrew) (Jerusalem: Yad Vashem, 1960), 37–38. But Eck rejected Steiner's interpretation in a *Ha'aretz* article of June 1966. Steiner's book never appeared in Hebrew.
66. Ibid., 277; this telling passage is, however, omitted from the English edition. For informed historical comment on this distinction during the Holocaust, see Yisrael Gutman, "The Sanctification of the Name and the Sanctification of Life" (in Hebrew), *Yalkut Moreshet* 24 (October 1977): 7–22.
67. Steiner, *Treblinka,* 284; not in the English edition.
68. Ibid., 136–37; English ed., 149.
69. Ibid., 313; English ed., 332.
70. Ibid., 309; English ed., 329.
71. Wiernik (1890–1972) authored one of the testimonies on which *Treblinka* depends: Jankiel Wiernik, *Rok w Treblince* (Warsaw: Nakł. Komisji Koordynacynej, 1944), an underground publication translated in the United States into Yiddish and English the same year: Wiernik, *A Yor in Treblinke* (New York: Unzer tsayt, 1944); *A Year in Treblinka: An Inmate Who Escaped Tells the Day-to-Day Facts of One Year of His Torturous Experience* (New York: American Representation of the General Jewish Workers' Union of Poland, [1944]).
72. Steiner's explanation for this is psychological: "The work had become his life. He was attached to it, like a captain to his ship, like a baron of industry to the empire created by his hands. So it is sometimes that our works bind us to them to the point where we become their slaves. . . . He knew, of course, that someday he would have to destroy it with his own hands, without leaving a single trace, but that day was still distant. In the meantime, its inevitable disappearance only increased his love for it." Steiner, *Treblinka,* 266–67; English ed., 286. In the book, Steiner chose to focus on Kurt Franz and marginalized Franz Stangl, the actual

commandant of Treblinka whom Gitta Sereny would a few years later make the subject of a well-known portrait after Stangl's extradition from Brazil in 1968 and Düsseldorf conviction in 1970. Steiner's justification for this approach is that Stangl "does not seem to have made much of an impression on the internees, except for a few instances of sadism which were not beyond the everyday norm of sadism in the camp." See Sereny, *Into That Darkness: From Mercy Killing to Mass Murder* (New York: McGraw Hill, 1974), and letter to Deborah Harkins of 28 March 1967 in Jean-François Steiner personal archives, Le Vésinet, France.

73. Steiner, *Treblinka,* 373–74; English ed., 395–96.

74. Wiernik, *A Year in Treblinka,* 42–44; Steiner, *Treblinka,* 373; English ed., 395. This discrepancy is noted in Miriam Novitch, *La Vérité sur Treblinka* (Paris: Presses du temps présent, 1967), 20–21, as well as in Morris Schappes's letter to the editor of the *New York Times,* 18 June 1967.

75. Steiner, *Treblinka,* 384; English ed., 406.

76. Among the arriving Soviet soldiers was Vassily Grossman, who immediately penned a propagandistic report on Treblinka and his experiences on the scene. Steiner acknowledged Grossman's book in the postscript to his own (referring to him only as "a war correspondent in the Soviet army who interviewed the first witnesses"). A French translation appeared in 1945 and was reprinted the same year (1966) that Steiner's own book was published. See Grossman, *Treblinkskii ad* (Moscow: Voennoe izd-vo Narodogo Komissariata Oborony, 1945); *L'Enfer de Treblinka,* tr. anon. (Paris: B. Artaud, 1945, 1966).

3. Nazi Criminality between Concentration and Extermination

1. Françoise Giroud, "Treblinka," *L'Express,* 11–17 April 1966; Pierre Joffroy, "Treblinka, une si petite jolie gare," *Paris-Match,* 9 April 1966; Jean-Laurent Bost, *Le Nouvel Observateur,* 16 March 1966; Philippe Labro, *Le Journal du Dimanche,* 20 March 1966; "*Treblinka,* par J.-Fr. Steiner," *Nouvelles littéraires,* 7 April 1966; René Chauvin, "Treblinka," *La Quinzaine littéraire,* 15 April 1966; Yves Durand, "Treblinka: la révolte d'un camp d'extermination," *L'Humanité,* 4 April 1966; Yvan Audouard, "La condition inhumaine," *Le Canard enchaîné,* 23 March 1966; Joseph Rovan, "Treblinka," *Esprit* 34, 6 (June 1966): 1271. See also Yrène Jan, "Un bouleversant document de J.-F. Steiner," *L'Aurore,* 19 April 1966. There were also many glowing reviews in the regional French press.

2. Pierre Vidal-Naquet, *Les Juifs, la mémoire, et le présent,* vol. 3, *Réflexions sur le génocide* (Paris: La Découverte, 1995), 12.

3. See Pieter Lagrou, *The Legacy of Nazi Occupation: Patriotic Memory and National Recovery in Western Europe, 1945–1965* (Cambridge: Cambridge Uni-

versity Press, 2000), esp. chaps. 2, 6, and 13, and Annette Wieviorka, *Déportation et génocide: Entre la mémoire et l'oubli* (Paris: Plon, 1992).

4. The camps purely for extermination were razed by the Nazis upon their departure in order to avoid discovery of what had transpired there. The Soviets liberated Majdanek (Lublin), which like Auschwitz had a labor component, before the Nazis were able to destroy it. On the Western liberations, see Robert Abzug, *Inside the Vicious Heart: Americans and the Liberation of the Nazi Concentration Camps* (New York: Oxford University Press, 1985). On photographs, but without the necessary distinction between concentration and extermination camps, see Barbie Zelizer, *Remembering to Forget: Holocaust Memory through the Camera's Eye* (Chicago: University of Chicago Press, 1998).

5. See Maud Mandel, *In the Aftermath of Genocide: Armenians and Jews in Twentieth-Century France* (Raleigh, N.C.: Duke University Press, 2003), chap. 2; and Donald Bloxham, *Genocide on Trial: War Crimes Trials and the Formulation of Holocaust History and Memory* (New York: Oxford University Press, 2001).

6. See Jean-Paul Sartre, *Critique de la raison dialectique,* vol. 1, *Théorie des ensembles pratiques* (Paris: Gallimard, 1960), in English as *Critique of Dialectical Reason,* vol. 1, *Theory of Practical Ensembles,* new ed., tr. Alan Sheridan-Smith (New York: Verso, 2002).

7. Simone de Beauvoir, "Préface," in Jean-François Steiner, *Treblinka: La révolte d'un camp d'extermination* (Paris: Fayard, 1966), 6; Steiner, *Treblinka: The Revolt of an Extermination Camp,* tr. Helen Weaver (New York: Simon and Schuster, 1967), xx.

8. Ibid.; English ed., xxi.

9. Simone de Beauvoir, *Tout compte fait* (Paris: Gallimard, 1972), 146, in English as *All Said and Done,* tr. Patrick O'Brian (New York: Putnam, 1974), 129.

10. Étienne Lardenoy, "Se faire complices pour être 'témoins'," *Rivarol,* 24 March 1966.

11. An associate wrote his biography: Émile Copfermann, *David Rousset, une vie dans le siècle* (Paris: Plon, 1991).

12. See David Rousset, "Les Jours de notre mort (premier fragment)," *Les Temps modernes* 1, 6 (March 1946): 1015–44, and "Les Jours de notre mort (deuxième fragment)," *Les Temps modernes* 1, 7 (April 1946): 1231–61. Rousset, *L'univers concentrationnaire* (Paris: Éditions du Pavois, 1946), and Rousset, *Les Jours de notre mort* (Paris: Éditions du Pavois, 1947). For the translations of the former, see *The Other Kingdom,* tr. Ramon Guthrie (New York: Reynal and Hitchcock, 1947), and *A World Apart,* tr. Yvonne Moyse and Roger Senhouse (London: Secker and Warburg, 1951). On the Rassemblement Démocratique Révolutionnaire, see Michel-Antoine Burnier, *Choice of Action: The French Existentialists on the Political Front Line,* tr. Bernard Murchland (New York: Random House, 1968), chap. 4.

13. Rousset, *Le Pître ne rit pas* (Paris: Éditions du Pavois, 1948). On Poliakov, see the next chapter.

14. The term "concentration camp" appears to date from 1901, and the consensus is that the institution itself dates from 1896. See Andzrej Kaminski, *Konzentrationslager 1896 bis heute: Gechichte, Funktion, Typologie* (Munich: Piper, 1990), and Joël Kotek and Pierre Rigoulot, *Le siècle des camps: détention, concentration, extermination: cent ans de mal radical* (Paris: Lattès, 2000). On the inception of the Nazi camps, see, in a large literature, Wolfgang Benz and Barbara Distel, eds., *Terror ohne System: die ersten Konzentrationslager im Nationalsozialismus 1933–1935* (Berlin: Metropol, 2001). Cf. Anne Applebaum, "A History of Horror," *New York Review of Books*, 18 October 2001, and Applebaum, *Gulag: A History* (New York: Doubleday, 2003), xxxiii–xl.

15. Eugen Kogon, *Der SS-Staat: das System der deutschen Konzentrationslager* (Berlin: Tempelhof, 1947). On Kogon's importance, see, for example, Jürgen Habermas, "On How Germany Has Come to Terms with Its Past," *Common Knowledge* 5, 2 (Fall 1996): 4–5. Cf. Naomi Diamant, "The Boundaries of Holocaust Literature: The Construction of a Canon" (Ph.D. diss., Columbia University, 1992), which studies Wiesel in comparison with Rousset to understand why the former became central to a Holocaust canon while the latter did not.

16. Wieviorka, "L'Expression 'camp de concentration' au 20e siècle," *Vingtième siècle* 54 (April–June 1997): 4–12 at 10, an article in which she contends that the lability of the term "concentration camp" makes it overly dangerous for historical use.

17. Rousset, *L'univers concentrationnaire*, 185; *The Other Kingdom*, 172; *A World Apart*, 111.

18. Ibid., 48–51; *The Other Kingdom*, 58–61; *A World Apart*, 25–27.

19. Ibid., 102; *The Other Kingdom*, 104; *A World Apart*, 61.

20. Rousset, *Les Jours de notre mort*, 587–88, cited in Georges Bataille, "Réflexions sur le bourreau et le victime: S.S. et déportés," *Critique* 17 (October 1947): 337–42 at 338, and Giorgio Agamben, *Remnants of Auschwitz: The Witness and the Archive*, tr. Daniel Heller-Roazen (New York: Zone Books, 2001), 27.

21. Rousset, *L'univers concentrationnaire*, 13, 184; *The Other Kingdom*, 29, 171; *A World Apart*, 2, 111.

22. Ibid., 186–87; *The Other Kingdom*, 172–73; *A World Apart*, 112.

23. In the United States, for example, aside from *L'univers concentrationnaire*, a portion of Rousset's next study appeared in a radical journal, and the young Irving Kristol discussed his work. See Rousset, "The Days of Our Death," *Politics* 4 (July–August 1947): 151–58, and Kristol, "Nightmare Come True," *Commentary* (October 1947): 390–93. Students of the Frankfurt School may be interested to learn that the University of California–Berkeley library's copy of *L'univers concentrationnaire* has the following in pencil on the frontispiece: "Für Leo [Löwenthal] zum Besuch, März 1949, Pacific Palisades, von Max [Horkheimer]."

24. Hannah Arendt, "Remarks to European Jewry" (1946), as cited in Martine Leibovici, *Hannah Arendt, une Juive: Expérience, politique et histoire* (Paris: Désclée de Brouwer, 1998), 147, the most judicious treatment of this whole question. Cf. Jean-Michel Chaumont, "La singularité de l'univers concentrationnaire selon Hannah Arendt," in *Hannah Arendt et la modernité* (Paris: J. Vrin, 1997). It is also important to remark, in Arendt's case, that the continuity between concentration and extermination is balanced by a separate argument (absent in Rousset's work) about why Jews in particular ended up the victims of the latter rather than simply of the former. A revised version of her overall view has most recently been presented by Enzo Traverso, *The Origins of Nazi Violence*, tr. Janet Lloyd (New York: The New Press, 2003).

25. Arendt, "The History of the Great Crime," *Commentary* 13, 3 (March 1952): 304.

26. In her depiction, as well as in her critique of human rights, Arendt also followed Rousset's stress on human nudity in the camp, an emphasis more recently taken up by Giorgio Agamben; see chapter 6 below. Arendt originally presented her interpretation of Rousset in "The Concentration Camps," *Partisan Review* (1948), and reprinted it in *The Origins of Totalitarianism*, 2nd ed. (New York: Meridian, 1958), chap. 12, esp. 436–37 and 441 n. 125; see also Arendt, "Social Science Techniques and the Study of the Camps," *Jewish Social Studies* 12 (1950), reprinted in Arendt, *Essays in Understanding*, ed. Jerome Kohn (New York: Harcourt, Brace, 1994). She also sent Rousset's book to her friends Karl Jaspers and Hermann Broch.

27. Lagrou, *The Legacy of Nazi Occupation*, and Wieviorka, *Déportation et génocide*. For generally negative readings of antifascist memory elsewhere, see, for example, Antonia Grunenberg, *Antifascismus: ein deutscher Mythos* (Reinbek: Rowohlt, 1993), and Jeffrey Herf, *Divided Memory: The Nazi Past in the Two Germanies* (Cambridge, Mass.: Harvard University Press, 1997).

28. Rousset, "Les menaces ne sont pas mortes," *Évidences* 1 (March 1949): 17–19.

29. Rousset, "Au secours des déportés dans les camps soviétiques: Un appel aux anciens déportés des camps nazis," *Le Figaro littéraire*, 12 November 1949.

30. Cf. François Furet, *The Passing of an Illusion: The Idea of Communism in the Twentieth Century*, tr. Deborah Furet (Chicago: University of Chicago Press, 1999), which sees antifascism as entirely the servant of communism, ignoring the role of antifascists in the critique of communism (including in the denunciation of the gulag).

31. See, conveniently, Rousset et al., *Le procès concentrationnaire pour la vérité des camps: extraits des débats* (Paris: Éditions du Pavois, 1951). During the Treblinka affair, Daix wrote a relatively positive review of Steiner's book. See Daix, "La vérité de Treblinka," *Les Lettres françaises*, 7 April 1966; on Daix, see the next chapter. Rousset's lawyer in the trial, Gérard Rosenthal, who had together with Rousset and Sartre cofounded the Rassemblement démocratique révolution-

naire, also wrote a critical article. Rosenthal, "La gloire et la honte des Juifs selon Jean-François Steiner," *Le Droit de vivre* (Bulletin de la Ligue internationale contre le racisme et l'antisémitisme), May 1966.

32. Sartre and Maurice Merleau-Ponty, "Les Jours de notre vie," *Les Temps modernes* 51 (January 1950): 1153–68. The title is a play on the title of Rousset's famous postwar novel based on his concentration camp experience.

33. See, for example, Rousset et al., *Les conditions de la liberté en U.R.S.S.* (Paris: Éditions du Pavois, 1951), in English as *Police-State Methods in the Soviet Union,* tr. Charles Joy (Boston: Beacon Press, 1953); cf. later Rousset, "Le sens de notre combat," in Paul Barton, *L'institution concentrationnaire en Russie (1930–1957)* (Paris: Plon, 1959).

34. Rousset, "L'affaire Tréblinka: les Juifs accusent," *Le Nouveau Candide,* 18 April 1966, and Rousset, "L'affaire Tréblinka: 'Nous ne sommes pas morts comme des moutons,'" *Le Nouveau Candide,* 29 April 1966.

35. Steiner, *Treblinka,* 277; English ed., 296. In one of the more important foreign reviews, Jean Améry wrote, citing this passage: "Das Alleinsein der Juden in diesem Krieg, ihre absolute Einsamkeit, ist . . . die große Wahrheit die Steiner meines Wissens als erster in voller Deutlichkeit ausgesprochen hat." (The solitude of the Jews in this war, their absolute segregation, is . . . the great truth that Steiner to my knowledge has expressed for the first time in total clarity.) Améry, "Erlösung in der Revolte," *Der Spiegel,* 7 November 1966. Lucy Dawidowicz later titled her significant history of the genocide *The War against the Jews, 1933–1945* (New York: Holt, Rinehart and Winston, 1975).

36. Billig's manuscript, titled *"Treblinka: le récit et la préface,"* is in the Jean-François Steiner personal archives, Le Vésinet, France, hereinafter Steiner files. The next year, he would publish his *L'Hitlérisme et le système concentrationnaire* (Paris: Presses universitaires, 1967); cf. the symposium on the book, with Rousset's contribution, in *Le Monde juif* 23, 13 (July–September 1967): 51–58.

37. On Rassinier's interwar and immediate postwar trajectory, see the meticulous biographical reconstruction by Nadine Fresco, *Fabrication d'un antisémite* (Paris: Seuil, 1999); for some comments on this book, see my H-Net review, online at http://www.hnet.msu.edu/reviews/showrev.cgi?path=3012924727570. In the postwar years, Rassinier usually presented himself as an anarchist, but he maintained close connections with the extreme right, which published his works.

38. See Rassinier, *Le Passage de la ligne: Du vrai à l'humain* (Bourg-en-Bresse: Éditions bressanes, 1949), and *Le mensonge d'Ulysse: Regard sur la littérature concentrationnaire* (Bourg-en-Bresse: Éditions bressanes, 1950). On Rassinier's postwar evolution, see Florent Brayard, *Comment l'idée vint à M. Rassinier: naissance du révisionnisme,* pref. Pierre Vidal-Naquet (Paris: Fayard, 1996).

39. Rassinier, "Les Juifs et les camps de concentration: Paul Rassinier répond à Jean-François Steiner," *Le Charivari* (June 1966): 5–6.

40. Brayard, *Comment l'idée vint à M. Rassinier,* esp. chap. 2, for his early expressions of this view of camp life in which the so-called *Häftlingsführung* takes center stage.

41. He elaborated that Léon Blum too, though "one of his preferred maxims" in the interwar years had been "better to die standing than live on one's knees," accepted his own wartime internment with passivity. "On a vu par la suite qu'il ne s'agissait que d'une clause de style," Rassinier venomously remarks.

42. Letter of 1 April 1966, cited in Valérie Igounet, *Histoire du négationnisme en France* (Paris: Seuil, 2000), 115. Neither Brayard nor Igounet mentions Rassinier's piece on *Treblinka,* hence the use of introducing it here.

43. Simone de Beauvoir, Claude Lanzmann, and Richard Marienstras, "Entretien avec Simone de Beauvoir: 'Ils n'étaient pas des lâches,'" *Le Nouvel Observateur,* 27 April 1966. On Marienstras, see also the next chapter. The editor's note of *Le Nouvel Observateur* made clear that Marienstras "has studied deeply the problems raised by the concentration camps."

44. "Pas fier," *Le Canard enchaîné,* 20 April 1966, and Steiner's angry letter to the editor in response, 27 April 1966.

45. Rousset, "Steiner est un raciste juif," and Beauvoir, "Rousset fait preuve d'une considérable arrogance," *Le Nouvel Observateur,* 10 May 1966. Rousset also repeated as evidence for his position that—contrary to Lanzmann's objection—Jews at Treblinka, like those in other camps, had tried to make themselves aware of the progress of the larger war, suggesting that they did indeed consider themselves part of a single conflict between fascist and antifascist forces. The communist reviewer Pierre Durand, while calling Beauvoir's preface "very beautiful," nonetheless deemed Steiner's theories "limited." Durand, "Treblinka," *L'Humanité,* 4 April 1966. Also critical of Lanzmann was Martine Monod, a communist writing in *L'Humanité Dimanche* later in the controversy, once the stakes were clearer: "It is as if these Jews," as Steiner and Lanzmann presented them, "came from nowhere, suddenly parachuting into Treblinka, springing from a mystical universe where there was no fascism, no world war, no Red Army, no Resistance, no occupied Europe, no nothing. . . . [Steiner] has developed the kinds of arguments most dangerous to the incessant combat that people must fight for their liberation, today as yesterday." Martine Monod, "À propos d'un livre dont on parle: *Treblinka,*" *L'Humanité Dimanche,* 12 June 1966, and the letters in response a few days later.

46. Louis Martin-Chauffier, "À propos de Treblinka," *Le Figaro littéraire,* 31 March 1966. Martin-Chauffier's testimony is *L'homme et la bête* (Paris: Gallimard, 1947).

47. Letter of Edmond Michelet to Constantin Melnik, 15 March 1966, in the Steiner files.

48. Michelet, "Treblinka," *Le Monde,* 2 April 1966.

49. Jacques Maritain, *Le Mystère d'Israël et autres essais* (Paris: Désclée de Brouwer, 1965), 224; for the origins of his interpretation in the interwar years, beginning with his flirtation with the right and proceeding through his attack on antisemitism, see Maritain, *L'impossible antisémitisme* (Paris: Désclée de Brouwer, 1994). In his preface to this book, Vidal-Naquet writes: "During and after the war, during what we call the Shoah, an event that, for many years after the victory, did not yet occupy a central place in our representation of the history of World War II, Maritain never stopped meditating on its immensity." Vidal-Naquet, "Jacques Maritain et les juifs: Réflexions sur un parcours," in ibid., 53. Maritain's key essays of 1937–38 on the Jews are available in English in Maritain, "The Mystery of Israel," in *Ransoming the Time,* tr. Harry Lorin Binsse (New York: Charles Scribner's, 1941), and *A Christian Looks at the Jewish Question* (New York: Longman's, 1939). For Michelet's own camp testimony, see Michelet, *Rue de la Liberté: Dachau, 1943–1945* (Paris: Seuil, 1955), esp. 106–8 for his reflections on Jews in the camps, already inspired by Maritain's Christian views.

50. See Steiner, *Treblinka,* 136–37; English ed., 149.

51. Here, it is worth noting that de Gaulle himself wrote a complimentary, if general, letter to Steiner thanking him for the book. Letter of de Gaulle to Steiner of 24 March 1966, in the Steiner files. Michel Debré also wrote him in a similar sense. Letter of Debré to Steiner of 7 April 1966, Steiner files.

52. These shifts were part of a more general reconciliation of Catholicism and modernity, on which see, for example, H. Stuart Hughes, *The Obstructed Path: French Social Thought in the Years of Desperation, 1930–1960* (New York: Harper and Row, 1966), chap. 3. On the *Bloc-Notes,* see now Nathan Bracher, *Through a Glass Darkly: History and Memory in François Mauriac's Bloc-Notes* (Washington, D.C.: Catholic University of America Press, 2004).

53. Elie Wiesel, *La Nuit* (Paris: Éditions de Minuit, 1959). Cf. Naomi Seidman, "Elie Wiesel and the Scandal of Jewish Rage," *Jewish Social Studies,* n.s., 3, 1 (Fall 1996): 1–19. It is to be noted, however, that it was several years after 1959 before *La Nuit* became canonized or even popular, and its initial print run of a few thousand copies, according to Wiesel's publisher, Jérôme Lindon, did not sell out until well into the next decade (personal communication).

54. François Mauriac, "Bloc-Notes," in *Le Figaro littéraire,* 5 May 1966, reprinted in Mauriac, *Bloc-Notes,* 5 vols. (Paris: Seuil, 1993), 4:255–58.

55. Bruno Ribes, "Les témoins de Treblinka," *Études* (June 1966): 782, citing Steiner, *Treblinka,* 182; English ed., 197.

56. Pierre Nora, "Mémoire et identité juives dans la France contemporaine," *Le Débat* 131 (September-October 2004): 24.

57. See, most importantly, the endorsement of the left-wing Christian *Esprit* of Steiner's book, written by a converted Jew who was also a Dachau deportee: Joseph Rovan, "Treblinka," *Esprit* 34, 6 (June 1966): 1268–74. While admitting

that more died at Treblinka than at Dachau, by an order of magnitude and for different reasons, Rovan affirmed that they were both part of the same universe. "I recognized the desert of Treblinka because I remember, and will remember my entire life, the desert of Dachau." See also the highly laudatory letter of *Esprit*'s famous editor, Jean-Marie Domenach, to Steiner of 16 April 1966, in the Steiner files. There also appeared, in a different left-wing Christian publication, another positive review. René Wintzen, "Une leçon qu'il ne faut pas oublier," *Témoignage chrétien*, 21 April 1966.

58. See, for example, the coverage of *La Voix de la Résistance:* an anonymous review and then an interview in light of the controversy. "Un récit de Jean-François Steiner: Treblinka," *La Voix de la Résistance*, 3rd ser., 109 (March 1966): 11; "Jean-François Steiner, auteur de 'Treblinka': un jeune à la recherche de la vérité," *La Voix de la Résistance*, 3rd ser., 111 (April 1966): 12.

59. "Treblinka Revisited," *Time*, 29 April 1966.

60. Letter to the editor by Steiner, *Le Nouveau Candide*, 25 April 1966.

61. See the report on the prize competition, "Le 5e Prix littéraire de la Résistance décerné à l'auteur de *Treblinka:* Jean-François Steiner," *La Voix de la Résistance*, 3rd ser., 111 (May 1966): 3, 11. The prize also made the news in *Combat*, 26 May 1966, *Le Figaro*, 26 May 1966, *France-Soir*, 27 May 1966, *Le Monde*, 27 May 1966, *Parisien Libéré*, 27 May 1966, and *Paris Presse*, 27 May 1966. The nine-member committee had one Jewish member (not counting one Jewish member who had converted to Catholicism), and Steiner's book won out over Charlotte Delbo's now highly regarded *Aucun de nous ne reviendra* (Geneva: Gonthier, 1965), in English as *None of Us Shall Return*, tr. John Githens (New York: Grove Press, 1968), and as part of *Auschwitz and After*, tr. Rosette Lamont (New Haven, Conn.: Yale University Press, 1995).

62. See M. Ackermann, "'Treblinka' divise la Résistance," *La Presse Nouvelle*, 1 July 1966.

63. "Il n'est point possible de faire deux blocs des déportes," *La Presse Nouvelle*, 26 May 1966; see also Roger Berg, "Au centre des débats: Treblinka," *Bulletin de nos communautés*, 17 June 1966. Similar sentiments were voiced in the UJRE's newspaper by the FNDIRP's vice president; see Jean-Maurice Hermann, "Treblinka: Comment? Pourquoi?" *Droit et liberté*, 15 April–15 May 1966. Paul later contributed a preface to Miriam Novitch's documentary dossier on *Treblinka*, which appeared the next year. See Novitch, ed., *La Vérité sur Treblinka* (Paris: Presses du temps présent, 1967).

64. For his attack on "negationism," see Vidal-Naquet, *Les assassins de la mémoire: "Un Eichmann de papier" et autres essais sur le révisionnisme* (Paris: La Découverte, 1987), in English as *Assassins of Memory: Essays on the Denial of the Holocaust*, tr. Jeffrey Mehlman (New York: Columbia University Press, 1992); most of his other contributions—which often took the form of prefaces to the most im-

portant books on the subject of the genocide—are gathered in his *Les Juifs, la mémoire, et le présent* series, partly translated as *The Jews: History, Memory, and the Present*, tr. David Ames Curtis (New York: Columbia University Press, 1995). For more focused treatment, see Samuel Moyn, "From *l'Univers Concentrationnaire* to the Jewish Genocide: Pierre Vidal-Naquet and the Treblinka Controversy," in Julian Bourg, ed., *After the Deluge: New Perspectives on the Intellectual and Cultural History of Postwar France* (Lanham, Md.: Lexington Books, 2004).

65. Vidal-Naquet later published his father's diary from this period. See Lucien Vidal-Naquet, "Journal, 15 septembre 1942–29 février 1944," *Annales E.S.C.* 48, 3 (1993): 513–44, with Vidal-Naquet's "Préface," ibid., 501–12, in English as "Presentation of a Document: The Journal of Attorney Lucien Vidal-Naquet," in Vidal-Naquet, *The Jews*.

66. Vidal-Naquet, *Mémoires*, vol. 1, *La brisure et l'attente, 1930–1955* (Paris: Seuil, 1995), 41–46 at 43, 113.

67. Vidal-Naquet, *Mémoires*, vol. 2, *Le trouble et la lumière* (Paris: Seuil, 1998), 33, and recently *Le choix de l'histoire: Comment et pourquoi je suis devenu historien* (Paris: Arléa, 2004), 58–59. For his contemporary books on the subject, see *Torture: Cancer of Democracy, France and Algeria, 1954–62*, tr. Barry Richard (Baltimore: Penguin Books, 1963), later published in French in 1972. See Vidal-Naquet's collection, *Face à la raison d'État: Un historien dans la guerre d'Algérie* (Paris: La Découverte, 1989), for his influential typology of intellectual response, including his own *dreyfusard* category. Vidal-Naquet's interventions are covered in the many works on French intellectuals and the Algerian war, such as Hervé Hamon and Patrick Rotman, *Les porteurs de valises: la résistance française à la guerre d'Algérie*, 2nd ed. (Paris: Albin Michel, 1982), or Jean-Pierre Rioux and Jean-François Sirinelli, eds., *La guerre d'Algérie et les intellectuels français* (Brussels: Éditions Complexe, 1991).

68. Vidal-Naquet, *Mémoires*, 1:167; Sartre, *Anti-Semite and Jew*, tr. George J. Becker (New York: Schocken, 1948), 93; cf. Vidal-Naquet, "Remembrances of a 1946 Reader," *October* 87 (Winter 1999): 7–23.

69. Letter of Vidal-Naquet to Steiner of 4 April 1966, in the Steiner files.

70. Vidal-Naquet, "Treblinka et l'honneur des juifs," *Le Monde*, 2 May 1966. Steiner allowed Vidal-Naquet to pore over the transcriptions of the testimony he had gathered in the course of researching the book.

71. Kerbourc'h et al., "*Treblinka*, de Jean-François Steiner," *Combat*, 10 June 1966. As for the appropriability of Steiner's book by antisemites, Vidal-Naquet clarified in this debate that "what antisemites say does not interest me."

72. He told me this in an interview.

73. Vidal-Naquet, *Assassins of Memory*, 14.

74. Ibid., 149–50 n. 24. Three years after the Treblinka affair, in 1969, Vidal-Naquet

documented the plagiarism of an earlier testimony involving another sensation-alistic book, Sylvain Reiner's *Et la terre sera pure* (Paris: Fayard, 1969), and suc-ceeded in having the publisher pull it from the market.

75. Vidal-Naquet, *Mémoires*, 2:246, cf. 242–43.

76. Vidal-Naquet, "Qui sont les assassins de la mémoire?" in *Les Juifs, la mémoire, et le présent*, 3:284; in this text, Vidal-Naquet repeated once again that it was "nonetheless the execrable book of Jean-François Steiner" that "led me to under-stand what a camp for pure extermination was." Cf. Wieviorka, "Pierre Vidal-Naquet face aux 'assassins de la mémoire,'" in François Hartog, Pauline Schmitt, and Alain Schnapp, eds., *Pierre Vidal-Naquet: Un Historien dans la cité* (Paris: La Découverte, 1998).

4. Jewish Identity in Question

1. Good, brief overviews in English are to be found in Esther Benbassa, *The Jews of France: A History from Antiquity to the Present*, tr. M. B. DeBevoise (Prince-ton, N.J.: Princeton University Press, 2001), chap. 13; Paula E. Hyman, *The Jews of Modern France* (Berkeley: University of California Press, 1998), chap. 10; and Bernard Wasserstein, *Vanishing Diaspora: The Jews in Europe since 1945* (Cam-bridge, Mass.: Harvard University Press, 1996), 61–70. For a popular account, see the relevant sections of Mark Kurlansky, *A Chosen Few: The Resurrection of European Jewry* (New York: Addison-Wesley, 1995).

2. Illustrative of this fact is Annette Wieviorka's recent reflection that the usual path, followed throughout modern French history, from the *Juif* to the *isra-élite*—including by her own group, children and grandchildren of East European immigrants—is only today, for the first time, by Sephardic North Africans, avoided. "Les Juifs ashkenazes ont adopté, en une seule génération, la voie de l'intégration républicaine." Wieviorka, "'Le judaïsme laïc n'a pas d'avenir,'" in Olivier Guland and Michel Zebib, eds., *Nous, Juifs de France* (Paris: Bayard, 2000), 27.

3. See Doris Bensimon and Sergio Della Pergola, *La Population juive de France: Socio-démographie et identité* (Jerusalem: Institute of Contemporary Jewry, 1984), 141 and chap. 6 in general.

4. Arnold Mandel and Jean-François Steiner, "Mourir à Treblinka," *L'Arche* 110 (April 1966): 28–31 at 28. On Dvorjetski, see the next chapter.

5. Steiner, "La jeunesse juive en quête d'elle-même," *L'Arche* 112 (June 1966): 18–19, 59, at 18.

6. Ibid., 19.

7. Steiner, "Notre destin collectif," *Les Nouveaux cahiers* 2, 6 (June–August 1966): 4.

8. Ibid.

9. Mandel and Steiner, "Mourir à Treblinka," 31.

10. Steiner, "La jeunesse juive en quête d'elle-même," 59.

11. Mandel and Steiner, "Mourir à Treblinka," 31.

12. Ibid.

13. Steiner, "Notre destin collectif," 6.

14. Ibid.

15. Steiner, "La jeunesse juive en quête d'elle-même," 59.

16. Jean Liberman and Steiner, "Renversement de valeurs à 'Treblinka,'" *La Presse Nouvelle*, 8 April 1966.

17. Mandel and Steiner, "Mourir à Treblinka," 30.

18. Edouard Roditi, "Voices from the Sephardic Diaspora," *Judaism* 16, 2 (Spring 1967): 220.

19. Steiner, "Notre destin collectif," 4.

20. Parisian Yiddishist Yitskhok Niborski, in a personal communication, speculates that their combined circulation in the mid-1960s may have been approximately fifteen thousand; all three, having lost subscribers and long since stopped daily circulation, discontinued publication within a few years of one another in the mid-1990s.

21. Borvine Frenkel, "A yidisher frantzoyzisher shrayber velkhn m'darf shteln tzum shand-slup," *Unzer shtime*, 18 March 1966.

22. On the Bund, see, for example, Henri Minczeles, *Histoire générale du Bund: un mouvement révolutionnaire juif* (Paris: Austral, 1995), which, however, contains little information on its spread westward with immigration.

23. Irène Kanfer, "A briv vegn Shtayners intervyu," *Unzer shtime*, 9–11 April 1966.

24. Ibid., citing Betti Ajzensztajn, *Ruch podziemny w ghettach i obozach: Materiały i dokumenty*, pref. Michał Borwicz (Warsaw: [Centralna Żydowska Komisja Historyczna w Polsce], 1946). For the anthology, see Kanfer, ed., *Le Luth brisé: Première anthologie en français de poèmes du ghetto et des camps* (Paris: Presses du temps présent, 1964). Kanfer, a poet in her own right, later published several volumes of verse. Kanfer added that she planned to translate Ajzensztajn's work into French, because the "shock" would be "useful," but this never occurred.

25. Frenkel, *"Treblinke, fun Zhan-Fransua Shtayner," Unzer shtime*, 30 April–2 May 1966. Actually, an Italian film director did buy the film rights to the book, but nothing came of it.

26. On the postwar Jewish communists, see Jonathan Boyarin, *Polish Jews in Paris: The Ethnography of Memory* (Bloomington: Indiana University Press, 1991), esp. chap. 5; the major study by Jacques Frémontier, *L'étoile rouge de David: les juifs communistes en France* (Paris: Fayard, 2002); as well as Annette Aronowicz's series of essays on Chaim Sloves, such as Aronowicz, *Haim Sloves: Jüdischer Kommunismus in Paris* (Berlin: Philo Verlag, 2002), and "Haim Sloves and the Soviet Union: An Essay on the Jewish People in One of Its Peregrinations," in

Gennady Estraikh and Mikhail Krutikov, eds., *Yiddish and the Left* (Oxford: Legenda, 2001), reprinted as "Haim Sloves, the Jewish People, and a Jewish Communist's Allegiances," *Jewish Social Studies,* n.s., 9, 1 (Fall 2002): 95–142. Also of much interest is Adam Rayski's autobiography, *Nos illusions perdues* (Paris: Balland, 1985).

27. G. Kenig, "Der oyter fun *Treblinke* hot alts farloyrn," *Di naye prese,* 21 April 1966. Kenig had himself authored several Holocaust-related books, most importantly *Unzere bafrayer: Fartseykhenungen fun a gevezenem krigs-gefangenem* (Paris: Oyfsney, 1952).

28. Boyarin, *Polish Jews in Paris,* 166.

29. Ibid., 41.

30. Cf. David Shneer's outstanding work, *Yiddish and the Creation of Soviet Jewish Culture, 1918–1930* (Cambridge: Cambridge University Press, 2004).

31. This information is from the biographical note in Charles Dobzynski, ed., *Anthologie de la poésie yiddish: Le miroir d'un peuple* (Paris: Gallimard, 2000), and the earlier, but longer, entry in Shmuel Niger and Yankev Shatsky, eds., *Leksikon fun der nayer yidisher literatur,* 8 vols. (New York: Alveltlekhn Yidishn Kultur-Kongres, 1956–81), s.v. "Szulsztein, Moshe," which includes references to criticism of Szulsztein's poetry by Jacob Glatstein, Nachman Mayzel, and others. See also Dobzynski's preface to Moshé Szulsztein, *L'or et le feu,* tr. Dobzynski (Paris: Cercle Bernard Lazare, 2001), a French translation of a selection of his poetry.

32. Moshe Szulsztein, "Der Kolumbus fun Treblinke (1–7)," *Unzer vort,* 14, 16, 17, 18, 19, 20, and 21 May 1966, cited below by part number.

33. On this shift, in addition to Frémontier's recent book, see Mojshe Salzman, *Di groyse enderung in yidishn lebn in Frankraykh: fun der zeks-togiker milkhomeh biz 1980* (Tel Aviv: Yisroel-bukh, 1980).

34. Szulsztein, "Der skhakl fun a polemik," *Arbeter vort,* 10 June 1966.

35. Szulsztein, "Der Kolumbus fun Treblinke," part 1.

36. Ibid., part 3.

37. On this, see the excellent study by Sarah Farmer, *Oradour, arrêt sur mémoire* (Paris: Stock, 1994, 2004), or the (subsequently published) English original, *Martyred Village: Commemorating the 1944 Massacre at Oradour-sur-Glane* (Berkeley: University of California Press, 1999).

38. Szulsztein, "Der Kolumbus fun Treblinke," part 4.

39. Ibid., part 6.

40. Ibid., part 1.

41. Ibid.

42. Ibid., part 3.

43. Ibid., part 4. Szulsztein either did not read, or did not deign to reply to, Steiner's discussion of the sanctification of the name in the text of *Treblinka* itself.

44. Ibid., part 3.

45. Ibid., part 7: "It is not right to say . . . that all Jewish youth have such a relationship to the tragedy of the destruction of the six million."

46. See the letter of Louise Alcan, secretary general of the Amicale des déportés d'Auschwitz et des camps de Haute-Silésie, to Steiner of 8 April 1966 and the circular letter of the Comité de vigilance pour le respect de la déportation et de la résistance of 22 July 1966, both in Jean-François Steiner personal archives, Le Vésinet, France, hereinafter Steiner files.

47. Henri Bulawko, letter to the editor of *Le Nouveau Candide,* 21 March 1966; Bulawko, "Un rescapé d'Auschwitz répond à Jean-François Steiner," *Amitiés France-Israël,* April 1966, summarized and reprinted under the same title in *La Presse Nouvelle,* 8 April 1966; as well as Bulawko's contribution to a collective article, Pierre Paraf et al., "Treblinka," *Notre Volonté* (Bulletin de l'Union des Engagés volontaires anciens combattants juifs 1939–1945), June 1966.

48. See Ralph Feigelson, "Treblinka: Un livre sujet à controverse," *France Nouvelle,* 11 May 1966, and "Le combat des cadavres," *Le Patriote Résistant* (Bulletin intérieur de la Fédération nationale des déportés et internés patriotes), May 1966. Feigelson also participated in the Salle Lancry debate.

49. Fourcade was a frequent addressee of these complaints. She received one from Novitch, undated, as well as a moving letter and lengthy point-by-point commentary on *Treblinka* from Henri Rudnicki, a Warsaw ghetto survivor, transplanted to France, who described himself as a "Polish resister." See Henryk Rudnicki, *Martyrologia i zagłada żydów warszawskich* (Łódź: Łódźki instytut wydawniczy, 1946); his letters, and the commentary, dated 1 July 1966, are in the Steiner files.

50. Novitch had herself written on the Treblinka uprising in 1966, in a piece in the house journal of the Centre de Documentation Juive Contemporaine. See Miriam Novitch, "Treblinka: le soulèvement," *Le Monde juif* 21, 7 (January–March 1966): 4–6. See later Novitch, *La Vérité sur Treblinka* (Paris: Presses du temps présent, 1967), the crucial source for considering the factual accuracy of Steiner's book.

51. Marceau Vilner, "L'opération *Les Juifs* numéro deux," *La Presse Nouvelle,* 25 March 1966. The title itself refers to Peyrefitte's book. Many other writers in Jewish publications condemned Steiner for either airing antisemitic sentiments or creating the circumstances for them to be aired. See, for example, the anonymous editorial in the Zionist newspaper *La Terre Retrouvée,* 1 April 1966.

52. Vilner, "Vivre à tout prix à Treblinka," *La Presse Nouvelle,* 8 April 1966; Vilner, "Le jeu de Machiavel," *La Presse Nouvelle,* 22 April 1966; and Vilner, "La marchandise et l'affaire," *La Presse Nouvelle,* 29 April 1966, referring to Steiner, *Treblinka: La révolte d'un camp d'extermination* (Paris: Fayard, 1966), 45, in English as Steiner, *Treblinka: The Revolt of an Extermination Camp,* tr. Helen

Weaver (New York: Simon and Schuster, 1967), 52. See also B. Ady-Brille, "Le roman de Treblinka," *La Presse Nouvelle*, 3 June 1966.

53. Vilner, "À l'intention de Mme Simone de Beauvoir," *La Presse Nouvelle*, 6 May 1966.

54. See Daix, "La vérité de Treblinka," *Les Lettres françaises*, 7 April 1966; the interview is in *La Presse Nouvelle*, 29 April 1966. Daix, a Mauthausen inmate during the war, published his novelized testimony years before: Daix, *La Dernière forteresse* (Paris: Éditeurs français réunis, 1950); later an ex-communist, he published his memoirs as *Tout mon temps: révisions de ma mémoire* (Paris: Fayard, 2001).

55. On Dvorjetski and Auerbach, see the next chapter.

56. Similarly, one might tentatively suggest that the shape of American post-Holocaust culture might look much different than it does in Peter Novick's well-known book *The Holocaust in American Life* (Boston: Houghton Mifflin, 1998) if Yiddish-speaking communities and newspapers were taken into account. For Novick's approach as applied to France, see Joan B. Wolf, *Harnessing the Holocaust: The Politics of Memory in France* (Stanford, Calif.: Stanford University Press, 2004).

57. Pieter Lagrou, *The Legacy of Nazi Occupation: Patriotic Memory and National Recovery in Western Europe, 1945–1965* (Cambridge: Cambridge University Press, 2000), 259–60.

58. In his ethnography, *Polish Jews in Paris*, Jonathan Boyarin recounts that Zionist immigrants sometimes asked him for news about their former compatriots who remained wedded to communism, to whom they had not spoken for years.

59. See Philip Friedman, "The Destruction of the Jews of Lwów, 1941–44," in *Roads to Extinction: Essays on the Holocaust*, pref. Salo Baron (Philadelphia: Jewish Publication Society, 1980), and Michael C. Steinlauf, *Bondage to the Dead: Poland and the Memory of the Holocaust* (Syracuse, N.Y.: Syracuse University Press, 1997), 55–56.

60. Aside from a number of works in Polish and Yiddish, including *Arishe papirn*, 3 vols. (Buenos Aires: Tsentral-farband fun Poylishe Yidn in Argentine, 1955), see his state thesis, Michel Borwicz, *Écrits des condamnés à mort sous l'occupation allemande (1939–1945): étude sociologique* (Paris: Presses universitaires, 1954). For his memories of internment, see Borwicz, "Ma pendaison," *L'Arche* (April–May 1963), reprinted in the 1996 Gallimard paperback edition of his thesis. For his collection, see Borwicz, ed., *L'insurrection du ghetto de Varsovie* (Paris: R. Julliard, 1966).

61. Jan-Claude Kerbourc'h et al., "'Treblinka,' de Jean-François Steiner," *Combat*, 10 June 1966.

62. Borwicz, ". . . Mais Michel Borwicz n'est pas d'accord," *L'Arche* 110 (April 1966): 30.

63. Simone de Beauvoir et al., "Entretien avec Simone de Beauvoir: 'Ils n'étaient pas des lâches,'" *Le Nouvel Observateur*, 27 April 1966.

64. See Wieviorka, *Déportation et génocide: Entre la mémoire et l'oubli* (Paris: Plon, 1992), 415–23, and Poliakov's memoir, *L'Auberge des musiciens* (Paris: Mazarine, 1981). Similarly, as noted, the slightly less prominent Jewish historians Joseph Billig and Georges Wellers circulated private manuscripts that went unpublished, except through David Rousset's citation of them in his pieces. Wellers also participated in the Salle Lancry debate and contributed to Paraf et al., "Treblinka," cited above (n. 47).

65. Poliakov, *Bréviaire de la haine (le IIIe Reich et les Juifs)* (Paris: Calmann-Lévy, 1951), in English as *The Harvest of Hate: The Nazi Program for the Destruction of the Jews of Europe* (Philadelphia: Jewish Publication Society, 1954). It is of interest, in light of the issue of the Christian contribution to the public emergence of the genocide discussed in the last chapter, that Reinhold Niebuhr wrote the preface to the American edition, and Jacques Maritain wrote a glowing review: Maritain, "Breviary of Hate," *Social Research* 20, 2 (Summer 1953): 219–29.

66. This six-page, page-by-page analysis is in the Steiner files.

67. Poliakov, "Treblinka: vérité et roman," *Preuves* (May 1966): 72–76 at 73. It is reprinted as "Les affabulations de M. Steiner," *La Presse Nouvelle*, 20 May 1966. This essay appeared in English in between the French controversy and the American translation and reception, but did not affect the latter. Poliakov, "The Murder Factory," *Atlas* 12, 2 (August 1966): 38–41. As noted in the prior chapter, Steiner had relied on testimony about this killing for the name of the weapon, and the expression "Sabbath knife," though hardly common, presumably refers to a challah knife. (Steiner recorded another of his witnesses calling it a "kiddush knife.") More than thirty years later, Vidal-Naquet could still recall that "one detail seriously outraged Léon Poliakov: an SS was killed by a Jew by means of a sacrificial knife. But there has been no sacrifice in the Jewish religion since the Temple's destruction." Vidal-Naquet, *Mémoires*, vol. 2, *La brisure et l'attente* (Paris: Seuil, 1998), 245. Of course, it was Poliakov who interpreted it as a sacrificial knife.

68. Poliakov, "Treblinka: vérité et roman."

69. Jean Liberman, "Léon Poliakov: 'Il n'y a pas de nature ni d'essence juives,'" *La Presse Nouvelle*, 27 May 1966. See also the critical note on *Treblinka* by another important historian, Olga Wormser, in *Éducation nationale*, 5 May 1966. Wormser, who participated in the Salle Lancry debate, had just published her *Quand les alliés ouvrirent les portes: le dernier acte de la tragédie de la déportation* (Paris: R. Laffont, 1965) and would soon publish own her thesis, *Le système concentrationnaire nazi 1933–1945* (Paris: Presses universitaires, 1968), most famous for distinguishing between concentration and extermination. See Wieviorka, *Déportation et génocide*, 201–4, and Donald Reid, "Germaine Tillion and the Resistance to the Vichy Syndrome," *History & Memory* 15, 2 (Fall/Winter 2003): 36–63. For her part, Tillion, the influential deportee and author of a well-known

memoir of Ravensbrück, and specially known for her analysis of women's experience in the camps (and for her engagement during the Algerian war), wrote in a respectful letter to Steiner that he had succeeded in "making vivid the most criminal period of this century," even as she doubted whether his thesis of Jewish specificity seemed "exact enough." Germaine Tillion to Steiner, 13 July 1966, in the Steiner files, along with his reply of 12 September. See Tillion et al., *Ravensbrück* (Neuchâtel: Éditions de la Baconnière, 1946), and later revisions of the same book; cf. Pierre Vidal-Naquet, "Réflexions sur trois *Ravensbrück*," in *Les Juifs, la mémoire, et le présent*, vol. 3, in English as "Reflections on Three *Ravensbrücks*," tr. David Ames Curtis, *South Atlantic Quarterly* 96, 4 (Fall 1997): 881–94.

70. Poliakov, "Treblinka: vérité et roman," 75.

71. "Jean-François Steiner, auteur de 'Treblinka': un jeune à la recherche de la vérité," *La Voix de la Résistance*, 3rd ser., 111 (April 1966): 12. See also, on this point, the interview with Steiner, "'Les cadavres de Treblinka un odieux marchandage,' dit Steiner," *Arts*, 4 May 1966.

72. Kerbourc'h et al., "'Treblinka,' de Jean-François Steiner."

73. Améry, ". . . wie eine Herde von Schafen? Kontroverse um ein französisches Buch über ein Vernichtungslager," *Die Weltwoche* (Zurich), 13 May 1966. He repeated these ideas, adding the analogy of black power in the United States, in the most prominent review of the German translation of Steiner's book. Améry, "Erlösung in der Revolte," *Der Spiegel*, 7 November 1966. Améry, who used a pseudonym for his real name, Hans Mayer, had just published his most important contribution to the Holocaust canon, but it would not become well known until somewhat later. See Améry, *Jenseits von Schuld und Sühne: Bewältingungsversuche eines Überwältigten* (Munich: Szszensy, 1966), in English as *At the Mind's Limits: Contemplations by a Survivor on Auschwitz and Its Realities*, tr. Sidney and Stella P. Rosenfeld (Bloomington: Indiana University Press, 1980).

74. Vidal-Naquet's affirmation, in the *Combat* debate, that Jewish singularity in revolt placed the Treblinka Jews in a religious history stretching back to the Jewish insurrection against the Romans strongly suggests that it is in the Treblinka affair that one might also seek the origins of perhaps his most famous study in classical Jewish history, his lengthy treatment of Josephus's *Jewish War*. See Flavius Josephus, *La guerre des Juifs, précedé par "Du bon usage de la trahison," de Pierre Vidal Naquet* (Paris: Éditions de Minuit, 1977). See also Vidal-Naquet's later essays on Josephus and Masada, in his *Les Juifs, la mémoire, et le présent* series. But cf. chapter 6 of this book, below, on Vidal-Naquet's evolution.

75. Letter of Wladimir Rabi to Mme Steiner, 8 March 1966, Steiner files, and Rabi, "Débat sur Treblinka," *L'Arche* 111 (May 1966): 46.

76. Nicolas Baudy, "La génération suivante," *Les Nouveaux cahiers* 2, 6 (July–August 1966): 8, 13. Baudy was the author, among other books, of *Les Grandes questions juives* (Paris: Editions planète 1965, 1968).

77. The latter fact is reported in a press release from the Comité de vigilance pour le respect de la déportation et de la résistance, undated, in the Rachel Auerbach file, Yad Vashem Archive, P.16/36.

78. David Lambert, "À propos de 'Treblinka,'" *L'Information juive,* May 1966.

79. He explains himself in a mimeographed "Note et réflexions suscités par le débat du 7 juin, aux Ambassadeurs, sur 'Treblinka,'" in the Steiner files.

80. Letter from Steiner to Michael Korda, 16 May 1966, Steiner files.

81. Letters of Reine Silbert and J.-P. Lévy to the editor, *Le Nouveau Candide,* 21 March 1966. Reine Silbert, however, was one of the friends whom Steiner acknowledged in his book for her help.

82. Letter from Hélène Roffé to Steiner of 21 June 1966, in the Steiner files. One can find similar sentiments, which Steiner's book provokes to this day, in the public reviews field at Amazon.com for the English translation of Steiner's book. "I couldn't put it down," one reader writes. "For two days I lived and breathed Treblinka, for two days I was beaten, starved, tortured, I saw my family gassed, I saw my fellow inmates hang themselves because death was better than this hell on earth. For two days I was an inmate of Treblinka because Jean-François Steiner put me there. *Treblinka* is quite possibly the most important piece of Holocaust literature ever written. It is non-fiction but it reads like a novel. It told me more about the death camps and Nazi regime than all of the books I have read combined. The most amazing thing about *Treblinka* though was the psychology behind it all. It gave answer to my question: Why did they not revolt before this? Why did they simply allow themselves to be led to death? On the third day I rose from the bottom of the abyss, I revolted, I left Treblinka along with 700 Jews, survivors of hell. I left but I didn't escape, no one escapes Treblinka."

83. Beauvoir et al., "Entretien avec Simone de Beauvoir," 16.

84. Editorial headnote to Steiner, "La jeunesse juive en quête d'elle-même," 18.

85. The Steiner files contain further information on these engagements.

86. "Il n'est point possible de faire deux blocs des déportés," *La Presse Nouvelle,* 27 May 1966.

87. Emmanuel Levinas, "Honneur sans drapeau," *Les Nouveaux cahiers* 2, 6 (July–August 1966): 1–3; reprinted as "Sans nom," in *Noms propres* (Montpellier: Fata Morgana, 1975), and in English as "Nameless," in *Proper Names,* tr. Michael B. Smith (Stanford, Calif.: Stanford University Press, 1996). All citations are from this source, with the translation often altered. Cf. the *Nouveaux cahiers* editorial correspondence of 26 May 1966 in the Steiner files. Later, see Levinas, "La mémoire d'un passé non révolu: Entretien avec Foulek Ringelheim," *Revue de l'Université de Bruxelles* 1–2 (1987): 13–14.

88. On this issue, see my "Emmanuel Levinas's Talmudic Readings: Between Tradition and Invention," *Prooftexts* 23, 2 (Fall 2003): 338–64.

89. It is to be noted, though, that Levinas, who for decades had worked in the field

of Jewish education, had often reflected on the problems of Jewish youth. See, for example, Levinas, "La crise de l'enseignement en France," *L'Arche* 1 (1957): 19–20; cf. later Levinas, "Le problème actuel de l'éducation juive en Occident," *Communauté* 12 (November 1960): 1–6. On the context for these writings, see my *Origins of the Other: Emmanuel Levinas between Revelation and Ethics* (Ithaca, N.Y.: Cornell University Press, 2005), chap. 6.

90. He also appears to be alluding here, as indeed he does directly at the end of the essay, to the Talmudic notion that after the destruction of the Temple the divine presence is confined to the "four cubits of the law," a metaphor in which spatial confinement has positive moral significance.

91. Emphasis added.

92. Beauvoir et al., "Entretien avec Simone de Beauvoir," 14–17. For Marienstras's most popular elaboration of diasporism, see his collection of articles, *Être un peuple en diaspora,* pref. Pierre Vidal-Naquet (Paris: François Maspéro, 1975); on his Cercle Gaston Crémieux, in English, see Hyman, *The Jews of Modern France,* 205–7.

93. Levinas explains: "[T]he fact that settled, established, humanity can at any moment be exposed to the dangerous situation of its morality residing entirely in its 'heart of hearts,' its dignity completely at the mercy of a subjective voice, no longer reflected or confirmed by any objective order—that is the risk upon which the honor of humankind depends. *But it may be this risk that is signified by the very fact the Jewish condition is constituted within humanity.* Judaism is humanity on the brink of morality without institutions."

94. Vidal-Naquet, "Treblinka et l'honneur des juifs," *Le Monde,* 2 May 1966.

5. The Revolt of the Witnesses

1. Jean-François Steiner, "J'ai retrouvé en Israël quatre rescapés; Ils m'ont raconté leur cauchemar," *Paris-Match,* 9 April 1966.

2. On this issue, see Sidra DeKoven Ezrahi, *By Words Alone: The Holocaust in Literature* (Chicago: University of Chicago Press, 1980), or David J. Bond, "Jean-François Steiner's *Treblinka:* Reading Fiction from Fact," *Papers on Language and Literature* 26 (Summer 1990): 370–78.

3. Daniel Jonah Goldhagen, "Motives, Causes and Alibis: A Reply to My Critics," *New Republic,* 23 December 1996. See also, for a sensitive recent consideration of the importance of victim testimony, its uses, and its limits, Mark Roseman, *A Past in Hiding: Memory and Survival in Nazi Germany* (New York: Metropolitan Books, 2001).

4. He added: "Kurt Franz is not the real Kurt Franz. I don't know who he really was, and this point didn't interest me. It would have been the subject of a different

book—*Treblinka* from the German point of view. Kurt Franz as I describe him . . . is the vision that the internees had of the real Kurt Franz." Letter of Steiner to Deborah Harkins of 28 March 1967, Jean-François Steiner personal archives, Le Vésinet, France, hereinafter Steiner files. Of course, if Steiner had always followed this principle, then he would not have narrated the interior monologue of Nazi contempt for Jews, passages that many took as straightforward evidence of an internalized antisemitism.

5. Annette Wieviorka, *L'ère du témoin* (Paris: Plon, 1998).

6. A third figure, Miriam Novitch, circulated at the time a manuscript titled "À propos du livre *Treblinka:* comment M. Steiner utilise les témoignages," in the Steiner files, and then set to work to prepare a "counterdossier" that, though it appeared a year after the controversy, remains the fullest and point-by-point attack on Steiner's work. See Miriam Novitch, *La Vérité sur Treblinka* (Paris: Presses du temps présent, 1967). She printed her circulated manuscript as the first dossier. On Novitch, see the previous chapter.

7. Steiner's source is Marc Dvorjetski, *Yerusholayim de-Lite in kamf un umkum: Zikhroynes fun Vilner geto (Lutte et chute de la Jérusalem de Lithuanie: Histoire du ghetto de Vilna)* (Paris: Yidisher natsyonaler arbeter-farband in Amerike un yidisher folks-farband in Frankraykh, 1948), in French as *Ghetto à l'est*, tr. Arnold Mandel (Paris: R. Marin, 1950), esp. 39–42, reprinted under a changed title and with a new preface recounting his service as a witness at the Eichmann trial as *La Victoire du Ghetto* (Paris: Editions France-Empire, 1962), esp. 41–44. I have used the French transliteration of his name (which he used in his French correspondence); it frequently appears as Mark (or, in Israel, Meir) Dworzecki in non-French sources.

8. Jean-François Steiner, *Treblinka: La révolte d'un camp d'extermination* (Paris: Fayard, 1966), 31; not in the English edition, for reasons described below.

9. Letter from Marc Dvorjetski to Steiner of 1 July 1966, Steiner files, as well as in the Meir Dworzecki file, Yad Vashem Archive, P.10/28.

10. In his diary, Ringelblum mentions Auerbach as "the director of the public kitchen at 40 Lezsno Street," but she also participated in the Oneg Shabbat underground archives group in the ghetto. See Emmanuel Ringelblum, *Notes from the Warsaw Ghetto*, ed. and tr. Jacob Sloan (New York: McGraw Hill, 1958), 201. Cf. Auerbach, *Varshever tsavoes: Bagegenish, aktivitetn . . . : 1933–1943* (Tel Aviv: Yisroel-Buch, 1974), and Samuel Kassow's entry in S. Lilian Kremer, ed., *Holocaust Literature: An Encyclopedia of Writers and Their Work*, 2 vols. (New York: Routledge, 2003), s.v. "Rachel Auerbach."

11. For her report, see Rachel Auerbach, *Oyf di felder fun Treblinke: Reportazsh* (Warsaw and Łódź: Centralna Żydowska Komisja Historyczna, 1947). On both the High Commission to Investigate Nazi Crimes in Poland and the related Central Jewish Historical Commission for which Auerbach worked before moving to

Israel, see Michael C. Steinlauf, *Bondage to the Dead: Poland and the Memory of the Holocaust* (Syracuse, N.Y.: Syracuse University Press, 1997), 47–48. When Steiner referred to Auerbach's book in his acknowledgments, he called it *The Camps of Treblinka*, evidently mistaking the French translation of the title word "champs" ("felder") for "camps."

12. On her decisive role in determining the character of the Eichmann prosecution, see Tom Segev, *The Seventh Million: The Israelis and the Holocaust*, tr. Haim Watzman (New York: Hill and Wang, 1993), 338–39.

13. Letter from Steiner to Rachel Auerbach, undated but apparently summer 1965, as well as a response from her to him, again undated but from the following fall, in Rachel Auerbach file, Yad Vashem Archive, P.16/36, hereinafter Auerbach materials.

14. Fifteen years later, when he interviewed some of the Treblinka survivors as part of his efforts in the Demjanjuk extradition, Allan Ryan of the U.S. Department of Justice's Office of Special Investigations notes, he learned that "a number of the Treblinka survivors . . . dispute vigorously the accuracy of Steiner's account," though he himself deemed it "accurate enough for the lay reader, and . . . certainly a gripping work." Allan A. Ryan, Jr., *Quiet Neighbors: Prosecuting Nazi War Criminals in America* (San Diego: Harcourt, Brace, Jovanovitch, 1984).

15. See esp. Steiner to Michael Korda, 16 May 1966, Steiner files.

16. Steiner, *Treblinka*, 395; Steiner, *Treblinka: The Revolt of an Extermination Camp*, tr. Helen Weaver (New York: Simon and Schuster, 1967), 414.

17. Steiner had been told of Rosenberg's continuing support by Félix Allouche of *L'Information d'Israël*, in a letter of 4 April 1966, Steiner files, and reported it to the public, for example, in his letter to the editor of *Le Canard enchaîné*, 27 April 1966. But unbeknownst to Steiner, Rosenberg soon came to change his mind.

18. Letter from Eliyahu Rosenberg to Steiner, 2 June 1966, in Auerbach materials.

19. Letter of Rachel Auerbach to Steiner, 27 April 1966, in Steiner files as well as in Auerbach materials.

20. Letter of Auerbach to Steiner of 27 April 1966, in Steiner files and Auerbach materials.

21. In a subsequent letter, she offered to underline, in different colored pencils, the different kinds of errors of fact and interpretation she thought Steiner had made. Letter of 21 May 1966, in Steiner files and Auerbach materials. She presented Steiner's failure as one not of moral transgression but of overambitious youth. "If you want to repair the wrongs that your book has inflicted, you must recognize that your lack of experience led to you make mistakes that you now must correct. Above all, you must stop acting like an ideologue and historiosopher of the Jewish people, so long as you do not have the necessary background."

22. The letter is signed by "Shmuel Willenberg in the name of Treblinka survivors" and appeared in response to the paper's earlier coverage. See "This Horror: 'Tre-

blinka'" (in Hebrew), *Ma'ariv,* 13 May 1966, and, for the letter, "A Shock and a Shame" (in Hebrew), *Ma'ariv,* 29 May 1966.

23. Letter of 14 May 1966 from Steiner to Auerbach, in Steiner files and Auerbach materials. In fact it is difficult to find an original copy of the book printed before the unannounced changes in subsequent printings. In the United States, the Yale University and Princeton University libraries hold one.

24. See letter of Steiner to Michael Korda of 18 May 1966, Steiner files.

25. Letter from Steiner to Dr. Henri Baruk of 8 September 1966, Steiner files. Baruk, likewise a medical doctor, served as an intermediary between Steiner and Dvorjetski.

26. Letter from Auerbach to Steiner of 14 May 1966, in Steiner files and Auerbach materials. Michel Salmon edited *L'Arche.*

27. Letter of Steiner to Korda of 16 May 1966, Steiner files.

28. See letter from Jacques Mercier to Auerbach of 20 June 1966 and her response of 24 June, as well as various telegrams between them, all in Auerbach materials.

29. This document, "Procès-verbal de la réunion tenue le 31 mai 1966 dans les locaux de Yad Vashem . . . ," is in the Auerbach materials; Mercier discounted *Rivarol*'s reaction by noting that "it is read by 3000 ex-Nazis and nobody else; we, former resisters, never respond to its attacks." A brief item in the "Register" section of *Der Spiegel,* 2 May 1966, which focused on Steiner's apparent challenge to the distinction between perpetrators and victims, also concerned the Yad Vashem negotiators, because of their fear that Steiner's book would reawaken German antisemitism. See also Steiner's letter to *Der Spiegel* of 8 September 1966, Steiner files, protesting the presentation of his book: "The executioners were those who imposed death and humiliation and the victims were those who suffered them. I believe that any other definition of the relations between the perpetrators and the victims would be a total confusion of moral values, the kind of confusion that generally leads to fascism."

30. See the documents "Points pour la négocation" (dated 6 July 1966), "Les résultats des discussions avec M. J.-F. Steiner" (dated 13 July 1966), "Desiderata" (dated 18 July 1966), and "Remarques et explication," undated, all in Auerbach materials.

31. Auerbach, "*Treblinke,* fun Zhan-Fransua Shtayner," *Unzer vort,* 19 February 1967, reprinted in French as "*Treblinka,* de J.-F. Steiner, en allemand," in the appendix to Novitch, *La Vérité sur Treblinka,* 123. On Melnik, Auerbach added, "A French newspaper drew attention to the fact that this person has the same name as a leader of the Ukrainian fascist bands, of terrible memory, who massacred Jews and Poles in Eastern Poland. The newspaper asked if, by coincidence, he is related to this Ukrainian bandit." Ibid. Of course, this seemingly reckless allegation had no foundation.

32. See letters of Auerbach to Mercier of 29 July 1966 and her follow-up of 1 August;

Mercier to Auerbach, 20 August 1966; Auerbach to Mercier, 19 September 1966; and Auerbach's final plea to Steiner in a letter of 25 September 1966, as well as her letter to Simone de Beauvoir of 26 September 1966, all in Auerbach materials.

33. Letters of Mercier to Auerbach, 29 September 1966 and 19 October 1966, in Auerbach materials.

34. See letter of Auerbach to Sassia Erlich, 21 December 1966, in Auerbach materials.

35. See the documents "Changements de noms" and "Corrections" in the Auerbach materials.

36. Sonia Grabinska, who had been particularly insulted by her cameo appearance in the book, became "Malka," and Steiner removed from his postscript any mention that she had survived. See letters from her husband Anatol Lewkowicz to Steiner of 9 May 1966, Steiner files and Auerbach materials, and of 6 June 1966, Steiner files, reporting her nervous breakdown and threatening suit.

37. Letter of Olga Imbert and Léon Czertok to Steiner of 11 October 1966 requesting suppression, in Steiner files and Auerbach materials.

38. Auerbach, "*Treblinke,* fun Zhan-Fransua Shtayner," in French in Novitch, *La Vérité sur Treblinka,* 124.

39. These examples are in Steiner, *Treblinka,* 94, 208, 67, and 250, and the equivalent pages in later French editions; English ed., 103, 224, 75, and 268.

40. The corrections were not always complete. As Alexander Donat observed in his English-language review, the passage referring to the town of Metzritch as "near Smolensk" was changed to read "near Bialystok," when it is in fact located in the Lublin district. Donat dryly writes, "Such a correction amounts to changing 'Yonkers near Chicago' to 'Yonkers near Washington, D.C.'" Donat, "Nazi War Victims on Trial," *Saturday Review,* 13 May 1967. When, a decade later, he published a collection of some of the essential testimonies from Treblinka—reprinting Wiernik's book and including Auerbach's in English for the first time as a whole—Donat mentioned Steiner only in his bibliography, but his principle of presentation is clearly directed against Steiner's example: "This book . . . consists mainly of the authentic eyewitness accounts of six survivors—undramatized, unadorned, without fabrications and hollow verbiage. The nightmare of Treblinka's hell is portrayed in simple words. Nothing can give a truer picture of Treblinka than Samuel Rajzman's conclusion: 'In writing about the Holocaust, we don't need authors with great imaginations. We need people who can depict the reality as it was. It was so overpowering that the facts speak for themselves.'" Donat, ed., *The Death Camp Treblinka: A Documentary* (New York: Waldon Press, 1979), 15–16.

41. Steiner, *Treblinka,* 108, 122; English ed., 118, 133.

42. See, in many versions over the months, Auerbach's list of "Passages à supprimer," in Auerbach materials.

43. One change Steiner did make was to delete the attribution of "monstrous complicity," but this alteration hardly mattered in the midst of the long string of such suggestions. See Steiner, *Treblinka*, 108; English ed., 118.

44. The best example, again, is the discussion of "the little despicable Jew, the little ghetto Jew, the vermin, the subhuman" who attacked "the beautiful edifice of the tall officer, blond and handsome and black who considered himself divine." Steiner, *Treblinka*, 283 (in the midst of an entire page omitted in the English edition).

45. "[T]he main thing is that it is a book about which one can be *honestly* enthusiastic, in which one *genuinely* believes." Letter of Michael Korda to Steiner of 20 April 1966, Steiner files. Unfortunately, according to Korda (personal communication), the American file on Steiner's book has been lost or destroyed. However, several letters Korda wrote at the time, available in foreign archives, refer to both of these readers' reports. Hilberg, who could not locate his report, testified to the "affinity" between Steiner's book and Hilberg's own work on the Nazi "machinery" and the problem of Jewish resistance, adding that he had endorsed the book because he felt "more tolerant of that kind of mix [of fact and fiction] in those days than I am now." He later met Auerbach, who remained bitter about the Steiner episode (personal communications). For his part, Javits responded to Auerbach's angry entreaty of 28 January 1967 with a reply of 13 February apologizing for blurbing the book without reading it carefully; both letters in Auerbach materials.

46. Letter of Korda to Steiner of 23 May 1966, Steiner files.

47. See letters of Korda to Walter Eytan of 20 September 1966 and to Steiner of the same day, Steiner files.

48. Letter of Korda to Auerbach of 20 December 1966, in Steiner files and Auerbach materials. Korda wrote to Steiner in forwarding him a copy of his reply to Auerbach, "Obviously, we cannot change the book to suit her wishes, and this business of 'purging' the book is idiotic. She has no right to censor a book."

49. Letters from Auerbach to Korda of 13 January 1967 and from Korda to Auerbach of 18 January 1967, in Steiner files and Auerbach materials, and from Korda to Steiner the same day, Steiner files.

50. Letter from Korda to Auerbach of 20 December 1966, in Steiner files and Auerbach materials.

51. A typewritten copy of this twenty-page document written in English, "Treblinka as Seen and as Described in Writing," is to be found, along with Glazar's cover letter of 29 June 1968, in the Richard Glazar files, Yad Vashem Archive, O.33/1152. Its existence is mentioned, and it is briefly cited, in Gitta Sereny, *Into That Darkness: From Mercy Killing to Mass Murderer* (New York: McGraw-Hill, 1974), 246.

52. Richard Glazar, *Die Falle mit dem grünen Zaun: Überleben in Treblinka* (Frank-

furt am Main: Fischer Taschenbuch, 1992), in English as *The Trap with a Green Fence: Survival in Treblinka,* tr. Roslyn Theobald (Evanston, Ill.: Northwestern University Press, 1995). Not all survivors whose testimonies postdate 1966, however, mention Steiner's book; Shmuel Willenberg, who had given his testimony to Steiner and signed the letter of protest during the Treblinka affair, is silent about it in his later *Rebellion in Treblinka* (in Hebrew) (Tel Aviv: Misrad ha-Bitahon, 1988), in English as Samuel Willenberg, *Surviving Treblinka,* tr. Naftali Greenwood (New York: Blackwell, 1989).

53. See "Treblinka-Chronist: zum Tod von Richard Glazar," *Frankfurter Allgemeine Zeitung,* 17 January 1998.

54. Letter of Melnik to Steiner, undated, Steiner files.

6. The Aftermath of the Controversy

1. Robert O. Paxton, *Vichy: Old Guard and New Order, 1940–1944* (New York: Knopf, 1972), in French as *La France de Vichy, 1940–1944,* tr. Claude Bertrand (Paris: Seuil, 1973). Cf. Moshik Temkin, "'Avec un certain malaise': The Paxtonian Trauma in France," *Journal of Contemporary History* 38, 2 (April 2003): 291–306, and Sarah Fishman et al., eds, *La France sous Vichy: Autour de Robert O. Paxton* (Brussels: Éditions Complexe, 2004). Henry Rousso, *The Vichy Syndrome: History and Memory in Postwar France,* tr. Arthur Goldhammer (Cambridge, Mass.: Harvard University Press, 1991); on France's incessant mourning, see Rousso and Éric Conan, *Vichy: An Ever-Present Past,* tr. Nathan Bracher (Hanover, N.H.: University Press of New England, 1998).

2. Donald Reid, "Germaine Tillion and the Resistance to the Vichy Syndrome," *History and Memory* 15, 2 (Fall–Winter 2003): 36–37.

3. See Olivier Mongin, "La réception d'Arendt en France," in Miguel Abensour et al., eds., *Ontologie et politique: Actes du colloque Hannah Arendt* (Paris: Éditions Tierce, 1989). On the German edition, see Shlomo Avineri, "A Banal Story," *New Republic,* 24 February 2003.

4. Hanna [*sic*] Arendt, "La banalité du mal," *Les Temps modernes* 21, 238 (March 1966): 1569–1602; Arendt, "Eichmann et six millions de juifs," *Le Nouvel Observateur,* 5 October 1966, 14–19; and Arendt, "Eichmann et les 'Conseils juifs,'" *Le Nouvel Observateur,* 12 October 1966, 20–25.

5. Hannah Arendt, letter to Léone Nora of 23 December 1966, Hannah Arendt Papers, Publishers—Gallimard—1960–75, Manuscript Division, Library of Congress, Washington, D.C., the source of all subsequently cited letters unless otherwise noted.

6. "Courrier: Hannah Arendt est-elle nazie?" *Le Nouvel Observateur,* 26 October 1966.

7. Hannah Arendt, *Eichmann à Jérusalem: Rapport sur la banalité dumal*, tr. Anne Guérin (Paris: Gallimard, 1966), 5–8. "C'est d'ailleurs [Poliakov] qui m'avait convaincu de la nécessité de faire le dossier de la polémique que j'ai publié en avertissement d'éditeur. Hannah Arendt en a été très mécontente car elle pensait que c'était déconsidérer *a priori* son livre que de faire état de cette polémique. Il m'avait paru impossible, comme à Léon Poliakov, de donner le livre au public français sans en faire état." Letter from Pierre Nora to the author. An essay by Robinson, "Les vertus des criminels et les crimes des victimes: Réplique à Mme Hanna Arendt," *Le Monde juif* 19, 1 (January–March 1964): 21–33, had appeared before the translation.

8. Letter from Pierre Nora to Denver Lindley, 12 December 1966, Library of Congress.

9. Letters from Lindley to Michel Mohrt, 30 November 1966 and 9 December 1966, Library of Congress.

10. Letter from Léone Nora to Arendt, 14 December 1966, Library of Congress. In reply, Arendt wondered: "It would be interesting, however, to learn who hit upon this idea if no one believed it." Letter from Arendt to Léone Nora, 23 December 1966, Library of Congress. For his part, Jean Daniel, the editor of *Le Nouvel Observateur*, who had written the headline, apologized to Mary McCarthy, who phoned him about it, for his "stupid error." Letter of Daniel to McCarthy, 6 March 1968, Hannah Arendt Papers, Adolf Eichmann File, 1938–68, Correspondence—Miscellaneous—German and French languages, Library of Congress.

11. Letter from Pierre Nora to Lindley, 12 December 1966, Library of Congress. Nora mentioned Steiner's book in this mode again in his letter directly to Arendt of 4 January 1967, Library of Congress. In both instances, Nora blamed Roger Peyrefitte's *The Jews* along with *Treblinka* for creating the difficult circumstances for the reception of Arendt's book.

12. It is perhaps worth noting that in his own emphasis on the bureaucratic genius involved in the Final Solution—he called its absent organizers "the Technicians" in his text—Steiner had also anticipated for French readers Arendt's far more subtle analysis of "the banality of evil."

13. Arendt, *Eichmann in Jerusalem: A Report on the Banality of Evil*, rev. ed. (New York: Viking, 1964), 11, 123, 125–26.

14. Pierre Démeron, "Le livre qui scandalise les Juifs et les non-Juifs," *Le Nouveau Candide*, 14–20 November 1966, 33–35 at 33–34.

15. Letter from Arendt to Léone Nora, 23 December 1966, Library of Congress.

16. Letter from Pierre Nora to Arendt, 4 January 1967, Library of Congress, and Arendt's slightly mollified response to him and his sister-in-law of 24 January 1967, Library of Congress.

17. Ernest Mandel, "Racines morales et raisons sociales des crimes fascistes," *La Gauche* 48 (1966): 7

18. Albert Memmi, "Autopsie d'un assassin," *Magazine littéraire* 3 (January 1967): 34–35.

19. Manès Sperber, "Le désastre incompris," *Le Monde,* 14 January 1967. Sperber had previously written about Arendt's book, before its French translation, in Sperber, "Hourban ou l'inconcevable certitude," *Preuves* 157 (March 1964).

20. Roger Paret, "Qui n'est pas Adolf Eichmann?" *Preuves* 191 (January 1967): 8–17. Avner Less, the Israeli major who had interrogated Eichmann, responded to Paret, who in turn responded to him. See Avner Less, "Lettre d'Avner Less," *Preuves* 193 (March 1967): 93–94 and Paret, "Post-scriptum sur Eichmann," *Preuves* 195 (May 1967): 92–93, cf. Lucien Steinberg, "Adolf Eichmann et son interrogateur," *Le Monde juif* 23, 13 (July–September 1967): 20–8.

21. Michel Borwicz, "Le 'roman' de Hannah Arendt," *Les Nouveaux cahiers* 2, 8 (December 1966): 2–7; Léon Poliakov, "L'histoire ne s'écrit pas avec des si . . . ," *Les Nouveax cahiers* 2, 8 (December 1968): 7–9 at 8. Poliakov had published the best available French translation of information on the Eichmann trial: see Poliakov, ed., *Le Procès de Jérusalem: jugement, documents* (Paris: Calmann-Lévy, 1963).

22. Vidal-Naquet, "La banalité du mal," *Le Monde,* 13 January 1967. A prior, multinational reception history, noting however only a few of the French discussions, usefully integrates them into thematic categories. See Richard I. Cohen, "Breaking the Code: Hannah Arendt's *Eichmann in Jerusalem* and the Public Polemic— Myth, Memory, and Historical Imagination," *Michael: On the History of the Jews in the Diaspora* 13 (1993): 29–86; see also Annette Wieviorka, *Le Procès Eichmann* (Brussels: Editions Complexe, 1989), 126–37, a treatment of "the trial of the trial" with some information on the French debate about Arendt's position.

23. Arendt, *Eichmann in Jerusalem,* 11–12.

24. Ibid., 122–23. She emphasized the distinction between leaders and masses later in her "Postscript" of 1964, in ibid., 283–84. In his recent memoir, Raul Hilberg writes that, though often mistakenly conflated with Arendt's position, *The Destruction of the European Jews* did not draw any genuine distinction between the Jewish councils and the communities they led: "I could not separate the Jewish leaders from the Jewish populace because I believed that these men represented the essence of a time-honored Jewish reaction to danger." Hilberg, *The Politics of Memory: The Journey of a Holocaust Historian* (Chicago: Ivan R. Dee, 1996), 151.

25. Arendt, *Eichmann in Jerusalem,* 11–12. Among the French reviewers, only Roger Errera specifically cited this crucial passage in defending Arendt against the calumny that she had indicted the passivity of the Jews as a whole. Errera, "Une analyse du totalitarisme," *La Quinzaine littéraire,* 1 December 1966. Errera, who had already reviewed the English-language edition in an article on books on the trial, continued the debate in an exchange with Wladimir Rabi. See Errera, "Eichmann: Un Procès inachevé," *Critique* 21, 214 (March 1965): 262–

74, and Errera and Rabi, "Le cas Hannah Arendt," *L'Arche* 118 (December 1966): 11–15. Errera became Arendt's main contact in France, and they pursued a correspondence through the next decade.

26. Vidal-Naquet, "La banalité du mal," *Le Monde*, 13 January 1967. He returned to Arendt a decade later on the occasion of the French publication of *The Origins of Totalitarianism*. See Vidal-Naquet, "Des juifs de cour à Eichmann," *Le Monde*, 20 October 1972, assigned by Roger Errera to review the section of the book on antisemitism.

27. Letter from Arendt to the Noras of 24 January 1967, Library of Congress.

28. See, for example, Steven Aschheim, ed., *Hannah Arendt in Jerusalem* (Berkeley: University of California Press, 2001).

29. M. Ackermann, "Les autres coupables," *Le Nouvel Observateur*, 26 October 1966.

30. Arendt, *Eichmann in Jerusalem*, 122.

31. Joan B. Wolf, *Harnessing the Holocaust: The Politics of Memory in France* (Stanford, Calif.: Stanford University Press, 2004), 26. Wolf's narrative begins with the Six-Day War. See also Henry H. Weinberg, *The Myth of the Jew in France, 1967–1982* (New York: Mosaic Press, 1987), and David H. Weinberg, "France," in David S. Wyman, ed., *The World Reacts to the Holocaust* (Baltimore: Johns Hopkins University Press, 1996). More generally, see Harold Marcuse, "The Revival of Holocaust Awareness in West Germany, Israel, and the United States," in Carole Fink, Philipp Gassert, and Detlef Junker, eds., *1968: The World Transformed* (Cambridge: Cambridge University Press, 1998).

32. Jean Daniel, "De Gaulle et les juifs," *Le Nouvel Observateur*, December 6–12, 1967, as cited in Paige Arthur, "Unfinished Projects: Decolonization and Philosophy of Jean-Paul Sartre" (Ph.D. diss., University of California–Berkeley, 2004), chap. 3. Daniel has recently offered reflections on the problem of contemporary Jewish identity. See Daniel, *La prison juive: Humeurs et méditations d'un témoin* (Paris: Odile Jacob, 2003) and "Les prisons de la pensée théologique: entretien," *Le Débat* 131 (September–October 2004):4–12.

33. François de Montfort and Steiner, "Les jeunes israéliens ne veulent pas que les politiciens viennent gâcher leur victoire," *La Dépeche du Midi*, 16 July 1967.

34. Apparently, however, the British publicity could have been slightly better organized, as a London *Times* item reported: "French author Jean-François Steiner can hardly be blamed for the flop of the press conference held yesterday by Weidenfeld and Nicolson to launch his book *Treblinka* in London. . . . There were so many to hear 29-year-old Steiner, a French Jew, talk about his controversial book that the conference had to be conducted on a split level basis, with questions and answers transmitted through a public address system to the second and third floors of the Wig and Pen Club in the Strand. Before the organizers realized that Steiner's English could not handle the questions being fired, and called on the

services on an interpreter, the conference fell to a *coup* of experts and raconteurs, anxious to expound on the events surrounding Treblinka. With only the occasional spotlight for a nod or a shake of the head on technical points in the book, Steiner was eased into the background, a rather confused figure. He was finally resurrected, as the conference drew to a close, to discuss his book publicly with Lord Russell of Liverpool—a discussion in which only Lord Russell took part." "A Confusion of Communication," *Times* (London) 27 May 1967.

35. Neil Ascherson, "Chronicles of the Holocaust," *New York Review of Books,* 1 July 1967.

36. See the serialization, Steiner, "Revolt at Treblinka," in *Saturday Evening Post,* 20 May 1966, and these reviews in the American and British press: "Variations on a Theme," *Time,* 26 May 1967; Michael J. Berlin, "After the Holocaust," *New York Post,* 17 May 1967; David Caute, "Final Solution," *Harper's Magazine,* July 1967; Josh Greenfeld, "Treblinka: Heroism or Fantastic Apology?" *Life,* 19 May 1967; Oscar Handlin, "Reader's Choice," *Atlantic,* June 1967; Christopher Lehmann-Haupt, "Holocaust Melodrama," *New York Times,* 22 May 1967; Robert Jay Lifton, "When We Dead Awaken," *Partisan Review* 35, 3 (Summer 1968): 475–83; Saul Maloff, "The Technics of Slaughter," *New York Times Book Review,* 14 May 1967; Maloff, "The Doll," *Newsweek,* 15 May 1967; Mordecai Richler, "Breaking the Silence," *Observer,* 28 May 1967; George Steiner, "Postscript to a Tragedy," *Encounter* 38, 2 (February 1967): 33–39; Lowell Streiker, "Painful Tattoos," *Christian Century,* 26 July 1967; Geoffrey A. Wolff, "Rebels against Nothingness" and "Telling Story of Death Camps Involves Author in Controversy," both *Washington Post,* 23 May 1967. Some of the local reviews are blurbed in later paperback editions of the book; George Steiner reprinted part of his essay in his famous collection *Language and Silence: Essays on Language, Literature, and the Inhuman* (New York: Atheneum, 1967).

37. As mentioned earlier, Alexander Donat published a highly negative review, "Nazi War Victims on Trial," *Saturday Review,* 13 May 1967, which is counterbalanced by Monica Sterling, "The Author," in the same issue. Bruno Bettelheim did as well: Bettelheim, "Survival of the Jews," *New Republic,* 1 July 1967. See also the negative article by Louis Harap, "The Holocaust: Myths and Facts," *Nation,* 3 July 1967, and the negative radio broadcast by Morris Schappes, "A New Controversy about *Treblinka,*" WBAI-FM, 23 May 1967, transcript in Rachel Auerbach file, Yad Vashem Archive, P.16/36. Both Harap and Schappes were well informed about the prior French controversy, by Auerbach herself.

38. There are in fact five such articles in Shneiderman's papers at the Diaspora Research Institute archives at Tel Aviv University (all P-73/Box 13, File 30)— "Shturem in Frankraykh vegn bukh *Treblinke,*" "Protestn fun lebn-geblibene heldn fun oyfshtand in Treblinke-lager," "Ven natzi-merder veren gerufn 'tekhniker'," "Felshungen vegn Treblinke un Vilner geto," "Dos bukh *Treblinke* un di

farloymdungen kegn yidshn folk" (the last two articles are identical contributions to different papers)—but I did not attempt a thorough survey of the Yiddish press outside Paris.

39. See Steiner, *Les métèques* (Paris: Fayard, 1970), and Steiner, *Varsovie 44: l'insurrection* (Paris: Flammarion, 1975). The latter deals not, of course, with the Warsaw ghetto revolt but rather with the uprising of elements of the dissolved Polish army in an attempt to take the city. So far as I know, Steiner's other books went largely unread, particularly by comparison to the earlier success.

40. See Jean-Michel Dumay, "Les derniers témoignages des partisans de Maurice Papon," *Le Monde*, 24 October 1997; cf. Steiner's afterword to Hubert de Beaufort and Michel Bergès, *L'affaire Papon: la contre-enquête* (Paris: Guibert, 1999). Steiner also assisted with Papon's brief and abortive 1999 flight from the country to avoid imprisonment. See Laurent Léger and François Labrouillère, "Les secrets d'une fuite soigneusement préméditée," *Paris-Match*, 4 November 1999. On the Papon trial, see the useful collection by Richard J. Golsan, ed., *The Papon Affair: Memory and Justice on Trial* (New York: Routledge, 2000).

41. See Didier Daenickx, "De 'Treblinka' à Bordeaux . . . ," *Revue d'histoire de la Shoah* 166 (May–August 1999): 89–99, and the entry by Samuel Khalifa in S. Lillian Kremer, ed., *Holocaust Literature: An Encyclopedia of Writers and Their Work* (New York: Routledge, 2003), s.v. "Jean-François Steiner."

42. Helen Epstein, *Children of the Holocaust* (New York: Putnam, 1978); see later Aaron Hass, *In the Shadow of the Holocaust: The Second Generation* (New York: Cambridge University Press, 1996); Marianne Hirsch, *Family Frames: Photography, Narrative, and Postmemory* (Cambridge, Mass.: Harvard University Press, 1997); and Froma Zeitlin, "The Vicarious Witness: Belated Memory and Authorial Presence in Recent Holocaust Literature," *History & Memory* 10, 2 (Spring 1998): 5–42.

43. See Eva Hoffmann, *After Such Knowledge: Memory, History and the Aftermath of the Holocaust* (New York: Public Affairs, 2004); Gary Weissman, *Fantasies of Witnessing: Postwar Efforts to Experience the Holocaust* (Ithaca, N.Y.: Cornell University Press, 2004); and, for an especially acerbic critique of the second-generation fetishism of their parents' experience, Ruth Franklin, "Identity Theft," *New Republic*, 31 May 2004.

44. Wieviorka, *L'Ère du témoin* (Paris: Plon, 1998), 13; in English, see Wieviorka, "From Survivor to Witness: Voices from the Shoah," in Jay Winter and Emmanuel Sivan, eds., *War and Remembrance in the Twentieth Century* (Cambridge: Cambridge University Press, 2000).

45. See Hayden White, "Historical Emplotment and the Problem of Truth," and Carlo Ginzburg, "Just One Witness," both in Saul Friedlander, ed., *Probing the Limits of Representation: Nazism and "the Final Solution"* (Cambridge, Mass.: Harvard University Press, 1989).

46. Cynthia Haft, "Écrire la déportation: Le sensationnel, avilissement du tragique," *Le Monde*, 25 February 1972. In the thesis she published soon after, Haft refused "to utilize material which is in any way dishonest or which does not acknowledge its sources. . . . In the case of Steiner, a book called *Treblinka*, by Vassili Grossman, was published several years before [but Steiner] omits reference to Grossman's book. We refuse to discuss any of these works further because they are part of a trend which we abhor." Haft, *The Theme of Nazi Concentration Camps in French Literature* (The Hague: Mouton, 1973), 190–91. Ironically, in both her article and in her important book, Haft failed to make the distinction Steiner did between deportation and extermination, which proved to be perhaps the most consequential result of the affair.

47. Franklin, "Speak Not, Memory," *New Republic*, 13 August 2001. Koeppen renarrated an early testimony by Jakob Littner. For a more recent "novelization" of the Treblinka revolt, see Ian MacMillan, *Village of a Million Spirits: A Novel of the Treblinka Uprising* (South Royalton, Vt.: Steerforth Press, 1999); cf. Zofia Smardz, "Hell with the Lid Off," *New York Times Book Review*, 21 November 1999: "The impact of *Village of a Million Spirits* is so forceful that it negates the question such a fictionalization of the Holocaust raises: Why turn to art to dramatize an already intensely dramatic factual event? Eloquently, MacMillan shows that the truth we can absolutely, factually know about the Holocaust is not the whole story. It is the experience only of those who saw and remembered and came back to tell us. But to understand completely, we must go beyond all this to the rest of the story, to the truth and the experience of the millions who died. The only way to get at that truth is to imagine it. And the only way to imagine it is through art." Smardz notes that Macmillan "has clearly culled much of the historical detail" from Steiner's book.

48. Dominick LaCapra, "A Poetics of Historiography: Hayden White's *Tropics of Discourse*," *Modern Language Notes* 93 (1978), reprinted in LaCapra, *Rethinking Intellectual History: Texts, Contexts, Language* (Ithaca, N.Y.: Cornell University Press, 1982), 79–80; cf., for a similar criticism, LaCapra, *History and Criticism* (Ithaca, N.Y.: Cornell University Press, 1985), 34–35.

49. LaCapra, *Writing History, Writing Trauma* (Baltimore: Johns Hopkins University Press, 2001), 35n., 37–42; cf. 102–4, and, more recently, LaCapra, *History in Transit: Experience, Identity, Critical Theory* (Ithaca, N.Y.: Cornell University Press, 2004), 64–66, 76–77, 133–37.

50. LaCapra, *Writing History*, 41–42.

51. Ibid., 212–13.

52. For more on the terminological and conceptual lineages of empathy, see my study of Levinas's philosophical development, *Origins of the Other: Emmanuel Levinas between Revelation and Ethics* (Ithaca, N.Y.: Cornell University Press, 2005). Edith Wyschogrod, one of Levinas's major disciples, has erected a theory

of historical representation on Levinas's Steiner essay, as her subtitle suggests; see Wyschogrod, *An Ethics of Remembering: History, Heterology, and the Nameless Others* (Chicago: University of Chicago Press, 1998).

53. Wormser-Migot, *Le Système concentrationnaire nazi, 1933–1945* (Paris: Presses universitaires, 1968); cf. Wieviorka's obituary, "Olga Wormser-Migot," *Le Monde*, 8 August 2002. Wormser-Migot claimed, in her attempt to distinguish between concentration and extermination, that there had been no gas chambers at Western camps, a mistake—since a few had them—that nevertheless did not compromise the overall distinction she helped introduce.

54. See esp. Stéphane Courtois, ed., *Le Livre noir du communisme: crimes, terreurs, répression* (Paris: R. Laffont, 1997), in English as *The Black Book of Communism: Crime, Terror, Repression*, tr. Jonathan Murphy and Mark Kramer (Cambridge, Mass.: Harvard University Press, 1999), and the debate provoked by it. In this context, several writers suggested in the 1990s that the focus on Jewish extermination had not only served to obscure what Nazism and Stalinism shared but had also led to the minimization of the suffering under communist regimes (and perhaps elsewhere as well). See also Catherine Coquio, ed., *Parler des camps, penser les génocides* (Paris: Albin Michel, 1999). But cf. Henri Raczymow, "D'un 'détail' qui masque le tableau," *Le Monde*, 21 January 1998.

55. See Alain Brossat, *L'Épreuve du désastre: le XXe siècle et les camps* (Paris: Albin Michel, 1996), and, for a critique, Robert Redeker, "Un autre révisionnisme? Alain Brossat et les camps," *Les Temps modernes* 53, 596 (November–December 1997): 125–32.

56. Vidal-Naquet, *Mémoires*, vol. 2, *Le trouble et la lumière* (Paris: Seuil, 1998), 242–43. Cf., for a similar point, Vidal-Naquet, "Réflexions sur trois *Ravensbrück*," in *Les Juifs, la mémoire et le présent*, vol. 3, in English as "Reflections on Three *Ravensbrücks*," tr. David Ames Curtis, *South Atlantic Quarterly* 96, 4 (Fall 1997): 881–94 at 888–89.

57. Omer Bartov, *Mirrors of Destruction: War, Genocide, and Modern Identity* (New York: Oxford University Press, 2000), 68–74. Bartov has written similarly of France in many other places, such as Bartov, "The Proof of Ignominy: Vichy France's Past and Presence," *Contemporary European History* 7, 1 (1998): 107–31; "Reception and Perception: Goldhagen's Holocaust and the World," in Geoff Eley, ed., *The Goldhagen Effect: History, Memory, Nazism* (Ann Arbor: University of Michigan Press, 2000); and his *Germany's War and the Holocaust: Disputed Histories* (Ithaca, N.Y.: Cornell University Press, 2003), chap. 4 and 160–71.

58. Bartov, "Reply," *American Historical Review* 103, 4 (October 1998): 1193.

59. Giorgio Agamben, "Qu'est-ce qu'un camp?" *Libération*, 3 October 1994, in English as "What Is a Camp?" in *Means without End: Notes on Politics*, tr. Vincenzo Binetti and Cesare Casarino (Minneapolis: University of Minnesota Press, 2000);

see later Agamben, "The Camp as Nomos of the Modern," in Hent de Vries and Samuel Weber, eds., *Violence, Identity, and Self-Determination* (Stanford, Calif.: Stanford University Press, 1997), reprinted as a chapter in *Homo Sacer: Sovereign Power and Bare Life,* tr. Daniel Heller-Roazen (Stanford, Calif: Stanford University Press, 1998).

60. Agamben, *Remnants of Auschwitz: The Witness and the Archive,* tr. Heller-Roazen (New York: Zone Books, 2001), 52.

61. Ibid., 17. This same sentence, not surprisingly, figured prominently in Georges Bataille's early review of Rousset's book: Bataille, "Réflexions sur le bourreau et le victime: S.S. et déportés," *Critique* 17 (October 1947): 337–42 at 338.

62. Agamben, *Homo Sacer,* 170.

63. Agamben, *Remnants of Auschwitz,* 76.

64. Ibid., 20, 26, 101.

65. Ibid., 34, 48, 51.

66. Ibid., 52, 45.

67. It is not out of an interest in setting victims against one another, but simply to distinguish categories, that it is worth adding that, however perceptibly akin to dead the "living dead" *Muselmänner* were, they were clinically alive, and some survived and, like those Agamben himself cites at the end of his book, bore witness. More important, their "living death" (and, when it occurred, their extinction) often occurred for different reasons and in a different way than the actual death of the European Jewish communities that were destroyed. Agamben, whose view on this matter is close to (albeit substantially more philosophically developed than) Wolfgang Sofsky's in his well-known study, is subject to Omer Bartov's criticism that studies of "the camps" in the end may penetrate only to "the penultimate horror." See Sofsky, *The Order of Terror: The Concentration Camp,* tr. William Templer (Princeton, N.J.: Princeton University Press, 1997), and Bartov, "The Penultimate Horror," *New Republic,* 13 October 1997, reprinted as part of Bartov, *Germany's War and the Holocaust,* chap. 4.

68. Agamben, *Remnants of Auschwitz,* 52; he likewise writes: "The *Muselmann* is not only or not so much a limit between life and death; rather, he marks the threshold between the human and the inhuman" (55).

69. It is true that Agamben begins his text with an allusion to Raul Hilberg as having established the "facts" of the Holocaust, but this acknowledgment does not, it seems to me, vitiate my claim, since Agamben then proceeds to ignore the factual difference between concentration and extermination in the rest of his text.

70. Agamben, *Remnants of Auschwitz,* 85.

71. Agamben, explaining his cancellation of an American teaching appointment, recently wrote: "Some years ago, I had written that the West's political paradigm was no longer the city state, but the concentration camp, and that we had passed from Athens to Auschwitz. It was obviously a philosophical thesis, and not his-

torical claim, because one could not confuse phenomena that it is proper, on the contrary, to distinguish. I would have liked to suggest that tattooing at Auschwitz undoubtedly seemed the most normal and economic way to regulate the enrollment and registration of deported persons into concentration camps. The bio-political tattooing the United States imposes now to enter its territory could well be the precursor to what we will be asked to accept later as the normal identity registration of a good citizen in the state's gears and mechanisms. That's why we must oppose it." Agamben, "Non au tatouage biopolitique," *Le Monde,* 11 January 2004.

72. For some such studies, all basically restricted to the American case, see Tim Cole, *Selling the Holocaust, from Auschwitz to Schindler* (New York: Routledge, 1999); Norman Finkelstein, *The Holocaust Industry: Reflections on the Exploitation of Jewish Suffering* (New York: Verso, 2000); Peter Novick, *The Holocaust in American Life* (Boston: Houghton Mifflin, 1998); Jeffrey Shandler, *While America Watches: Televising the Holocaust* (New York: Oxford University Press, 1999); cf. Alan E. Steinweis, "The Holocaust and American Culture: An Assessment of Recent Scholarship," *Holocaust and Genocide Studies* 15, 2 (Fall 2001): 296–310.

73. Patrick Wajsman, "Notre jeunesse retrouve son âme," *L'Arche* 124 (June 1967): 21–22.

74. Already in January 1965, the Centre de documentation juive contemporaine had organized an exposition on the theme of Jewish resistance; see the special issue on it, which includes a report on the inauguration, of *Le Monde juif* 20, 3–4 (September 1964–May 1965). In the pages of the *Le Monde juif,* resistance garnered further attention throughout 1967 and 1968, notably in connection with the Warsaw rebellion's twenty-fifth anniversary; the journal printed many of the French contributions to a Yad Vashem conference of 1968 on the subject, also available as Meir Grubsztein, ed., *Jewish Resistance during the Holocaust* (Jerusalem: Yad Vashem, 1971). See also the work of CDJC collaborator Lucien Steinberg, *La révolte des justes: les Juifs contre Hitler* (Paris: Fayard, 1970), in English as *Not as a Lamb: The Jews against Hitler* (Farnborough: Saxon House, 1974). In America, see Yuri Suhl's *They Fought Back: The Story of Jewish Resistance in Nazi Europe* (New York: Crown Publishers, 1967), which appeared around the same time as the English translation of Steiner's book—and many, many other works. In a more scholarly mode, see Salo W. Baron and George S. Wise, eds., *Violence and Defense in the Jewish Experience* (Philadelphia: Jewish Publication Society, 1977); Amos Funkenstein, "On the Passivity of Diaspora Jews: Myth and Reality" (in Hebrew) (Tel Aviv University, 1981); and David Biale, *Power and Powerlessness in Jewish History* (New York: Schocken, 1986).

75. In a substantial literature on later years, see, for example, Michael Shurkin, "Decolonization and the Renewal of French Judaism: Reflections on the Contemporary French Jewish Scene," *Jewish Social Studies,* n.s., 6, 2 (Winter 2000): 156–76.

76. Pierre Nora, "Mémoire et identité juives dans la France contemporaine," *Le Débat* 131 (September–December 2004): 20–34 at 28–29.

77. See Tzvetan Todorov, "The Abuses of Memory," *Common Knowledge* 5, 1 (Spring 1996): 6–26; *Les Abus de la mémoire* (Paris: Arléa, 1998); "Je conspire, Hannah Arendt conspirait, Raymond Aron aussi," *Le Monde*, 31 January 1998, a response to Raczymow's article, cited in n. 54 above; and *Mémoire du mal, tentation du bien: enquête sur le siècle* (Paris: R. Laffont, 2000), now available in English as *Hope and Memory: Lessons from the Twentieth Century* (Princeton, N.J.: Princeton University Press, 2003). In what follows, I draw on my review of the latter book, "The Ghosts of Totalitarianism," *Ethics and International Affairs* 8, 2 (Fall 2004): 99–104. See also Todorov's conversations with Alain Finkielkraut and Richard Marienstras, *Du bon usage de la mémoire* (Geneva: Éditions du Tricorne, 2000).

78. Todorov, *Hope and Memory*, 162.

79. Of course, Todorov is quick to warn against measuring every garden-variety wrong against past crimes; but what he more fundamentally opposes is the restriction of a crime like the Holocaust to such a singular status that people who supposedly hate evil will stand by as roughly comparable wrongs are repeated, simply because they do not see them as similar.

80. Todorov, *Hope and Memory*, 174.

81. Ibid., chap. 3. See also the recent collection of essays on Rousset by Brossat, Coquio, Todorov, and others in *Lignes*, n.s., 2 (May 2000): 5–232.

82. Todorov, *Hope and Memory*, 150–51.

83. Paul Berman, *Terror and Liberalism* (New York: W. W. Norton, 2003).

84. See Avishai Margalit, *The Ethics of Memory* (Cambridge, Mass.: Harvard University Press, 2002).

Index

Agamben, Giorgio, 55, 160–63, 209n.67, 209–10nn.70–71
Ajzensztajn, Betti, 94–95
Algerian war, 21, 79–80, 108–9, 174n.29, 186n.67
Alliance Israélite Universelle, 89, 110
Amazon.com, 194n.82
American Jewish Committee, 58
Améry, Jean, 109, 182n.35, 193n.73
Amif, 22
Ansky, S., 176–77n.56
antifascism, and construction of World War II past, xvi, xviii, 2, 11–12, 46–7, 52–53, 56–58, 73, 77–78, 82, 166; and Jewish identity, 87, 102–4. *See also* Rousset, David
Anti–Semite and Jew (Sartre), 80, 91
antisemitism: and French culture, 27–29, 51–52, 99, 148; perceptions of in Jean–François Steiner's text, 7–8, 33–35, 39, 59, 61–63, 94, 96, 104, 107, 190n.51, 195–96n.4, 200n.44; and philosemitism, 27–29; Steiner's response, 7–8, 183n.44, 198n.29; Vidal–Naquet's response, 186n.71. *See also* Rassinier, Paul; *Rivarol*
Aranovich, Pessia, 32–33, 125
Arbeter vort, 97–98
Arche, L', 89, 92–93, 98, 110, 112, 163
Arendt, Hannah, xx, 4–6, 11, 128, 181nn.24, 26, 202n.10, 203n.24; on concentration versus extermination, 56–67; as follower of David Rousset, 56–58, 147; French

controversy around *Eichmann and Jerusalem*, 142–49; on *Judenräte* (Jewish councils), 145, 203n.22; on sensationalization, 142–44, 146; on *Sonderkommandos* in death camps, 147; source for Giorgio Agamben, 160, 162; stress on elite rather than mass compliance, 4, 147, 203–4n.24. *See also* complicity
Aron, Raymond, 79, 149
Arthur, Paige, 149
Ascherson, Neil, 151
Assas, Chevalier of, 92
Auerbach, Rachel: assistance to Jean–François Steiner, 25, 127–28; as critic of Steiner and organizer of campaign against his book, 125, 128–30, 200n.45; as Holocaust historian, 103, 126, 196–97nn.10–12; intervention in publication and reception of American edition, 130–37, 151

Bartov, Omer, 159, 209n.67
Baruk, Henri, 130, 198n.25
Bataille, Georges, 55, 209n.61
Baudy, Nicolas, 110, 130
Bayard, 92
Beauvoir, Simone de, 5, 34, 102, 106–7; book preface for Jean–François Steiner, 1, 48–50; defense of Steiner in universalist terms at variance with his message, 68–71, 76, 78, 147; on Jewish youth, 112; targeted by others, 72, 74, 80, 82, 95, 103

213

20; image of Nazis of, 34–35, 37, 107; interview that sparked Treblinka affair, 1–8, 13, 24, 27, 35, 89, 94, 98, 101; narrative of Treblinka camp and revolt, 34–44; narrative of Vilna ghetto, 32–33; opinions about Zionism, 21, 91–92, 150; as paratrooper in Algerian war, 21; participation in trial of Maurice Papon for war crimes, 151, 206n.40; relations with Jewish youth, 89–90, 93, 111–12; research trip to Israel, 25, 125, 127; self-presentation to Jewish community during controversy, 89–93; trajectory after controversy, 151

Steiner, Ozias, 14, 20
Stern, Israel, 100
Streicher, Julius, 107
Stroop, Jürgen, 170n.11
Szulsztein, Moshe, 97–101, 103, 106

"Technicians, the," Jean-François Steiner's label for perpetrators, 33, 37, 60, 123, 138, 202n.12
Temps modernes, Les, 1, 21, 49, 53, 58, 94, 142
testimony, belief in importance or self-sufficiency of, 25, 122–24, 154–55, 199n.40, 207n.47
Théâtre des Ambassadeurs, public debate at, 77, 111
Theory and Practice of Hell, The (Kogon), 57
Tillard, Paul, 29
Tillion, Germaine, 192–93n.69
Time, 76
Todorov, Tzvetan, 164–68
Treblinka (book), xv–xvi; American edition of 134–37, 151; conception, research, and writing of, 22, 25, 124, 126; cover and dust jacket of, 20, 43; literary and popular success of, 45, 77; post-publication revisions of, 129–34; reader's report on, 106–7; sales figures for, 151, 169–70n.2; summary of, 32–44. See also Steiner, Jean-François
Treblinka camp, xv, 7, 12, 33–44, 82, 159, 161

Ubu the King (Jarry), 54
Ulysses's Lie (Rassinier), 63
Union des Juifs pour la Résistance et l'Entraide (UJRE), 77, 185n.63
uniqueness, of the Holocaust. *See* comparability, of crimes or suffering
univers concentrationnaire, concept of, 2, 49, 53–59, 71, 77–78, 82, 159, 162–63. *See also* concentration camp; Rousset, David
univers concentrationnaire, L' (Rousset), 52–53, 55, 58, 82
universalist humanism, compatibility of Jewish particularity with, 14, 20, 40–41, 63, 91, 100, 118, 121, 164
Unzer shtime, 93–96
Unzer vort, 97, 131–32

Vallat, Xavier, 18, 173n.18
Vatican II (Catholic reform council), 75–76
Vercingetorix, 92
Vichy regime, 18–19, 141
Vichy syndrome, xviii, 4, 141
Vidal-Naquet, Pierre: and Algerian war, 79–80, 108–9, 186n.67; difference with Marxist interpretation of genocide, 80; on distinction between concentration and extermination, 46, 82–5, 158–59, 161; early life and Jewish identity, 79–80, 91; engagement in Treblinka affair, xv, 9, 79–85; on Jean-François Steiner's concept of Jewish particularity, 82–83, 86, 108–9, 148, 193n.74; on Kadmi Cohen, 16; response to Holocaust denial, 79, 84; reviews of Hannah Arendt's works, 144, 147–48, 204n.26; on sensationalism in Holocaust memory, 10, 148, 186–7n.74; shift of opinion about Steiner's book, 83–85, 148, 187n.76, 192n.67; on shifts in Holocaust memory, 84–85, 184n.49
Vilna, ghetto, 23–24, 32–33, 103–4, 125; Jean-François Steiner's depiction of Jewish behavior in, 34–35; partisan movement around, 22–23

2